D1498301

ALL THE MOVES

ALL THE MOVES
(but none of the licks)

Clive Selwood

Peter Owen
London and Chester Springs

PETER OWEN PUBLISHERS
73 Kenway Road, London SW5 0RE
Peter Owen books are distributed in the USA by Dufour Editions Inc.,
Chester Springs, PA 19425-0007

First published in Great Britain 2003
© Clive Selwood 2003

ISBN 0 7206 1153 9

A catalogue record for this book is available from
the British Library.

Printed in Croatia by
Zrinski SA

To beloved Shurley who made it all possible; to Sam, Bee, Chet and Brod who made it all worth while; to John and Sheila who made it all a bit of a laff; to Petals who made it all ridiculous; to sister Joan and to Michelle who supplied the family pictures; to the staff of Peter Owen Publishers who tried to put all of this into some kind of order and without whom you wouldn't be reading this; and to the many artists who never quite made it. But most of all to the tens of thousands of hopefuls who know that with a little support, encouragement and advice there is an exciting and glamorous life waiting for them out there.

FOREWORD BY JOHN PEEL

Sheila Gilhooly 2002

It wasn't all that long ago that I sat in a BBC theatre and listened as a man told a simply hilarious story about the late John Walters and myself. Members of the audience rocked in their seats at the telling of the tale. I even laughed myself. It *was* a really good story. The trouble was that it was almost completely untrue. Did the teller, I wondered as I chortled unattractively, know that the story was untrue? Had he decided to sacrifice veracity in the search for a winning anecdote – something Walters himself might, on occasion, have done? I wanted to leap to my feet, to tell the truth, to let the other people in the room know that I had never, ever in all of my life dressed as Tom the cat, although Walters and I did spend an evening in mouse costumes at a party at which we were the only people in fancy dress. But who would have believed me?

I don't know what stories Clive is about to tell you in this, his book. Perhaps it is better that I don't. But if he tells you anything other than that I am kind and generous and good and, in certain lights, not unattractive, I should treat what he has written with a pinch of salt. I have asked him to underplay my heroism on the banks of the Imjin River all those years ago, though.

I understand, too, that there are sections of Clive's narrative that contain no mention of me at all. I have asked him to ensure that the book will appear in the shops with these sections clearly marked so that you can hurry by them.

Clive and his Shurley have, for thirty-five years now, encouraged me in most of the correct decisions I have made and attempted to persuade me against making most of the incorrect decisions. It is because of them that I declined the chance to play a role in a production of *The Rocky Horror Show* in Stoke-on-Trent.

I owe them much more than this foreword.

AUTHOR'S PREFACE

A balloonist floated gently towards earth and enquired of a passing stranger, 'Excuse me. Can you tell me where I am?'

'Certainly,' replied the stranger. 'You are in a hot-air balloon, about thirty feet off the ground.'

'Tell me,' said the balloonist, 'do you work for a record company?'

'I do,' said the stranger. 'But how did you know that?'

'Because', came the reply, 'what you told me, while technically correct, does nothing to help me in my present difficulty.'

'Then you must be a recording artist,' responded the stranger.

'It's true. I am' was the proud reply. 'But how could you tell?'

'Well,' said the stranger, 'you don't know where you are or what you are doing, but now that you have told me, you think it's my fault and my problem.'

But his words were lost in the air as the balloonist fired up the flame and floated off into the atmosphere – unaware of the dark clouds on the horizon . . .

CONTENTS

ILLUSTRATIONS BETWEEN
PAGES 112 AND 113

INTRODUCTION

So. There you are, dear reader. Not an original line, I fear, but one I discovered inside the flap of a letter from the greatly missed Viv Stanshall of the Bonzos. Still, if it got your attention . . .

The late John Walters, who produced the Peel shows for many years on BBC Radio 1, tells of the time that Vivian deputized for Peel for a couple of weeks one summer. Walters claimed that it was an 'interesting' experience but not one he ever wished to repeat. The programmes were an exhilarating mix of music and surreal humour, written and performed by Viv with assistance from his chum Keith Moon of the Who.

Having booked studio time, Walters and Moon – who was at the peak of his fame at the time – waited patiently for the great man to arrive. After an hour or so a call to Viv's wife established that he had indeed left home and should be at the studio within minutes. A further call half an hour later drew the same response, as did a third and fourth. The fifth call established that our man had in fact only just left home but should arrive at any moment. All this time Mr Moon, who could have been forgiven a tantrum, sat quietly waiting without complaint.

With very little studio time left Mr Stanshall eventually arrived and, setting down a carrier bag that clinked ominously, apologized for his lateness with the explanation that he had been driving around trying to find an off-licence that would cash a cheque. Almost speechless with relief – and rage – Walters hurried the pair down to the studio where he asked Viv to speak the opening lines of his script in order to establish a level. 'Oh, hang about, old boy,' was the response in that wonderfully fruity voice. 'I've got to write it first.'

The shows were in fact ground-breakingly funny. Years later, with Viv's approval, I tried to release them as spoken-word cassettes, but by then there were no master copies left. Both Keith and Viv died young and in tragic circumstances. They were each unique and great British eccentrics who can never be replaced.

My editor is threatening to add 'some cohesion' to this collection of chapters. I wish him luck and hope that he can. In my limited experience life is just a collection of chapters, good and bad, interesting and dull. A series of accidents without a plan. Take a look at the biography that's printed on the cover of this book. Would anyone plan that mess? The great patrician Prime Minister Harold Macmillan is said to have described his period in office as 'responding to events', and that is most likely true for all of us as we stumble through life.

For some of you there may not be enough specific information on dates and times and other finer points of fact. I guess whether something happened at a specific time on a given day wasn't so important to me that I committed it to memory. The way you see it here is the way that I remember it, and if it seems a little jumbled at times, well, life's like that. So, while every effort has been made by the author, editor and several dedicated experts to ensure the accuracy of dates, places and spellings, please remember that these were heady and exciting times. We were all busy doing it and being there rather than keeping a diary, so it is possible that there may be a few minor discrepancies. Should you find one, please keep it to yourself, and it will be your secret.

If you've stayed with me this far then you, too, are probably fascinated by the mystique of the record business. This is a book for everybody interested in popular music in general and the machinations of the record business in particular. Every business has its own traditions or tricks of the trade, and I, working at the heart of the music business, have seen most – and invented rather more than my fair share. It is not, however, an exposé. It is rather more a chronicle of how a sometime wannabe crooner – who filled in time at various chores such as washing lampshades, working as a welder's apprentice and selling toffee apples at the Nottingham Goose Fair – came to be offered the top jobs in the British and American record industries.

On the way the reader may learn how to record, manufacture, distribute, market and promote that record into the charts; how to manage the careers of successful artists; how to create and launch one of the world's most successful independent record labels; and what it is like to deal with such superstars as Bruce Springsteen, Paul Simon, Andy Williams, Abba, Jim Morrison and the Wombles on a daily basis.

The author was there when 10CC were spirited away from Jonathan King's record company; when at different times both Elton John and Freddie Mercury were convinced that their careers would never get off the ground; when Rod Stewart 'depped' for a drunken singer and made a smash hit record for just £15 worth of nuts and bolts; when David Bowie pulled all Three Degrees; and when the then head of BBC Radio 1 instructed John Peel to stop playing Marc Bolan because 'he will never be popular'.

I hope this book will provide some insights into the seemingly casual and amateurish behaviour of many record company executives that masks a collection of highly skilled, ambitious, greedy, devious and often charming rascals, who spend millions finding, grooming, recording and 'hyping' the talent that so many love to hate.

The enduring fascination of the music business to millions of new believers every year is the notion that anyone can do it. And it's true! The rags-to-riches tale of this year's hot property is well documented – and usually fictitious – but few people outside the magic circle are aware that the same applies to those somewhat shadowy figures who pull the strings behind the big names. No qualifications are required beyond enthusiasm, dedication, a degree of common sense, a lot of persistence and a great deal of luck.

In artist management it is doubtful that anybody had greater success than Colonel Tom Parker, who was successful long before his time with Elvis. The Colonel had little education and spent his formative years working fairgrounds. By contrast Jonathan King, with no commercial experience, had a smash hit record and recorded Genesis while still at Cambridge. On sheer charisma and bravado he went on to found UK Records, which, during my time in charge, enjoyed four records in the Top Twelve simultaneously while JK himself was away on an extended holiday.

Jac Holzman founded Elektra Records and signed megastars Queen, the Doors, the Cars and dozens of equally successful acts. His influence still reverberates through-out the music world, but he began by recording his friend Theo Bikel on a domestic recorder and bicycled across Europe setting up a distribution network.

When Herb Alpert and Jerry Moss started A&M Records, they sold their wares out of a Volkswagen, and Berry Gordy created Tamla Motown by selling records door to door. It just happened that two of the early doors he called on housed the Temptations and the Supremes. At least he never had to deal with failure, as did the Ertegun brothers who, between them, had several dud ventures before hitting pay dirt with Atlantic Records.

Closer to home, even the ubiquitous Mr Branson launched Virgin Records initially as a cut price mail-order operation that had great difficulty paying its bills. Steve Mason bought a bankrupt company called Pinnacle, turned it into the leading independent record distributor and became a multi-millionaire in the process. Steve is proud to speak of his beginnings as a bouncer at the Greyhound in Croydon and has not lost the common touch despite his mansions and fleet of expensive cars.

The great broadcaster John Peel, with whom I have been associated for over thirty years, left school with just four O-levels and went to America to seek his fortune, where he became, in turn, a computer programmer and storm-insurance salesman.

This writer was expelled from school with too few qualifications and the head-master's prediction that I would end up working in an amusement arcade. He was right. I ended up working in the world's largest amusement arcade – the one known as the music biz. It has given me an exhilarating life and bought me homes and property on both sides of the Atlantic.

It's true. Anybody can do it. Two of my children, Bee and Chet, worked for me briefly in the eighties then left to set up their own record operation. With no financial assistance – and just the increasingly rare word of advice from me – they now employ a couple of dozen staff and have a turnover of millions.

This is not a 'how to' book. The business of music changes so rapidly that even if it were possible to write such a book it would be out of date before it appeared in print, but it is to be hoped that this modest tome will serve as a guide to some of the oppor-tunities and pitfalls that await the determined but inexperienced entrepreneur.

The music business is wide open; more so now than at any time. It may not be easy, but this working-class lad achieved just about all he ever wanted to in a career that has included international travel, working closely with world-famous stars, helping to shape musical tastes, making a lot of money and, most importantly, having a whole lot of fun.

Trust me. There's still plenty of room at the top.

1. YOU TOO?

YOU TOO?

Let's face it, for the majority of the population life can be pretty boring. Apart from those fortunate few prancing about in the 'meeja', life is a dreary progress from cradle to grave, punctuated by the odd holiday, affair or minor achievement. It's no wonder that so many get out of their heads on drink or drugs or look wistfully at the antics of people in show business who apparently lead a glamorous life of adulation, achievement, parties and luxury travel. And they do!

Having worked with many of the world's top entertainers I can tell you that at the top of the heap life can be wonderful. Naturally, almost none of them sees it like that. They see it as just deserts for their monumental talent. It is a constant struggle to remain at the top, which involves fights with all the people who aided their progress: the record company, which still expects to make a profit; the manager, who tries to retain a home life; the promoter, who hopes to stay in business; the publisher, late with royalties from far-flung places; the tour manager; the publicist; the producer; the video director; every member of the band; the accountants; the lawyers; and, of course, the taxman.

It sure is tough at the top, but it's a thousand per cent tougher for thousands of hopefuls with a toehold on the bottom rung and even tougher still for the millions of hopefuls who can only dream.

Actually getting into the music business as a performer has become relatively easy over the past few years and even easier yet with the arrival of the internet, though it remains to be seen if this route can provide the rewards. Even achieving a modest degree of success is now possible for anybody with a hint of talent, a few hundred pounds and the determination to succeed against all odds. If you don't already know, I'll lay out a few ground rules as we go. It's a lot cheaper than a drug habit or even spending your leisure hours in a pub or taking exotic holidays – and you never know!

Getting started in the administrative side of music is rather more difficult but still possible for anybody reasonably intelligent, presentable, prepared to start at the bottom and claw their way viciously up the corporate ladder.

I was fortunate enough to get an early foot in the door and go on to work with some of the most creative, inspirational, stimulating, weird, ruthless, amusing and infuriating people outside of a novel. Stay with me and you'll meet some of them. All too many, unfortunately, are dead, but that, too, is part of the glamour of the music biz. Jimi, Janis, Jim and John went to early graves simply because of who they were and how they lived. Like Marilyn and James Dean, they had to go, and, for that reason alone, they will always be with us.

Every year tens of thousands of young people leave schools, colleges and universities all over the world trained as academics, scientists, computer programmers or whatever and sharing a burning ambition to get into the music business. Why? It may be that they know, or at least sense, that the music business offers virtually unlimited opportunities to do your own thing and, for the successful few, it can be an exhilarating life in which creativity can combine with commercial ability to produce fulfilment, riches, excitement, glamour, travel and even a place in history. It can also guarantee early burn-out, life without sleep, massive disappointments and, all too often, a dependence on drugs or liquor.

The artists probably have the toughest task. With over a hundred records released every week, only one or two achieve any measure of success. For the others it usually means the end of the road. A road that involved years of trekking around the country, packed into smelly, unreliable vans, turning up and laying out your heart for people who neither know nor care, walking off stage to the sound of your own footsteps and then packing up the equipment for yet another drive to yet another town where, with luck, you might be paid enough to cover the cost of your petrol. For every overnight sensation there are thousands of crushed former hopefuls. It's hardly surprising that a high proportion of those precious few who eventually make it indulge in the kind of excesses that so often lead to a swift return to obscurity and poverty.

Some good friends of mine began their professional careers in a group called Band of Joy, whose line-up in those early days included two members who later went on to form Led Zeppelin. The original group split up, and the two who went on to form Zep earned millions, with adoring fans throughout the world. My chums formed another band, signed a recording contract and were taken to America where, halfway through a tour, they were dumped, penniless. They tried to continue playing, but with no backing, money or American reputation they ended up living for weeks on a daily handful of dry porridge oats and a glass of water. They were eventually forced to sell their instruments to raise the cash for the return fare. Are they bitter? Not really. It takes a special kind of madness even to start down that road – but to have come so close! It's never – repeat – never simply a question of talent. To achieve any success as a performer requires dedication, a huge amount of luck, excellent timing and, almost invariably, the commitment of a responsible and knowledgeable manager. The support and deep pockets of an aggressive and well-staffed record company helps. Without all that backing the talent is just a curse.

And what of those who make it to the top before disappearing almost immediately back into unfulfilled obscurity? Those one-hit wonders who have to go back to operating a lathe or stacking supermarket shelves. Those few months of fame and seeming prosperity are very seductive. Launching Strange Fruit Records brought me into contact with literally hundreds of musicians and artists who'd had a taste of fame but, for whatever reason, found it impossible to sustain. Character, luck, judgement or simply an unwillingness to continue to grow all played their part.

Clifford T. Ward and Sting were both schoolteachers with a talent for writing and performing wonderful songs. Cliff refused to tour and just wanted to stay home and write. Sting took his talents around the world, honing his craft, first with the Police and later as a solo act. Sting is a fantastically wealthy man, who can afford to 'mislay' the odd few million, while Cliff, before his death in 2001, lived on a fast-diminishing income of royalties from over a quarter of a century ago and battled daily with a wasting disease. In terms of pure talent it is too close to call, but in terms of character the answer is clear.

At a sales conference in Ontario I had a conversation with a young man on the brink of making a fresh start. He had enjoyed enormous success with a song called 'Mister Piano Man', about which he complained he had not received the rewards he felt he was due. Rather than sitting back bemoaning his fate and the fickleness of the public, he was back on the trail with all guns blazing – albeit as an unheralded addition to an entertainment menu featuring Paul Simon, who was himself launching his second solo career. That was several million albums and singles ago for Paul but also for Billy Joel, for it was he, and they both continue to flourish and entertain.

2. ALL I EVER WANTED TO BE WAS THE SINGER IN THE BAND

– I STILL DO

CS THE CROONER

ALL I EVER WANTED TO BE . . .

Even after four decades in the music business, working at the highest levels, selling millions of records and dealing at close quarters with superstars, there is nothing to compare with the sheer joy and elation of performing in public.

The early days at primary school were promising. I had a good voice and, while evacuated to Reading during the Second World War, sang solo with the school orchestra and even broadcast on the BBC Home Service. Returning to London during the Blitz I was forced to entertain relatives with my soprano rendition of 'The Minstrel Boy' to my huge embarrassment. Eventually a posse of experts arrived at the school to assess my potential. Can you imagine a small, scruffy ten-year-old boy singing unaccompanied to a group of middle-aged experts? They concluded that I tried too hard and should have performed in a more relaxed fashion. The story of my life.

The Blitz must have been hell for adults, but kids quickly adapt to almost anything. We played in the streets while the dreaded doodle-bugs zoomed overhead, pausing only when the engines stopped to dash through quickly opened front doors to the comparative safety of the Anderson Shelters buried in the backyards. As soon as the explosion came we would resume our street games, unless, of course, the explosion had been very close, in which case we would go along to investigate the carnage. Occasionally a second bomb would land only minutes later on the same spot in an effort to kill off or maim the rescue services. That caused a few narrow escapes.

Sailing through the eleven-plus exam I was awarded a scholarship to Christ's Hospital School, which was, so I believe, one of the best in the country. Unfortunately it was for boarders and required the wearing of a very strange uniform consisting of breeches and white stockings. This was obviously out of the question for a working-class lad, so I applied to, and was accepted by, another very good school. Latymer Upper School had very high standards and a magnificent record for sending students to Oxford and Cambridge. The entrance exam was not a problem but, on arrival at the school, I was the proverbial fish out of water and very much intimidated by the upper-class accents and smart clothes of the other boys, many of whom had already spent a couple of years there as fee-payers.

Knowing nothing of Latin or even proper English grammar – so no change there – I quickly sank from being a star entrant to languishing at the back of the D form. The staff were a motley crew. One master in particular, a badly disfigured war veteran with a tin leg, soon got our attention by leaping up on to the front desk and proceeding to march around the classroom on our desktops giving each pupil a smart crack around the ear with his swagger stick. Today he would probably be arrested. Another master loathed me with a passion and, having spotted me flicking a chum with my soft rubber book strap, beat me with it in front of the class until he was soaked in perspiration and was forced to remove his jacket and tie. In fact it didn't hurt at all, but he was not to know that, and it must have been a dreadful thing to watch. The Divinity master carried a collection of several canes, each of which he named and, upon being chosen for punishment, we were expected to select a cane by name. God moves in mysterious ways. The French master administered punishment with the sharp edge of a large ruler on the back of the culprit's hand. Boy, that still smarts. The headmaster enjoyed fondling small boys in short trousers and, if sent to his room for detention, he would insist that they stood on their heads. One quickly learned to avoid such situations.

My poor father attended countless meetings at the request of the various masters and must have wondered why he ever bothered. I don't recall the precise reason for my eventual expulsion, but it had something to do with smoking and a couple of ladies occupying a houseboat on the nearby Thames. I didn't inform my parents and left home at the usual time, spending the days catching up on schoolwork in the local library. I did manage four O-levels, which was rather more than I deserved, and the headmaster predicted that I would end up 'working in an amusement arcade' – which turned out to be a pretty good guess.

Leaving school with no money and few prospects, I was determined to be a singer and took a job at the Eldorado Ice Cream factory to earn enough to buy some clothes. It was a truly dreadful job, which entailed standing in several inches of hot, greasy water and lifting hundred-pound tins of lard from floor level to shoulder height all day and every day. The tins were ripped open by hand with a triangle of steel that left a sharp and jagged edge, which we gripped with a wet cloth to heave upwards. The trick was to try to keep your footing on the greasy floor, but I managed to spill plenty of blood and saw the occasional finger severed and dropped into the steaming cauldrons, which were only shut down at the end of the day. Before leaving at the end of the shift we were expected to climb into the vats to clean them out. A favourite game for the old hands was to wait until one of the new boys had dropped into one of the eight-foot-high stainless-steel cookers before turning the heating back on and removing the ladder. Our screams as we burned fingers on the scalding metal provided much merriment. Workers of the world, unite.

I also spent several weeks working with my father as a fitter's mate. At the time he was employed on a school site in Ruislip, which involved a journey of two bus rides and several stops on the Underground to arrive at eight in the morning. The work was relatively well paid but arduous. On one occasion we worked right through a complete weekend, without any sleep, stripping out the school heating system, which was, of course, packed with asbestos. No masks or protection were offered, but it was a lot of welcome overtime. On another occasion we were required to carry a bundle of lengths of copper tubing across the site: my father took the front end, hoisting it up on his shoulder, and I did likewise several yards behind. Copper tubing is very whippy and, pausing to light a cigarette, I dropped my end to the ground causing the tubing to vibrate at high speed, so almost decapitating my poor father. He murmured a few appreciative comments.

Another example of the unity of the workers occurred when we finished the job and returned to the factory where I was immediately banned by the union as a non-member. I offered to join the union but was refused and was effectively thrown out of the job by my workmates. It didn't matter to me – but suppose I had needed the work?

I applied to join the Merchant Navy but blew it at the first interview when ordered to stand to attention. If it was like that even before joining I had no chance. There followed a series of silly jobs such as working in a plant contractor's office and even as a clerk in a firm of solicitors, where I manned the switchboard and accidentally disconnected all the conversations, which resulted in an early dismissal. There was never any thought in my mind of a career other than as a singer, but meanwhile I was expected to earn my keep, and dole was non-existent if you refused any of the totally unsuitable jobs that were offered at the Labour Exchange.

It was still a great time to be young and single, however. I managed to get the odd job singing in pubs and attended all too many disastrous auditions. The weekends were spent at all-night parties. At one of these it snowed heavily, which prompted one of my chums to walk out of the house and about two miles up to Putney Common on his hands through the virgin snow just to leave tracks to confuse any early risers. He was a few years older than me and seemed very dashing and sophisticated. Sadly, he ended up doing time for indecent exposure. Perhaps a clue was, when leaving the house, he would ask his dear old mum to 'knit him some French letters'. I never thought my mum knew what they were until I arose one morning to find the contents of a packet that I had left in a shirt pocket laid out on the kitchen table. The matter was never referred to.

The mother of another pal owned and ran a very smart coffee bar close to the London Coliseum, which was frequented by actors and chorus boys. We were forbidden to visit but, of course, did when she was not there. One play at the theatre was *Mister Roberts* starring the screen legend Tyrone Power. The gossip was that the star was making such a nuisance of himself with the chorus boys that they were sabotaging the show. This seemed entirely possible when the gentleman came on to me in the coffee bar and I was forced to flee with one of my early heroes in hot pursuit. Another customer was Diana Dors, who would arrive in the company of a grotesque dwarf whom she would lift up on to the counter before engaging in bawdy banter with the other customers. Pretty dangerous and heady stuff for a teenager. That reminds me that I also managed the odd day as a film extra on a Diana Dors picture. It was excruciatingly boring just standing around for hours, but the money was good.

My cousin was engaged to an American sailor whom she subsequently married. He was a very nice man, but I abused his friendship on all too many occasions by breaking into his London flat and stealing his cigarettes and liquor. In fact I became addicted to Southern Comfort and in my early teens was knocking back a couple of bottles a week. At the US forces' shop, the PX, that liquor cost the dollar equivalent of five bob (25p) a bottle and Lucky Strikes were about a shilling a pack! By late teens I was perilously close to becoming an alcoholic but was saved when my sister introduced me to her Sikh boyfriend, who claimed never to be affected by drink in any quantity. I took up the challenge one evening, after a visit to the theatre, and between us we cleared a cabinet full of assorted booze. He drove us home, but I was paralytically drunk for three days. I was working in the shoe department of Selfridges at the time and somehow managed to stagger into work before collapsing into a heap, whereupon the staff assumed that I was suffering from some dread illness and sent me home in a taxi. It was ten years before I could drink even a half-pint of shandy, which probably saved my liver and possibly my life.

When I was thirteen or fourteen years old I met my first wife, Patricia, with whom I went steady until she became pregnant at the age of eighteen. In those times marriage was automatic, and we were married the day before I was due to travel to Scotland to take up a position as a Butlin's redcoat entertainer. I was married in a borrowed suit, and the honeymoon was a miserable night in a London hotel. We were just a couple of silly kids who somehow managed to produce and raise three wonderful, happy and successful children. With barely a thought for the overwhelming responsibilities of marriage, I set off for Butlin's in Ayr and my first regular engagement as a professional entertainer.

3. BUTLIN'S

BUTLIN'S

Anyone who did time at a Butlin's holiday camp, either as a camper or on the staff, will know that the sitcom *Hi-de-Hi* on BBC television got it exactly right. It was still an age of innocence in the mid-fifties when I was hired on as a redcoat for the princely wage of £8 a week all in. Believe it or not, this was an opportunity to save a considerable sum of money, and I jumped at it.

I set off for Ayr full of hope that I might follow the paths of other redcoats who had gone on to greater things – after all, my immediate predecessor in Ayr had been Des O'Connor. Upon arrival at the camp in the pouring rain my first glamorous task was to knock holes in the tennis courts with a hammer and a large nail to allow them to drain. I was allocated a chalet to be shared with a grumpy old traditional North-Country comic, exactly as played by Paul Shane in the television sitcom.

Some of the other redcoats were old hands who treated it as a summer season between pantomime and idleness, but I quickly made friends with Jackie, a small but colourful character who had been an amateur British boxing champion, a commando during the war and was now making a stab at becoming an entertainer. Unfortunately, he was intermittently mad and, since he hated kids, was immediately dubbed 'Uncle Jackie' and put in charge of keeping the children entertained. One of the weekly rituals was the children's treasure hunt in which Jackie, in a variety of disguises, cycled around the campsite collecting a train of youngsters who would pursue him to the point where he would ride his bicycle off the top diving board and into the pool. The spectacle was captured on film and shown to the parents in the theatre at the end of the week. Imagine the gasps of horror and outrage when the film showed Jackie kicking out at the kids and smiting them with his bicycle pump as they pursued him. Fortunately there was no sound or my chum may have been lynched. He was quickly given another title and different duties – one of which was to beat the stuffing out of any drunks who became too troublesome. One of my enduring memories is of Jackie donning black leather gloves and escorting a drunken lout to his chalet where, it was said, the troublemakers often literally climbed the wall to escape his attentions. They were then thrown off the camp with their belongings chucked after them. Rough justice – but it worked.

Though it is fashionable to believe that anti-social behaviour by youngsters is a recent phenomenon, it was rife – if less organized – in the fifties. The dread period at Butlin's was when the 'wakes weeks', or holiday periods, of both Glasgow and Newcastle coincided and the camp became a battleground for the two warring factions. Minor skirmishes developed as the week progressed, culminating in a pitched battle in the ballroom when the bars emptied. The participants were left to it and locked in for the rest of the night. In the morning the ballroom doors were opened to a scene of absolute devastation, with smashed mirrors and floors liberally sprinkled with blood. Those who could still walk were escorted out of the camp by burly security men; those who could not were literally thrown over the camp fence, followed by their belongings, and left to make their own medical and travel arrangements. Summary justice again, but I understand that for most of the combatants it was a cherished annual event.

The security guards were formidable and dressed in quasi-military uniforms. They were ostensibly employed to keep gatecrashers out, but many of the 'Happy Campers' believed them to be guards to keep them on the site and would occasionally offer them bribes to help them escape. We would dream up escape routes that entailed the camper crawling face down across waste ground to tunnel under the perimeter fence. A number of campers eagerly adopted this route just to do a little shopping in the local town – or perhaps it was to escape the organized physical jerks that took place every morning. And for these pleasures they were paying the equivalent of a month's wages.

Another Jackie escapade was 'Penny-on-the-Drum'. Each night the redcoats would parade around the camp at bar-closing time singing and chanting to the accompaniment of a big bass drum. Oddly enough, it worked, and the booze-sodden campers would follow the parade into the ballroom where they would be encouraged to perform various silly and energetic activities in order to sweat out the alcohol and belligerence before retiring to bed. On one infamous night Jackie persuaded all the drunken miners into the centre of the ballroom with their wives and girlfriends lining the perimeter. Following a series of loony exercises such as getting them to hop around like rabbits or kangaroos and climb on one another's backs, he persuaded them to remove their heavy boots and hurl them at their loved ones! Stupid and drunk they may have been, but all too many were very good shots and there were some nasty casualties resulting in another change of duties and job title for my friend.

Jackie had a beautiful wife who worked elsewhere, but, like so many in the entertainment business, he regularly fell in love with another woman. When things got desperate he would call his wife, who would arrive the following day and cradle him in her arms murmuring, 'Ah, has my Jackie fallen in love again? Never mind.' A couple of hours of this and she would depart, leaving a few pairs of fresh drawers which they apparently shared. Jackie went on to become a huge hit on Australian television, which is probably about right. He was a great comic, and together we performed a double act which was very well received – often to the extent that members of the audience actually wet their pants with laughter. I would be on stage singing when Jackie would interrupt, saying that I was not delivering sufficient emotion. He would then demonstrate what was required, which somehow entailed me ripping off his shirt and covering him with an assortment of eggs and flour. It sounds awful but in the hands of a master it worked.

The food at the camp was spectacularly awful, and on a number of occasions campers and staff went down with food poisoning. Any staff who did not make it into work were docked wages and warned to be more responsible. Many of the workers rebelled and threatened to strike. The response of the management was to inform them that, in the face of strike action, staff from other camps would be flown in to replace the dissidents within twenty-four hours. I have a hunch that Billy Butlin and Margaret Thatcher would have got on famously.

At the start of the season the entertainment manager, 'Knocker' White, gathered all the redcoats together to warn of the dangers of over-participation in the very available sexual opportunities. On purely business terms it was pointed out that any over-indulgence leading to a fall in work rate would incur instant dismissal. We were, after all, a collection of healthy and presumably attractive young people and, as I discovered, the campers tended to leave all moral restrictions behind as they entered the gates. To my astonishment, the first wave of arrivals on the first day surrounded the redcoats and begged to be allowed to perform personal chores such as washing shirts and underclothes. I had been advised that this was code for sexual liaisons and, like my colleagues, chose only the prettiest girls to grant these privileges. As the season went on one became even more selective by doling out socks to this young lady, shirts to another and underwear to a third or fourth. In general the redcoats were reasonably discreet – aided by the fact that, as I discovered, a major function of the security staff was to patrol the camp at night, paying particular attention to the redcoat chalets, where a powerful torch beam would often pick out an energetic backside or two. On several occasions the male redcoats enjoyed the favours of both mother and daughter singly or together. I often wondered if the women concerned discussed the experience with each other when they got home.

As the singer with the band, the opportunities open to me were considerably more than I could handle and, given my recent marriage, I took some time to adjust to this new-found freedom. Any activities of mine, however, paled into celibate insignificance compared to those of the camp football coach, who almost literally shagged himself to death. At the conclusion of a night on the bandstand he invited me along to meet a couple of his 'friends' who were waiting in their chalet. Having no other plans, I joined him and we visited two attractive young women, had our wicked ways with them and left without, as far as I can recall, even being introduced. The whole episode took no more than fifteen minutes, whereupon my footballing friend suggested we make a further visit to another two receptive females. I demurred but suggested that I wait outside while he concluded another romantic episode. Sure enough, about fifteen minutes later he emerged and suggested yet another liaison, whereupon I left him to it, marvelling at his stamina if not his style. Within a month he could barely walk, let alone coach football. After five weeks he could barely see, and it became a morning ritual to awaken him, carry him up to the barber shop and pack ice on to his eyes until he could open them. He was one of the first casualties of the morality code, and I never discovered whether he ever returned to professional football where he had been a star player with one of the leading Scottish clubs.

Affairs between the redcoats were rare, and I never knew of any. If the male reds were in demand with guests you can imagine how the glamorous girl redcoats were pursued, courted and showered with gifts. They simply had no time for romantic attachments with staff – though it was rumoured that the Radio Butlin announcer had a bit of a thing going on with the entertainment manager. The real beauty on the site was a former Butlin's Holiday Princess, Aileen, a truly stunning girl who was required to parade around in a swimsuit and arrange the beauty competitions. Aileen had to fend off suitors with a stick, and the truly persistent were told that she and I were a couple – on the grounds, I guess, that it would be difficult to compete for favours with the singer in the band. We were in fact only mates, with never anything more between us than mutual friendship. It worked for Aileen and made me look good. All that changed, however, when my new wife came to stay. I will never figure out the female mind. On the second night of my wife's visit Aileen came calling at around midnight, ostensibly for a cup of tea since mine was the only chalet boasting tea-making facilities. In fact the facilities consisted of an electric ring balanced on top of a wardrobe, and it could be operated only from a standing position on the bed, but its presence had created a popular late-night meeting-place for the musicians and entertainers. On that night Aileen wore a raincoat and it became apparent that beneath it she was nude. A somewhat strained conversation ensued, and after Aileen left my wife quizzed me about the relationship. Despite my protestations of total fidelity to her she had obviously heard the rumours and made a connection. The chalet had single beds, and I eventually went to sleep to be awakened hours later by the sound of a bread-knife swishing through the air towards my heart. Fortunately I was able to dodge the blade but never able to establish my innocence.

Another sexual non-event occurred when I took a very attractive young Irish girl for a walk along the beach. We lay down for a while, but she complained that the sand was troublesome and suggested that we go back to my chalet. Lying together on the bed in the darkness, she became concerned that her blouse was becoming creased and 'would I think badly' of her if she took it off? Being a gentleman, how could I refuse? She following this by worrying that her skirt, too, was becoming rumpled and would I mind terribly helping her off with it. And that was it. Nothing further occurred despite my mumbled entreaties and blandishments. After about an hour of wrestling and muttering, the North-Country comic, who was occupying the other single bed, roared out of the gloom, 'Either fuck or fuck off. I need some sleep.' Very romantic. The surprising thing was that a day or two later one of the other redcoats told me that he had enjoyed a very satisfying night with the young lady marred only by the fact that in the heat of passion she had insisted on calling out my name. I've never worked that out.

The most potentially dangerous situation occurred following a night spent with a red-headed Scottish girl who insisted on biting my tongue after each climax. It was quite painful and eventually my face was covered in blood, my tongue was swollen and I was virtually unable to speak, let alone sing. Despite the fact that it obviously worked as a stimulant I do not recommend it. Masochism was never my thing, and I spent the next few days hiding out in the shower and generally trying to avoid her. Not very gallant, I know, but I was only eighteen. Imagine my horror when, shortly after my wife arrived, I saw the two of them deep in conversation while I was on the bandstand. That night I sang everything in the book in an effort to avoid the impending confrontation. In fact nothing was said, and for that I'll always be indebted to the lady to whom I behaved so badly.

For those not engaged in sexual exploits, fighting, trying to escape or avoiding food poisoning, there was bingo and professional wrestling. Some of the older hands among the redcoats managed to supplement their meagre wages by fiddling the bingo proceeds, but I was fascinated by the entertainment prospect and teased the audiences with long-drawn-out calling of the numbers in a way that could drive some of the dedicated players into a frenzy.

The bingo calling took place in the ring where, once a week, a troupe of professional wrestlers entertained. It was all fairly well choreographed but nevertheless a very tough business. Towards the end of the evening things would get somewhat out of hand and I would be called on to enter the ring and separate the combatants. This inevitably resulted in me being picked up and hurled out of the ring into the laps of the delighted ringsiders. Choreographed it may have been but, trust me, it still hurt like hell.

For reasons that I am quite unable to recall we were visited by one of the original screen cowboys, Bill Boyd, who played the hero Hopalong Cassidy to the delight of countless young customers of Saturday-morning pictures. To encourage campers to enjoy evenings free of the worries of parenthood, it was Butlin's policy to monitor the chalets in the evenings listening for crying babies. The parents would then be informed over the PA and make appropriate arrangements. Over dinner one evening, following the usual announcement, Hopalong suggested that he make the trip to the youngster concerned. It is hard to imagine the experience for the children of being greeted in the middle of the night by the famous cowboy in full Western kit. The next day, at a civic ceremony on the steps of the Town Hall, the silver-haired star was presented with the keys to the city by the Provost of Glasgow in ceremonial regalia complete with gold chains. Hoppy thanked him kindly and in return presented the Provost with a tin Hoppy button.

The very best times for me were the hours spent in the theatre after the show, singing with a few of the musicians who shared my enthusiasm for jazz. I was having fun, but it couldn't last. My wife hated the place and, after just a few weeks, insisted that we leave less than halfway through the season. She was, after all, still very young, pregnant and unable to eat any of the food or join in the physical activities. It was for me a time of wonderful freedom and self-expression without even the responsibility of providing food and shelter – probably the last such period in my life. I recommend it to any young man and in fact encouraged my eldest son Brod to do a season at Butlin's. He has never disclosed any of the details, and I think I know why.

4. STRUGGLING

STRUGGLING

Back in London with no job, nowhere to live and a pregnant young wife to support, the future looked bleak indeed. My new brother-in-law offered to rent us a couple of rooms in his house and fixed me up with a job as lampshade cleaner at the Cumberland Hotel where he worked as an electrician. The job, for the most part, entailed finding somewhere quiet to hide and sleep, though occasionally we would venture out to change the odd lightbulb.

One of the many places we found to snooze was on the parapet that ran around the roof of the hotel. This was a ledge about one yard wide, approximately two hundred feet above the traffic of Marble Arch, where we would sleep for hours with nothing but the occasional floodlight between certain death and us. These days I get dizzy standing on a brick. One of our little gang was a young Irishman, who, after settling his debts every payday, spent what was left of his wages in the pub. He would return to the hotel in a drunken stupor, which often prompted him to tiptoe around the parapet with his back to the traffic and his heels out in space. There were more than a few startled guests surprised by the sudden appearance of a young man outside their window, several storeys above the traffic and seemingly about to fall backwards, but they probably dismissed it as an illusion. He eventually emigrated to Australia to pursue a career as a cowboy.

The time at the Cumberland was useful to me because the hotel is not far from Denmark Street, where most of the music publishers were located, and within walking distance of Archer Street, where musicians met to be hired. Here I picked up the occasional job and got to meet Sid Green, who was one of the great publishing fixers. Around the wall of his office were dozens of pictures of him with music greats such as Nat Cole and Sinatra. I was in awe and determined that one day I, too, would have such a collection. Years later I did, but I never displayed them and they seem to have got lost somewhere along the line. Sid arranged for me to take classical singing lessons and arranged an appearance on *In Town Tonight* on BBC radio, where I was supposed to be a visiting Australian singer. For Sid this was just another way to get radio exposure for 'Stowaway', the song he was currently working. It was eventually a hit, due in no small way to his efforts, and is an illustration of the lengths it was then necessary to go to in order to get exposure for a song. I knew nothing of this and anyway failed to capitalize on the opportunity.

Shortly after my son Brod was born I was sacked from the hotel but managed to get employment in a radio and television shop in Richmond. With another mouth to feed and no money for bus fares, I walked several miles each way to work and rationed myself to five hand-rolled fags a day and an apple for lunch. We were so poor that we could not even afford milk for cups of tea and had to make do with the free powdered milk that was available for the baby. My dear mother made several mercy trips bringing bags of food, which she would leave on the doorstep.

I was still desperate to earn a living as a singer and managed to get a residency with the house band at the Richmond Hotel at weekends and the occasional gig at the Bull in Sheen, both of which places featured prominently in the early career of the Rolling Stones a few years later. They, however, went on to glory. A possible break occurred when I auditioned for a new record company and was offered the chance to record a cover of the Everly Brothers' US hit 'Bye Bye Love'. This was a brand new sound at the time and very strange to someone steeped in Chet Baker, Sinatra, Peggy Lee and Lena Horne. I nevertheless persevered, learned the lyrics and turned up at the studio to be faced with the complete Geraldo Orchestra. That alone gives an indication of how misunderstood was this new music from America. I was uncertain and terrified. To make matters worse, a group of portly middle-aged men arrived in matching blazers to be my backing group. They were the hugely professional Peter Knight Singers. The leader handed them music scores and blew on a pitch pipe whereupon they burst into a perfect rendition of the song I had taken two weeks to learn. I was devastated and squeaked alarmingly while the orchestra stared up at the vocal booth in disbelief and the backing group shuffled their feet. I took to my heels and fled, but not before Geraldo most kindly tried to reassure me that he, too, had been nervous on his first recording. A true gentleman.

Life back at the shop in Richmond began to improve and, though I was expected to sweep up and clean the equipment, I began to make some extra money by foisting sets with high commission values on unsuspecting customers; more money in fact than the store manager was making, which gave him some cause for concern. Also at the store was Reg Smoothey, who was the brother of half of one of the great comedy double acts of a few years before, Lowe and Ladd. Reg had some of their old scripts, and together we performed them at different venues to considerable acclaim. They were truly terrible, but audiences seemed to like the act, a fact which mystified me, and I soon tired of it.

The rooms above the shop were let to a photographer who appeared to specialize in pictures of young men in gladiatorial poses. I got to know him quite well before he was arrested. It seemed that his main source of income was from blackmail. At that time homosexuality was still illegal, and he distributed thinly disguised magazines by mail order, which included an offer to supply photographs posed to customer's requests. When he received the more outrageous requests he blackmailed the customer with threats of exposure. This may seem abhorrent behaviour, but some of the letters he received were truly disgusting. The one that particularly sticks in my mind was from a bishop, written on official paper, requesting pictures of choir boys being lashed upon bloody buttocks with explicit detail of the pain and horror on their faces. Who was the sinner?

An earlier job as door-to-door salesman for the Kleen-E-Zee Brush Company had offered some insight into this strange world. Selling things door to door is a tough, precarious business and not one at which I showed any promise, though it did allow the freedom to attend those damned auditions even if it didn't pay the rent. I managed to make a rare sale to an apparently single man in Barnes and celebrated with a bit of sunbathing on the local common, where I was surprised to meet the customer again.

He asked if he might join me and confided that he was a part-time professional wrestler and would I like to arm-wrestle him? Murmuring that it was too hot for such activities, I began to collect up my samples and clothes, whereupon he confessed that our meeting was not an accident. It appeared that he had friends in high places who were more than happy to pay for the company of young men, and one very well-known band leader would supply an apartment and a sports car of my choice just for the privilege of a weekly visit. I was thankful to be in a long-term relationship and declined the offer – but if I hadn't? He then went on to tell me of another of his clients, who had recently returned from a trip to Austria where he had been beaten and tortured to within an inch of his life, including a spell locked in an Iron Maiden. Though close to death, he had enjoyed the experience so much that he was anxious to return as soon as his health improved, and would I care to join him as his chauffeur?

Another part-time job was selling vacuum cleaners to people who had responded to advertisements for cleaners offered at less than £5. It was known as 'switch selling', and the trick was to demonstrate that the cheap job was secondhand and useless and switch the customer to a £30 model. A lot of money in commission could be made but not, it would appear, by yours truly. My father thought this looked like an easy route to riches and demanded to be allowed to accompany me on a sales demonstration. We arrived at a rather grand house by appointment and my dad went through the routine of emptying rubbish on to the carpets prior to demonstrating how much better was the more expensive model than the advertised bargain. You can probably guess the rest. The cheap job blew up, fused all of the lights and we fled in panic leaving the occupants to clear up in darkness. Dad never forgave me and firmly believed that I had deliberately set him up.

Training for that job consisted of accompanying the sales manager on a couple of sales demonstrations and learning from him. He had remarkable ability and never failed to make a sale. When the time came for the customer to stump up the money, if the husband demurred he would ask what the man did for a living and point out that he needed tools for his job and surely his wife was not to be denied the tools needed for hers. It never failed. When I asked a customer what he did for a living I was told to mind my own fucking business.

Earning more money from commission than the shop manager in Richmond failed to endear me to him or his wife the cashier, and it was time to move on. I accepted a job in Wimbledon at a shop that sold radios and televisions but also stocked records. My father was horrified by the move and suggested that, at £8 per week, I was probably biting off more than I could chew. There's a confidence-builder. It was only a small record department, but it opened up a whole new world to me. This was still a time of shellac 78s, and I remember when I first heard about the new 45s that were soon to become popular.

My assistant took an order for a record by somebody called Annabella Fantez, which didn't appear in any catalogue, but eventually I tracked it down as 'Mary's Boy Child' by Harry Belafonte, which has become one of the all time best-sellers and is still heard every Christmas. A small event but the start of a lifelong love affair.

Occasionally salesmen would visit us from the record companies, and they seemed to me to have one of the most glamorous jobs in the world. I determined that if I could not make a career of singing then this would be the next best thing. And it was.

Learning that the salesman from Vogue Records was leaving, I applied for and got his job. I was ecstatic. The position carried a decent salary and expenses, a van that I could have for personal use and a supply of the latest records. The down side was that my territory excluded London but covered the rest of the country as far north as Manchester, which meant that I would need to spend four nights a week away from home. Vogue Records was owned by Decca Records and was essentially a wholesaler of various catalogues including London American, Coral, Brunswick and a wonderful collection of jazz labels such as Contemporary and Blue Note. The job was a snap. I travelled the country averaging a thousand miles a week and, since the previous incumbent had been a lazy bugger, managed to treble the business. It was a cinch. All I needed was a case full of record sleeves with a few samples of the latest releases and I was welcomed in hundreds of shops that had never seen a record-company rep.

On Saturday mornings I was required to spend time in the office submitting expenses, sales reports and collecting new-release information. It was here that I began to meet some of the oddballs who populate the music biz. The general manager was a Labour councillor and a Catholic, who chased all the girls in the office to their considerable discomfort. The managing director, who worked from Decca and appeared only on Saturdays, was an apoplectic Protestant with a lousy temper. They hated each other and would rant and shout to the obvious amusement of the staff. The director addressed the manager as an idol-worshipping bastard and was in turn referred to as a buttoned-up shit. Somehow they managed to survive each other.

The records were racked in blocks of tall shelves, and the copies for the shops were picked to order. One Saturday, while perambulating through the racks, I encountered a beautiful black girl whom I had long fancied but had never approached. Seizing the opportunity, I made a flirtatious remark whereupon, with a low animal growl, she thrust me up against one of the racks and stuck her tongue several inches down my throat. I was, to say the least, a trifle disconcerted and, in true tabloid fashion, made my excuses and left somewhat hurriedly. I felt less of a fool a few weeks later when I learned that the young woman concerned had been dismissed for having it off in the back of a van with four warehousemen on their way to the factory.

As a healthy young man working in one of the glamour industries and on the road four nights a week, however, I have to confess that I was not indifferent to the many sexual opportunities that arose. It didn't always work out, though, and once, at a boarding house in which I stayed in Coventry, I invited the daughter of the landlady out for a drink only to discover that she was banned in every pub in the city. I also made many good friends and within a year or so was promoted to the London area, but not before I crashed and wrote off the little company van by turning it over three times on an icy road. It was difficult to believe that I had escaped without even a bruise, and on the way to hospital for a check-up I asked the ambulance driver to stop by the wreck, convinced that I had crossed the threshold and would see my crushed body still in place. What was extraordinary was the number of people who had suddenly gathered to peer at the carnage in the middle of the deserted Salisbury Plain.

The London area was a whole new ball game with new opportunities. Some of the major shops could order in thousands, and those that supplied the jukebox trade would order many thousands of copies of sure fire hits such as a new Presley. I recall helping Joanna Smith open the first W.H. Smith record department, unaware that this would begin the slow decline of the specialist record shop. In those days record shops were run, in the main, by experienced and knowledgeable staff who memorized labels and catalogue numbers; if they didn't have the record you wanted they could find it for you. There were over five thousand such stores across the nation, but now there are less than a thousand. Still, this is no different, I suppose, to the demise of the small grocer or fishmonger – and we are all guilty of patronizing supermarkets.

By this time I was on first-name terms with the managers and buyers of just about every major record shop from London to Manchester and knew which of them made regular returns to the compilers of the charts. I didn't then know how valuable this information was to become. What was apparent was that I was still out on the fringes of the record business and it was time to move closer to the action. Not only that, but I learned that there was a job available at Philips Records, which came with a real car as opposed to a little van.

Who could resist?

5. PHILIPS

CS AND ELDEST SON BRODERICK WITH 1961 UK EUROVISION ENTRY, THE ALLISONS

PHILIPS RECORDS

First, there was EMI and Decca controlling the UK record business. Then in the 1950s they were challenged by a newcomer, Philips Records. Philips was owned by the Dutch electrical giant, and it entered the British market with the rights to the mighty American Columbia catalogue. In the early fifties its artists dominated the charts, and releases by Doris Day, Frankie Laine, Guy Mitchell, Johnny Ray and others were automatic and instant quarter-of-a-million chart-toppers. The only problem was that Philips viewed records as loss leaders to promote the brandname of their electric light bulbs and, in those early days, were losing about sixpence per disc sold.

I grew up in awe of these acts and have indelible memories of seeing both Johnny and Frankie at the London Palladium. Johnny, in particular, was an extraordinary performer – outrageously camp, partially deaf with a very visible hearing aid, he moved awkwardly but had an almost mystical aura on the stage. I know many seasoned professionals who toured with him and watched every move of every performance from the wings. Very few acts can muster that kind of respect from colleagues. Towards the end of his career I was asked to promote a revival show at the Palladium featuring Johnny Ray, Billy Daniels and other fifties acts. Our cleaning lady was a devoted Johnny Ray fan, and I took the opportunity to introduce her to her hero. He was gracious and charming, but his devoted fan never uttered a word nor ever mentioned the event over the following years. Perhaps I did her a disservice. Meeting idols rarely matches our expectations.

By the time I joined Philips as a salesman, rock and roll had all but thrown out the old guard of the catalogue, and the company was busily trying to build a roster of British acts. It was a mixed bunch led by Marty Wilde, Shirley Bassey, Frankie Vaughan and Anne Shelton. A short, rather pompous American named Lesley Gould, who was not noted for his humour, ran the company. He reportedly redeemed himself in this respect when asking Johnny Mathis's female manager to allow her artist to appear at a Royal Variety Command Performance. When informed that no fee would be forthcoming, since it was considered a great honour to appear before the Queen, the manager is reported to have said, 'Well, fuck your Queen', to which our man is said to have responded, 'And fuck yours, too.' (Johnny was affectionately known as the 'African Queen' at the time.)

Johnny once explained to me that he walked, talked and acted like a man in every respect but had his own sexual agenda, which seemed fair enough. Later in that conversation he spoke all of the complete lyrics of 'Witchcraft' to me in a low, as they say, thrilling voice and invited me to spend the night. He was one of the most devastatingly attractive men you could wish to meet and if ever I was going to cross that line . . . but I pointed out that it wasn't for me and the matter was dropped with no hard feelings, to use a rather unfortunate phrase.

As a sometime singer I was in awe of Frank Sinatra, who was on the Capitol label.

I had collected his albums, seen all his movies, watched him in concert at both the high and the low points of his career and, of course, tried to ape his unique singing style without any success. Imagine my shock when I actually took a phone call from him.

The call was in fact for Johnny Mathis, who was staying at the Mayfair Hotel while on a British tour in 1962, and I was spending a lot of time with him arranging promotion. John was in the bathroom when the phone rang.

'Who shall I say is calling?' I quavered, as if there could possibly be any doubt.

'Frank' came the reply. And Johnny would not take the call. He suggested that I ask the legend to call back.

'Just tell him that we are having a party upstairs in my suite and he should come up,' said my idol. I was beside myself. A conversation with my all-time hero and an invite to his party! But Mathis would have none of it. The telephone rang several more times that afternoon, and each time my host refused the call. Very disappointing, but Frank and I got pretty matey on the phone at least.

That evening Johnny and I went to the Hippodrome theatre where the star of the show, a brilliant American club act whose name I have completely forgotten, performed part of her set sat at our table with Mathis sharing the spotlight – run-of-the-mill stuff for Mathis but a touch of pure Hollywood to me. We then went on to the Pigalle in Piccadilly, which had just started a season of top US singers in cabaret. The star that week was Peggy Lee. Another of my faves, and another whose style I had copied. The place was packed with all seats having been sold months in advance – but, of course, room could be found for a star of Mr Mathis's eminence and a table was cleared for us just in front of the stage. Minutes before the show was due to start there was a small commotion outside and all heads turned to see Frank Sinatra, Dean Martin, Sammy Davis and assorted members of the Rat Pack being escorted to the front where some poor patrons were turfed off their table to allow it to be joined to ours.

Peggy was truly divine and sang only a few inches away from our enthralled company. You really have to see her in a club setting to appreciate fully her subtle changes and nuances. The evening was somewhat marred by the loutish behaviour of Sammy Davis who was very drunk and who insisted on trying to duet with Miss Lee, who was most gracious and, of course, completely cool. 'Have a little more wine, Sam' was as agitated as she got, while Sinatra suggested that he 'shut the fuck up'. I was stunned. Sammy was yet another of my heroes, and it was distressing to see him behaving so boorishly, particularly during a semi-whispered version of 'Bye Bye Blackbird' when he leaped on to the table and tried to ape Peg's exquisite hand movements.

After the show Mathis and I returned to his hotel and a continuation of the telephone invitations, which were once more refused. By now it was close to dawn and the party was evidently in no danger of winding down. I asked John why he didn't at least put in a token appearance, and he told me that that party had probably started some months before in Hollywood and would likely carry on around the world to Australia, which was the next stop. He simply did not choose to get involved in that lifestyle where day merged into night with no breaks, even for sleep, since the party went relentlessly on with the participants snatching the odd few hours on a bed or couch while the party and the music played on.

I returned to the hotel at about eleven that morning and peeked into the Sinatra suite. Sure enough, the room was full of bodies, with loud music and Anthony Newley dancing with Sammy Davis who was wearing nothing but a pair of skimpy shorts. Davis looked, in truth, both ugly and deformed. What a tragedy. He was truly a gifted performer, a fabulous dancer, fantastic mimic and a very exciting singer. But only a short, one-eyed black Jew can know how hard you need to try to be liked. He even bought a Rolls-Royce in an effort to gain respect, but the rest of the Clan just thought that was funny.

By contrast Mathis was astonishingly handsome, superbly fit and perfectly at ease with himself. One of the great masters of microphone technique, he managed to keep his cool when a BBC producer went to great lengths to explain just how important it was to move his mouth away from the mike for the high notes and come in closer for the quiet passages. At another session for a television show he tried to explain to the drummer that a particular passage should sound 'like a four-alarm fire'. When the session man couldn't or wouldn't understand Johnny took over his seat and demonstrated exactly how the rhythm should be, which drew applause from the rest of the orchestra.

I never made it to the party, and John informed me that at some point in the proceedings a clutch of young women would arrive to put on a sex show since most of the assemblage were too wasted by booze and debauchery to perform the usual physical acts themselves. So much for idols.

Since first scribbling these notes the great man has died, and what I have written now seems a bit cheap and shallow. That is nevertheless what happened and has no bearing upon the majestic talent of Frank Sinatra. I was lucky enough to see him at the London Palladium in the early days of his career when he drew screams from the audience with – literally – a movement of his little finger. He was magnificent. I saw him again at the Trocadero some years later when he was having personal and career problems. His voice was not what it had been, and when he sang 'Nancy' Ava Gardner got to her feet and flamboyantly left the theatre. But he was still superb and the bitter edge to his announcements just showed that he had grown up. It is doubtful that the world will ever see another entertainer of his ability and stature; the training grounds are no longer there. He is terribly missed and won't be forgotten – and if I close my eyes I can still see those astonishing blue eyes from the back of a dark theatre.

Another great star who stayed at the Mayfair was Eartha Kitt. As a very young man I watched her on *Sunday Night at the Palladium* and was enthralled; so much so that I phoned her and asked if we could meet. She agreed to meet me in the lobby of the hotel the following night and arrived a little late but swathed in mink and diamonds. Spotting me lurking among the ferns she must have guessed that this was the cheeky little sod who had called her, since she beckoned me over and invited me up to her suite. She was at the time one of the world's biggest stars and by God you knew it. When she entered or left a room it was as if the lights had been turned on and off. Eartha, who had a dreadful childhood, was astonishingly kind to a scruffy adolescent and gave me the best advice: 'Be yourself and trust your instincts.' I do try, Eartha – and thanks.

At Philips I discovered I had a knack with singles, and within a short time I was specializing in this area even to the extent of presenting a hospital radio show and joining the executives at the weekly board discussions where I received an early lesson in corporate politics. Gould, the pompous boss, announced his intention to sign an act that, in my opinion, was well past its prime. Despite their obvious misgivings, all of the assembled executives, in turn, approved the move except yours truly. The managing director, in a display of pettiness that I saw repeated in various forms by various chief executives over many years, said, 'I don't think we need this person at any future meetings.'

Despite being drummed out of the inner sanctum I continued to concentrate on singles sales and chart success with a range of activities including presenting the company radio shows recorded for hospital patients. One of my proudest achievements was to suggest the release of 'Take Five' as a single from Dave Brubeck's *Time Out* album. It was a huge hit, which, as a modern jazz single, makes it virtually unique. When the musician came to England we discussed the follow-up release, making notes on the back of an album that Dave signed with a very personal message. A few years ago I lost that album and several thousand others in a burglary. They were all special, irreplaceable and probably sold for pennies at a boot sale. Still, I imagine the perpetrators had unhappy childhoods. I certainly hope so.

Touring with Brubeck was fun. He had only to remove his trademark spectacles to pass through any crowd unnoticed. Most jazzers are pretty cool, but my work partner Arnie Kosky, another salesman at Philips, was not overly thrilled when he toured with Miles Davis, who seemed to resent everything and everybody. When asked to sign a poster for Arnie's girlfriend, Miles refused, saying that he was sick of white girls masturbating over pictures of him. Nice. He was a genius and his music will live for ever – but did he have to go out of his way to be so obnoxious to the people around him? By contrast Errol Garner presented Arnie with a gold watch as a memento of another, happier tour.

Touring with pop acts was another thing altogether. Usually the bill featured one of the top names, such as Bobby Vee, supported by half-a-dozen lesser artists each doing a twenty-five-minute spot. The Bobby Vee tour included Clarence 'Frogman' Henry, the Springfields – just before Dusty left to go solo – and Tony Orlando, who was a dynamic showman. Tony's big US hits, 'Bless You' and 'Halfway to Paradise', were covered by Billy Fury, who scooped the UK chart honours. Tony eventually had one of the all-time international best-selling singles with 'Tie a Yellow Ribbon' and is now a very successful music publisher in America.

Dusty was as blind as a bat without her glasses but great fun to be with. She gained a reputation for being difficult in later years, but on that tour she was kind enough to allow me to introduce my future brother-in-law to her. Shurley's brother Barrie had just moved to London from his native Yorkshire and was young and very impressed, despite coming from a showbiz family. He was even more impressed when, some months later, while gazing into a jewellery shop window, Dusty appeared at his side and addressed him by name. A great lady and one who is greatly missed.

One night, after a show at the Tooting Broadway Granada, Arnie and I were waiting in the limo outside the stage door where hordes of female Bobby Vee fans were assembled. When the stage door opened and Arnie's girlfriend emerged, somebody shouted, 'That's Bobby's girlfriend – let's kill her', and in an instant the poor girl went down beneath a frenzy of screaming scrubbers. We bolted out of the car and, using elbows, fists and knees, punched and clawed our way to the rescue. I was reminded of this scary incident years later when taking Michael Nesmith to an interview at BBC Broadcasting House. Bay City Roller fans, replete in tartan gear, besieged the entrance. Michael flung himself to the floor of the car and began to shake with fear. He begged me not to stop and, though aware that the BCR fans probably would not recognize him, was ashen-faced and trembling. If that was what it was like for an ex-Monkee, what could it have been like for the Beatles? Derek Taylor, who organized their publicity, once referred to them as being 'beatled to death'. Fortunately I was never part of that madness, though I did just happen to be in Savile Row when they performed on the rooftop. I was showing one of the Elektra executives around Swinging London at the time and it did not appear to be a particularly special event – certainly not the last public performance of the Fab Four.

At Philips I devised the scheme of taking artists around the chart shops for brief personal appearances. We would appear at up to a dozen stores in a day, where the additional sales and local coverage often made the difference in the all-important lower end of the charts. It didn't always work, but Marty, Frankie, the Springfields, the Allisons and many more felt the benefit of a little extra push.

Driving Frankie Vaughan around was an unusual experience, a little like being in the company of a scoutmaster. He was a big star at the time and he had recently completed the movie *Let's Make Love* with Marilyn Monroe, though most of his scenes were consigned to the cutting-room floor. When pushed, he revealed how Marilyn had always appeared late, belching, breaking wind and groping him in the close-ups; the latter would have been heaven to a large percentage of the male population but was anathema to Frank who telegraphed his beloved wife Stella to come to the rescue. She was immediately banned from the set and the screen goddess transferred her attentions to Yves Montand, who was somewhat more sophisticated. Frank also told of his first visit to Las Vegas, where the party that was thrown in his honour lasted through the night and all of the following day until he found it was time to do another show and his head had yet to touch a pillow. Following that show, he found himself at the centre of another party set to continue the pattern of the first, so he made his excuses and went to bed. Frank was quick to point out that he was simply another excuse for another party rather than a special person. That kind of lifestyle has killed a lot of careers – but what a way to go.

An altogether different animal was Jimmy Dean, who had a huge hit with 'Big Bad John'. Jimmy was in the UK to appear on *Sunday Night at the Palladium*, which was the top-rated television show, but he was not too big-time to get out and push our limo through the snow to a garage when we ran out of petrol. When he stayed at one of London's small, exclusive hotels I would wake him up mid-morning whereupon he would immediately light the first of many cigarettes and drain a glass of bourbon before springing into action. Many of the very British residents hated him and were very rude, but he thought they were cute enough to take home and put on his mantelpiece. He followed 'Big Bad John' with an 'answer' record, which was also a hit, then appeared in a couple of James Bond movies as a mad Texan millionaire before making another fortune in the meat trade, selling sausages and cooked meats under his own name. He was Big Bad John and a rare larger-than-life character.

It was at a reception for somebody or other at Philips that I first saw the astonishingly beautiful Shurley, whom I pursued with a kind of madness. There were a number of stars at the reception, including Dusty when she was a member of the Lana Sisters, but I had eyes for only Shurley who was – and is – the coolest, most intelligent person I have ever met. She was there in her role as an operator of jukeboxes and, with my responsibilities for singles, I was legitimately able to badger her into changing my life. By this time my first marriage had lasted ten years, following a long period of teenage infatuation. Quite simply, Patricia and I had married too young and, as the years passed, we became increasingly unfulfilled, apart from overseeing the lives of three cherished children. For the next fifteen years, with the approval – and considerable sacrifices – of Shurley, who had given up a millionaire lifestyle, we managed to sustain two families and shield the kids, to a large degree, from the agony of a broken marriage.

Because it was the time I met Shurley, and for many other reasons, I have fond memories of Philips and its associated label Fontana Records, which later merged with Polydor to become Phonogram, which in turn bought Decca and Island and A&M on the way to becoming the biggest record company in Europe, before being taken over by MCA, which is a division of Seagram's, the liquor company.

It was a circuitous route, beginning as a loss-making offshoot of a major international electrical corporation to becoming a division of a major distillery. How many artists have flourished or died on the journey? How many executives ruined their lives and relationships in pursuit of success at almost any price? Down here near the bottom of the food chain we should have known better. A few months into the establishment of Polydor Records in Britain the German masters sent over a team of 'experts' to try to work out a dynamic plan for success. After a couple of weeks of meetings with the management and study of relevant papers, they called a final meeting at which they announced the solution to the problem. With a kindly but firm voice they enquired of the managing director, 'Vhy don't you only release hits?' Now that is true corporate mentality and an indication of how a host of creative individuals end up as pawns in a never-ending game.

SALVO

Meet the Disc Jockey — 28
CLIVE SELWOOD

THERE is a very fresh look about our DJ feature this week, for we concern ourselves with a new announcer who introduces a new 208 programme for a new record company. The disc jockey is Clive Selwood, and he can be heard every Thursday at 7.45 p.m. introducing "Sounds Like Salvo". The first programme in this series sponsored by Salvo Records is broadcast this week.

Selwood has some special ideas for presenting disc shows on the air. One, which will be a regular feature of his programmes, is to have bassist Brian Jones playing rhythmic figures in the background while Clive announces the records.

Clive Selwood was born on 2nd July, 1935, in London, and educated at Latimer Upper School. Unfortunately, Clive and school parted company rather suddenly when the headmaster decided that the young pupil was taking too much time off from his studies to attend auditions.

He had set his sights on a show business career, and since his somewhat hurried departure from school he has never wavered in his ambition to make good in the entertainment world. At first he tried his luck as a singer.

He toured on some of the top one night-stand concerts in the country, but although he was always very well received by the audiences on his personal appearances, Clive didn't quite make the grade as a vocalist.

In between his many show business jobs, he took on a wide variety of other employment to make ends meet. He was a door to door brush salesman, sold vacuum cleaners, and was a representative for a firm which manufactured washing machines.

At another time Clive became a Redcoat at Butlin's Holiday Camps, but this eventually led him back to his career as a vocalist, for he wound up the season entertaining the visitors in the theatre and dance hall.

Today, Clive no longer thinks of his future in terms of a singing career, but as an A & R manager. He likes Modern Jazz and the good singers, but would like to record 'soul' music, being of the opinion that there is a wealth of undiscovered talent in this field.

FOR THE WEEK
25th MARCH to 31st MARCH

RADIO LUXEMBOURG

★ The Station of the Stars

208 metres Medium Wave

DAILY FROM 7.00 p.m. till 3.00 a.m.
(And on 49.26 metres short wave)

SUNDAY, MAR. 25th

ckson's
BOX
est, up-to-date,
records
Co Ltd)

ers'
on
d

9.30   **THE HELEN SHAPIRO SHOW**
A Tune-Filled fifteen minutes in wh.ch Helen sings her favourite songs
(The Toni Co—White Rain)

9.45   **MATT MONRO SINGS**
with accompaniment of the Johnny Spence Quartet
(Peter Stuyvesant Cigarettes)

10.00   **THE SAM COSTA SHOW**
in which Sam invites teenager Carol Lorimer to assist him in a
(Cerveld Ltd)
(Guards Cigarettes)

[Everite Time Check]

MacDonald Hobley
invites you to
MAKE A TAPE
which you can hear yourself on the air and win a luxurious day air to Para, Rome and New York a personal and starred appearance in city and record company. Other g record an audition with e given weekly competition. Listen for this exclusive competition. for dio and Cycle Stores.

TWENTY
week's best selling dance with the Musical Express by dia
Ltd)
(tdingpool)

10
De

SALVO

While still working as a salesman for Philips Records, I answered an advertisement in the industry trade paper *Record Retailer* for the directorship of a new record label. My chum Arnie Kosky and I both applied and were appointed joint managing directors, which was something of a feather in our collective hats as we were still in our twenties.

In fact we knew virtually nothing about the nuts and bolts of the industry at that time and even less about our new employer. Looking back, our naïvety was breathtaking. Starting from scratch, we were expected to find and license in hit singles from America, arrange manufacture and distribution, organize marketing and promotion, plus, of course, design labels and bags for the product and set up all the royalty and accounting procedures, and so on.

We were, however, a couple of hotshots and divided our responsibilities between us, with Arnie taking care of sales, distribution and manufacture while I initially tried to license in the American product without either a good company track record or any reasonable funds for advances. The label, incidentally, was unaccountably called Salvo Records, which, at best, sounded like a brand of lavatory cleaner, as our former colleagues were kind enough to point out.

Today to be designated an indie label carries a degree of cool, since it stands for rugged independence free of the restraints and commercial considerations of the major multinational conglomerates. In those innocent times it was just dumb – unless one had very deep pockets. The UK industry was entirely controlled by just four companies: Decca, EMI, Pye and Philips. Even the mighty Columbia Records from the USA was licensed to Philips and some years short of becoming CBS in Britain, while Rank Industries had lost millions in trying to establish Top Rank Records before being effectively frozen out by the Big Four. Still, Arnie and I were young and idealistic enough to believe that we could take on the big boys.

Our employer was a somewhat shadowy figure whose name I now forget, but this is hardly surprising since we later discovered that the name he gave us was false, and we only ever met him in rented hotel rooms or when he chose to appear at our hastily rented office. We were, however, paid on time and somehow managed to acquire enough material to initiate a first release. The major labels then distributed their records themselves and through a chain of wholesalers across the country. Now they would be called one-stops, where dealers could order every label. Arnie had set up manufacture through Pye and distribution through the wholesalers, so we were ready to go.

At that time Radio Luxembourg was the only commercial radio station broadcasting to the UK, and Radio 1 had yet to be even a twinkle in the eye of the BBC. At Broadcasting House pop records were something to be, at best, tolerated a couple of times a week in dedicated programmes with the very occasional spot in 'request' programmes, which were fought over by extremely experienced 'pluggers'.

Without radio exposure we would have no chance, but plays on Lux were limited to those companies that bought complete programmes, such as the Decca Hour or the EMI, Pye or Philips shows, which were produced by the companies and, of course, played only their own product. We managed to scrape together enough money to buy half an hour of time a week for three months and pay the studio costs but not enough to pay for one of the 'name' disc jockeys to present the show. Having produced a weekly hospital radio show at Philips for some time I was pressed into service as the presenter of our rather limited extravaganza.

In the early sixties British disc jockeys were a pretty lame bunch, and my heroes were the cool presenters on American Forces Network (AFN) rather than the 'zany' efforts of Jack Jackson or the studied indifference of David Jacobs. In the absence of any obvious hit product I determined to be at least interesting in my few minutes a week. I asked a musician friend, Brian Jones, to play his string bass as an accompaniment to the introductions to the records and to vary the pace and mood as the music dictated. The shows were all prerecorded at Radio Luxembourg's London studios and shipped over to the principality for later transmission. We had a lot of fun doing them, but reception was so bad in many parts of Britain that many people, if they heard the programme at all, probably thought that thrumming noise behind the disc jockey was just interference. After recording one show we had some time over, and I used it to record myself singing a fairly jazzy version of 'Love Me or Leave Me' with just a string bass accompaniment that owed a lot to Lena Horne. Imagine my delight when, returning to the studio a couple of weeks later, the engineers played me the same recording overdubbed by Britain's best jazz drummer, Phil Seaman, and a pianist. God, I wish I had kept a copy of that final version.

Despite our best efforts, the label had no success, and the time came to wind it up. It was then that we discovered that our employer was in fact a pretty famous person in the world of classical music as the conductor or leader of the London Symphony Orchestra. This was revealed in a final meeting with Lord Goodman QC, who was the Prime Minister's personal counsel – a truly Dickensian and extremely powerful person. We never discovered who was really behind the venture or where the money had come from or even why. Tax laws were complicated then, so we assumed it was simply tax evasion. Twenty years later I had a call from a collector offering me £25 each for as many Salvo Records as I could supply. I had, of course, kept none, but it is worth noting that the fewer copies you sell first time round the higher the price collectors will pay. So all you budding record producers should hang on to a few hundred copies of your failures as a pension.

Meanwhile, back in the real world, I was again out of work. That faded into insignificance, however, as all hell was about to break loose when I fell foul of a prominent person with criminal connections and was forced to go into hiding and on the run for a year.

7. ON THE RUN

ON THE RUN

Checker was the local tearaway when I was growing up in south London. A big fellow who worked out regularly, he had already served time in a Borstal for stealing handbags from old ladies and would proudly display the scars he carried from an official birching whenever he appeared at the local baths. He was not a man to tangle with if it could be avoided. It was, in truth, no great surprise when, following the obligatory ''Oo you bleeding looking at?' one night, he punched me in the mouth and dislodged a tooth before ambling back up Putney High Street followed by his cackling acolytes. I do not recall just what I was doing hanging around the high street that particular night in my new wide-brimmed trilby hat – probably hoping to pick up girls rather than a smack in the mouth. What was clear was that my teenage dignity had been shattered along with my tooth, and I made a point over the next few weeks of tracking down each member of the gang and offering to re-enact the scene one on one. Nobody accepted the offer and even Checker, to my unutterable relief, just grinned and patted me on the head.

Still, a little pride was restored, though this was somewhat tarnished when I returned home one day to discover my dear old mum plying one of the gang, Fatty Longman, with cups of tea in the scullery. It seems that Fatty, who was employed by the council, had been mowing the grass on the common land outside of our house and looked so hot and sweaty that my dear innocent mum had invited him in for tea. She would do things like that. Fatty was always a bit of a wimp despite his size, so he gulped down the tea and left.

All fairly innocent stuff, you might think, but the next time I came across Checker he was holding back a crowd of onlookers in Soho while his boss, a notorious gangster, chased another leading gangster along the street, slashing at him with an axe. There was, literally, a trail of blood criss-crossing the street and splashed up the shop windows. The victim, Jack Spot, was rushed to hospital and eventually made a partial recovery with the help of a few hundred stitches. He was never the same force, however, and he relinquished his territory to his assailant, who looked like a gangster from central casting and was known and feared throughout London's underworld as Albert Dimes. Gang warfare was fairly rampant at that time but usually limited to 'their own'. It never occurred to me that I, too, would be hunted by said Albert and in fear of my life.

It started with a call from a friend who knew that I had incurred the wrath of a certain millionaire to whom Albert owed a favour or two. He told me that Albert was on his way to collect me and bring me back to, as it were, face the music. Fortunately I had recently moved house and Albert went to my old address, but this bought only a little extra time as 'The Man' had contacts in the police who quickly provided the new destination. Within a short time there was a knock on the door, and a peek through the curtains revealed two black limos with engines running, containing a posse of well-dressed gentlemen.

Fearing for the safety of my three young children, who were asleep in bed, I went quietly into the night and was taken for a ride in the good old-fashioned way – thankfully not by Albert, who had by this time lost interest and gone to wherever gangsters go at that hour. If you saw it in a movie you would be hard pressed to believe that a person could so easily succumb to that kind of situation, but, at the time, you hope that by facing the music and being logical, things can be resolved. They weren't. I was whisked away to an exclusive block of flats in Mayfair where a madman wielding, of all things, a hand grenade and a knife confronted me. I think the grenade was just for show, but the knife was only too real and only too close to my face. It really ain't like the movies. When a knife is that close you don't remember all those self-defence techniques. It's hard enough just trying to stop your knees buckling. We have all seen the hero shrugging off the chair that is crashed over his head, but in real life, I promise you, you go down. If the chair is a solid antique and lands with force on your head there tends to be a degree of blood and concussion.

Somehow I managed to get away from the flat and past the porter who studiously ignored my head wounds, and I began the long walk back to south London. Out of cigarettes I stopped off at an all-night café in Earls Court where nobody turned a hair as I dripped blood all over the establishment. The wounds were so bad that I was forced to book into Putney Hospital for a few days under an assumed name, which may have saved my life since The Man subsequently decided to finish the job and called all the hospitals in London looking for me.

London was no place to be for a while, so Shurley and I went on the run for a year or so staying in cheap hotels and flats in Manchester, Bolton, Leicester and Yorkshire. The Man had many contacts around the country, and all too often we would overhear a conversation or possibly misinterpret a remark that had us packing up and moving on. It was a very difficult period both emotionally and financially, since I had to keep sneaking back to London to see the kids, who were living with their mother, and try to continue to maintain them and pay the mortgage without any visible means of support. Shurley was, as ever, a rock and somehow juggled our meagre finances to enable us to survive. I took on a number of fairly low-key jobs based in various parts of the country until we felt it was safe to return to London and try to pick up the pieces.

During this uncertain period I met up with a number of, shall we say, unusual characters, including a Canadian millionaire named Marcel Rodd, who owned a huge range of classical and children's material, and for whom I worked briefly. Marcel was known to be eccentric, and I recall his production manager's despair when he discovered that a crucial recording, which was due to be given away as the spearhead of a very large advertising campaign, 'went down in the bath'. In those days of vinyl this meant that it was not available. He tried to relay this information to Marcel, who simply feigned deafness and allowed the campaign to run, which is an interesting way to deal with a problem.

Another millionaire, an Asian named Sayed Mohammed Ali, had a most unusual calling card. He would announce his arrival in the offices of major record companies by brushing past defensive secretaries, throwing open the usually closed doors of the executive he wanted to see and hurling on to the desk of the astonished executive a huge roll of used banknotes. He would then withdraw and await a response. It was a remarkable man who could resist investigating the source of this bonanza, since the roll of notes was always, as they say, big enough to choke a horse.

A small, excitable man, Ali began his commercial life in Britain by making furniture from soapboxes that he sold in street markets around Manchester. I was aware of Ali's reputation, and by the time we first met he had become the leading dealer in Britain in overstocked or deleted records and a millionaire several times over. Deletions and overstocks, particularly of vinyl, were always a problem to successful companies. One dramatic appearance on *Top of the Pops* could create an overnight demand for a hundred thousand copies of a single, and that demand had to be satisfied fast before the fickle public lost interest. Even allowing for just a 10 per cent misjudgement of the demand could result in twenty-five thousand copies of a hit left unsold – and few things are deader than last year's hit. Add to this a degree of over-enthusiasm on the part of the pressing plant, combined with a few returns from dealers, and, with just ten hits in a year, it was possible to end up with a warehouse full of unsaleable records taking up valuable space and earning nothing. In fact, they were just useless lumps of plastic, since the cost of removing the labels and sleeves to recycle the vinyl was prohibitive. Which is where Ali came in.

He had built up a network of secondhand stores, market stalls, fairground suppliers and other outlets that were prepared to buy deletions and overstocks at knock-down prices. The main hurdle was the attitude of the major companies, which were reluctant to allow their product to disposed of in this way despite the growing mountains of unsold stock. Cash was the answer, and Ali gave every appearance of being awash with the stuff.

For a good few years Ali had the market virtually to himself, and many a sales or marketing director was salting away tokens of Ali's gratitude in Swiss bank accounts. There were, of course, rumours of midnight meetings at lonely spots where truck-loads of supposedly redundant stock would change hands in return for a few of Ali's calling cards. It is just possible that the occasional mistake occurred whereby good current stock found its way into the boxes. When one of the major Irish distributors was audited it was discovered that several thousand boxes of the then best-selling album actually contained very old and completely useless twelve-inch shellac discs. How this happened was never established but everybody assumed that somebody in that organization had received a calling card.

I met Ali at a particularly low ebb in my business and personal life, being jobless and living in cheap digs in Manchester where Ali headquartered. Like so many entrepreneurs who had made it on their wits and achieved a degree of security, he was possibly looking for Establishment acceptance and respectability within the music industry. I can think of no other reason why he offered me the post of sales manager at a hugely inflated salary. Out of work, broke and with a family and mortgage to support, it is hard to be choosy and I was sorely tempted. Shurley, in her wisdom, pointed out that, following such an association, it would be even more difficult for me to pick up a career in the 'legit' industry, so with some reluctance I declined the offer. Ali went on to become a highly respected businessman with a string of successful shops, so it worked out well for both of us – but it was a tough choice.

Eventually many other companies got into the business of buying and selling deletions or overstocks, so the pickings got slimmer and the temptation to cut corners became greater. There was one infamous incident in which it was discovered that the chairman of one of the great companies also owned a clearance company to whom he was selling vast quantities of the then top-selling album at considerably less than cost price. He agreed to resign – in some comfort, naturally.

After a period in the wilderness I found a legitimate job with a Leicester-based company called Thorpe and Porter, whose main business was supplying what were known as 'action' magazines through a chain of twelve thousand newsagents. The magazines were considered pretty racy for the period, with pictures of scantily dressed women on the covers being threatened by Nazi officers; barely worth a raised eyebrow by today's standards, but at that time the company was keen to diversify into the rather more respectable business of music. (It remains one of the sadder facts of life that during a national miners' strike, when presumably money was tight for them, the sales of these repellent mags increased dramatically because, it seems, the miners had more time to spend on beer and dirty books. Salt of the earth, eh?)

We thoroughly enjoyed living and working in Leicester, but the company was ambitious and decided to relocate to London. By this time my former adversary had found other people to intimidate, so our biggest problem with the move was finding accommodation. With a very limited budget, and needing to be within commuting distance of the West End, we sought cheap digs in Croydon. One of the first adverts we answered was for a room in the basement of a house that was currently home to a pig; not a large pig, and the owner assured us that we could have sole occupancy. We spent a few weeks in a room in a house otherwise occupied by very old and sick ladies who monitored, and commented on, our every activity. Eventually we wound up renting a room at the top of a house in Sanderstead that gave us some insight into what goes on in suburbia.

Within a couple of days of our arrival we were instructed not to flush the toilet after 11 o'clock at night. We soon discovered that the lady of the house was having a fairly torrid affair with 'Old Tom', who would arrive on his bike and canoodle with Madame in the porch while her husband watched the telly. When both parents were out the teenage son would turn his short-wave radio to the fire fighters' frequency and, whenever a fire was reported, don a fireman's hat and dash around the house ringing a handbell and shouting 'Fire'. Left alone in the house, the husband, who collected butterflies, played recordings of Hitler's speeches and German military music at top volume. Somehow we managed to scrape up enough money for a deposit on a maisonette in Camberley and returned to some kind of sanity. As a going-away present I secreted a dozen eggs in various inaccessible places through-

out the house to remind them of the tenants who were not allowed to flush the loo after 11 o'clock.

For Thorpe and Porter I was engaged to start up a record division and began with a catalogue of cheap cover albums of shows and popular classics, which were handled by Monty Lewis as Pickwick Records. Monty had the rights to the label from the USA, and we worked closely to evolve a price and packaging policy that enabled us to sell over a million albums in the first year through newsagents and supermarkets. These were excellent results for a start, but there was a considerable demand for more contemporary material, and one of the directors hit upon the idea of supplying ex-jukebox records at bargain prices. Having purchased a few thousand copies from old contacts, I arranged a test sale at a supermarket in St Albans and was astonished by the results. We placed the records in a sturdy cardboard dumper bin and, within just a few hours, all had sold and the bin was completely destroyed. We had a new business.

With such an obvious hit product the immediate problem was supplying demand. When Pickwick were unable to supply the demand for new titles that we had created I decided to approach Marcel Rodd to try to obtain further catalogue. All went well for the first few minutes of our meeting at his rather scruffy offices when suddenly, without warning, Marcel began to scream obscenities while accusing me of trying to usurp his authority. He leaped from his desk and chased me around the office literally foaming at the mouth. Fearing for my life, I picked up a chair and fended him off as best I could. As suddenly as he had started this rampage he stopped, apologized for his behaviour and explained that he always did that once every day and I had just happened to be there at the wrong time. (Years later Marcel called me offering the job of managing director of his companies. What would you have done?)

However, we eventually came up with a solution to the problem of supply. Shurley, who had been in the jukebox business, had a list of contacts that, along with my own lists from my days in promotion, pretty much covered the country, but these were people who dealt in cash and were not about to change their ways. The answer was to try to find someone trustworthy who could travel the country with satchels of cash, negotiating with jukebox owners and operators in each region. I gave the job to my dad, who had worked hard throughout his life for next to nothing and was close to retirement on a pittance. What a mistake. We provided him with the capital, the lists of contacts and a contract that allowed him to earn more money in a few months than he had ever seen. He performed well enough, without managing to satisfy the ever-growing demand, until one of the directors told me that having my father in such a position of trust was a 'conflict of interest' and I must either fire him or resign. Well, you can't fire your own dad, so I resigned in the belief that we could perhaps work together to find and supply even more records for which I knew there was a ready market. He refused. I shall never know why, but perhaps this is an illustration of why it is a common belief that families should never work together.

I eventually found another outlet for the records, and for a few months became a competitor to my own father and my former employers. It was a grand time spent travelling around the country loaded with cash, buying old records, packing them into apple boxes and delivering them to our customer. We worked eighteen- and twenty-four-hour days but only three or four days a week and prospered right up until our customer went bust owing us just about everything we had earned.

8. ILLU

ILLUSIONS

It is barely conceivable in these days of multinational branding and marketing overkill but, back in the innocent and considerably less affluent early sixties, the only records available in Woolworth's were cheap cover versions of the Top Twenty. Of course, no self-respecting teenager would be seen dead buying one of these abominations, which were sold under the Oriole brand, but their parents, who just wanted a few hit tunes to play at parties, bought them in their millions.

These records, which were never played on radio or promoted in any way, except as inexpensive copies of the originals, nevertheless sold in sufficient quantities to encourage competitors. With the advent of EPs four cover versions could be crammed on to one disc under the banner 'four hits for the price of one'. There were no throwaway B-sides, so it looked pretty good value if you didn't look or listen too critically. In fact, when the mighty Columbia Records chose to enter the UK market they purchased the Oriole factory and facilities as a starting base.

The recordings were pretty shabby affairs, usually made in batches of four in one session of three hours, using tired old session musicians, a hurried and often scaled-down copy of the hit arrangement and a 'sound-alike' singer who would be paid £15 per song recorded. There were no royalties paid nor prestige attached to the recordings, but a number of subsequently successful singers were very happy to earn a bit of cash in this fashion. My friend Muff Murfin, who now owns a clutch of studios and produces jingles and station idents for radio stations around the world, fondly recalls his days as a session singer, when he and Elton John – who was still called Reg at the time – would compete to earn a few quid from these recordings.

One of these new companies was run by a handsome and elegant young Canadian, whom I shall call Rip, since he is now a famous and wealthy film producer and no doubt has a battery of lawyers at his disposal. Rip was, and may still be, the best con man I have ever met. His clear, unflinching baby-blue eyes and effortless sincerity could ease the contents, and possibly the lining, from your pocket without you being aware of it until your suit fell apart.

I was brought into the organization and first met Rip at the start of his record company venture. It was impossible not to be impressed by the swish offices just off Piccadilly Circus, the cultured receptionist, the array of expensive racks, carousels and display material and not least by Rip, who was obviously wealthy, ambitious and knowledgeable. How was I to know that the premises were in fact just the one rented office rather than the whole floor, that the receptionist was employed by the landlord, the materials were samples from manufacturers eager to make a sale and that Rip was living in a bedsit in Bayswater with three months' rent overdue?

With the grand title of 'Sales Director' I signed on to organize national distribution for what appeared to be a reasonable range of these cover EPs. Because the major labels controlled distribution and they were not about to give any help to a small company trying to steal some of their business, Rip had devised a plan to appoint a network of local agents who would both sell and deliver the records, on a purely commission basis, with a view eventually to becoming managers employing other sales agents. It was an early version of the pyramid selling that became the foundation of a number of multinational companies. What I did not know was that Rip never had any intention of paying anybody anything – and that included yours truly.

Flushed with ambition, and in a rented vehicle to accommodate the stock and sales literature, I set off around the country to interview the hundreds of applicants who had responded to the series of small adverts I had placed in newspapers in key cities offering a 'business opportunity with huge potential profits in the exciting music industry to anybody with sales ability and the will to work'. This was a period of considerable unemployment and the response was overwhelming. With far too many applicants to interview individually, I was forced to conduct group interviews and appoint agents with overlapping areas in the fairly certain belief that there would be a high proportion of drop-outs. There were, but the initial responses were so strong that we were forced to rent an additional warehouse to cope with the orders and reorders.

It seemed we had clicked in a big way, and I began to count the commission due. Needless to say, I have absolutely no idea where the money went, but within a very short while I joined a long and growing list of people demanding to be paid. These included all of the salespeople, the landlords, the printers, the studios, the record pressing plant, the box suppliers, the hotels where the interviews had taken place and heaven knew who else. I should have bailed out when it became apparent that Rip had developed a routine with creditors' calls. He would accept the first few calls and respond to their pleas with a few soothing assurances that the bill would be paid shortly and that 'the current difficulty had been brought about by too much early success resulting in a short-term cash-flow problem'. When the calls became frantic he would remain cool and urbane but cut the caller off in the middle of a sentence. When the creditor called back the receptionist was instructed to apologize and say that our hero had been inadvertently cut off by the switchboard and had subsequently been called out to an urgent meeting. Rip fielded dozens of calls a day in this fashion. It was just business to him, and I watched in increasingly penurious amazement.

On one occasion two burly and blustering gentlemen forced their way into the office and declared that they intended to stay there until their bill of several thousand pounds was paid. Rip was not at all fazed by their presence or demands. He offered them coffee, professed ignorance of their account and suggested that they make themselves comfortable since, even as he spoke, the company accountant was returning by taxi from the City where a massive facility had just been finalized to cover the recent shortfall. He spoke airily and convincingly of the immediate expansion plans we had and how this would benefit all of our suppliers. He even hinted that our two visitors might wish to make a pitch for further business when this little difficulty was resolved. As some of the tension began to ebb, he was interrupted by the telephone and exploded to his 'secretary' that he had left strict instructions that he was not to be disturbed. Grudgingly he accepted a call from 'Bernie'. There then followed a series of exchanged pleasantries and enquiries about family, followed by an assurance that he was in fact too busy to meet at such short notice and could it wait a day or so? After some protestations he agreed to meet the caller immediately on the strict understanding that the matter was too urgent and important to delay and that he would only be needed for no more than a half-hour.

'Better get your coat, Clive,' Rip said on replacing the receiver. 'Bernie has a proposition for us, and he'll only hold it open for the next hour.'

As if scripted I asked, 'Bernie who?'

'Delfont,' Rip snapped and apologized to our visitors, assuring them that we would be no more than an hour and anyway the accountant would be with them shortly and had full authority to sign cheques for such relatively small amounts. Since Bernard Delfont was the single most important person in the UK entertainment business at that time, our visitors recognized the urgency of the situation and were in fact quite keen to hear the outcome of our meeting. As we sped down the hall I wondered aloud what the mighty Bernard Delfont might want with us with such urgency. 'Don't be daft,' said Rip. 'I made the whole thing up. You know the receptionist calls me to make me look busy whenever we have visitors. Let's just go across the road and have some coffee until those two bozos leave.' And we did.

As the situation worsened, Rip placed a small advertisement in the personal column of *The Times* along the lines of 'successful young entrepreneur needs £50,000 investment'. To my astonishment he received several replies and proceeded to conduct meetings with various eager investors on the basis that he was about to build a new and much needed record-pressing plant. To build up the project he advertised for, and found, an experienced factory manager, to whom he promised the job of running the proposed factory once a suitable site had been found – ignoring the fact that to do it the man would need to uproot his family and home. Amazingly, the talks progressed and Rip got his £50,000 and immediately spent it on a Ferrari! As there was enough left to pay me some of what I was owed I took the opportunity to leave before the gendarmes arrived. In fact, a factory was eventually built under Rip's guidance and, as far as I know, still operates.

A few months later Rip called me with news of a massive cash injection and an exciting new business venture. I agreed to meet him, but this time I had the good fortune to have Shurley with me. I was again completely taken in, but Shurley's good sense prevailed and probably saved my house. A year or so on I again met Rip strolling along Upper Brook Street in Mayfair looking very well off. He explained that his fortunes had changed. He was now wealthy and in the process of decorating and furnishing his new apartment just off Park Lane. Would I like to see it? With an hour to kill, I accompanied him to a truly superb apartment where the interior-design expert from Harrods, who happened to be a very attractive young woman, was busy taking measurements and offering suggestions about the furnishing. I particularly recall her suggestion of a 'jungle motif' for the master bedroom complete with fake tiger-skin bed cover. While Rip considered her recommendations I left, feeling that there was no justice. I had always believed that Rip would eventually hit the big time, but this was stratospheric.

At a chance meeting later I enquired about the apartment. With a pitying look Rip explained that it was only ever a ruse to get into the Harrods girl's knickers and, with that in mind, he had obtained the keys to the apartment from the letting agents for just that afternoon. He was in fact still living in a Bayswater bedsit where the landlady carefully screened all calls. I wish I could say that I had learned my lesson, but he could probably still work his magic on me. I did see a report in a local paper that a young man with the same name had been convicted of swindling a lot of old ladies out of their pensions, which is entirely possible since con artists are not choosy about their victims. What is true is that, when last heard of, our flawed hero had become a big movie producer with millions at his disposal. He was working his magic upon one of the screen's greatest and most protected actors, who is now almost certainly less wealthy than he was before Rip came into his life.

It is possible that the entire popular music industry, in fact all of showbiz, is a giant con. It is certainly an illusion well exemplified by the magnificent Garry Shandling who, in the *Larry Sanders Show* – which appeared all too briefly on BBC television – presented the two faces of a showbiz star. On camera he is a warm, witty, caring person, happy to share the applause with the guests on his television chat show. Off camera he is foul-mouthed, vain, shallow, paranoid and entirely self-absorbed. It is a perfect portrayal, and in the show the people around him accept this in its entirety. They know, as just about everybody in the business knows, that it takes a very special personality to offer oneself up to the public every night – being aware each time that failure is imminent. The talent may dry up, public taste can change overnight and, worst of all, the performer may be found out. That fear lurks secretly in the souls of most artists. I mean, does anybody really believe that the latest pimply-faced adolescent discovery is truly a sex god with the key to all the secrets of the universe? It's a game we all play from time to time, and most artists come to recognize the rules in time.

9. CENTURY 21

CS, MONTY PRESKY OF PYE AND KEITH SHACKLETON OF CENTURY 21
LAUNCHING CENTURY 21'S MERCHANDISING OPERATION

CENTURY 21

With the demise of the ex-jukebox records business I was again out of a job but happened to see a Gerry Anderson programme on television and was sufficiently impressed to call him and suggest that he release some of the soundtracks on disc. He suggested a meeting, at which he showed me the pilot of his new series *Thunderbirds*. I was completely bowled over and certain that it could become as successful on disc as it was bound to be on television. Gerry agreed and gave me the task of setting up a new children's label, operating out of his studios at Slough in Berkshire.

Century 21 Films, as the company was known, was largely financed by the television company ATV, which also owned, among many other things, Pye Records, and Gerry was keen not to upset any in-house apple cart. He insisted that the record series first be offered to Pye. The ATV empire was controlled by Sir – later Lord – Lew Grade, who in effect held the purse strings for Gerry's projects, and, since Gerry in fact hated working with puppets and had ambitions to work with real actors, he was at great pains not to cross His Lordship or any of his immediate subordinates. Louis Benjamin, who ran Pye Records, was thought to be very close to Lord Grade, which meant that any negotiations for the distribution of the record label had to be handled with great delicacy; such delicacy, in fact, that at the meeting with Louis 'Benjy' Benjamin at Pye I did all the talking while being prompted in whispers by Gerry, who had taken a seat immediately behind me.

In the event we needn't have worried, as Benjy informed us that there was no sale for children's records and we should feel free to make whatever alternative arrangements we chose. Benjy had apparently had a miserable time with the Hanna–Barbera label, which was made up entirely of American cartoon soundtracks.

With some relief we began to assemble the catalogue and decided on a first release of six titles. These included two or three adapted soundtracks from *Thunderbirds*, a couple from *Stingray* plus some older material and one soundtrack with the voice of the lead character removed to enable the listener to read along with the other actors from a supplied script. We decided to release them as what we called Mini Albums. These were seven-inch EPs played at LP speed, which was then unusual if not unique.

Without any finished product, just a list of the first six titles and mocked-up sleeves for four of them, I visited Selecta Records, which was the distribution arm of Decca. By this time *Thunderbirds* had just been aired and, to my astonishment, Selecta ordered forty thousand copies of each title – almost a quarter of a million copies, which probably stands as a record opening order for a new series to this day.

On learning this, Benjy decided that he had erred and insisted that Pye also distribute the series. As a result Selecta halved their order and asked me to guarantee that Pye, who were also pressing the records, would play fair and not try to supply the major retailers such as Boots and Smiths in advance of supplying Selecta. After seeking assurances from Benjy, like a fool I gave my word. You've guessed it. Come the day of release Pye supplied all of the major shops first and made Selecta wait two weeks for their supplies, claiming that there were 'production problems'.

Having given my word, I felt bound to resign, which must have had the Pye lads in hysterics. What a blue-eyed twerp I was in those days. Not least for creating possibly the most successful children's label ever for just wages and no percentage but then resigning just as the series took off. I agreed to stay to oversee the official launch of the series and, at the press launch, was amused to hear Benjy explaining to the scribes how he had always believed in the strength of the children's market and how proud he was to have started this series. In the event the initial response from the public was total lack of interest.

The display boxes of records sat on the counters of Boots and Smiths and were ignored; this despite the appearance of a full-page advert in *Century 21*, which was then the best-selling children's comic in the country and the appearance on television of my son Chet, then about eight years old, playing the part of the 'missing' actor to the specially prepared soundtrack on the top-rated BBC television *Braden Show*. How I would like a video of that performance.

I relayed the bad news to Gerry, who, with his flair for the unexpected, suggested that we take a full-page advertisement in the *Daily Mirror* at a cost of several thousand pounds. Owing to the enormous cost, no record company had ever previously attempted this, but Gerry reasonably argued that a brand new approach was needed. He was right and, amazingly, within hours of the advert appearing the shops were sold out and reordering.

I stayed within the Century 21 set-up for a while working on 'character merchandising', which was essentially licensing various manufacturers the rights to use the names and pictures of characters from *Thunderbirds* and *The Man from U.N.C.L.E.*; boring stuff, but things were livened up by a couple of fantastic parties Gerry threw to publicize his activities. The first took place at a grand house in Belgravia that invitees were only able to discover after a series of meetings and whispered conversations with shady-looking characters posted around London, who would direct them on to the next contact. Upon arrival at the house, which was presented as an Embassy, the guests were searched by armed guards and shown into the ballroom to meet Gerry and mingle. At an arranged time Gerry stood up to address the sizeable crowd in front of a large portrait of Lady Penelope. As he began to speak, shots were fired and Lady Penelope herself crashed through her portrait and dashed through the crowd pursued by armed guards firing, I hope, blanks. Now that is an entrance.

Another party took place on an ocean-going liner, kindly supplied by Ellerman Lines. It was to encourage exports of Century 21 toys and, thinking about the potential shipping business, Ellerman's gave us access to one of their great liners moored in London Docks. The party began at midnight, an intriguing time in deserted dockland, with the liner all lit up and throbbing with activity. To this day I have never seen catering on that scale either on cruises to the USA or even in the movies. There were whole hogs turning on spits, wonderfully sculpted ice dishes and just about anything one could fancy on a buffet table at least as long as a cricket pitch. One's every need was catered to by a fleet of wraith-like waiters, who appeared as if by magic at every turn. It was a huge success and it cost us nothing.

It seemed that everything Gerry Anderson touched turned to gold. He had the most popular children's television series, a fabulously successful range of toys, the best-selling collection of comics, a highly profitable character merchandising company second only to the James Bond set-up – and, of course, the record label. Oddly enough, his real ambition was still to make feature movies with real actors, and for this he needed the support of the ATV board of directors, who were invited to the Slough studios to watch the *Thunderbirds* series being filmed. As the day of the visit approached, Gerry became increasingly agitated, insisting that the offices and studios were cleaned and polished to military standards and generally driving the creative staff crazy. The phalanx of executives eventually arrived in a fleet of black limousines and began to tour the premises in a black-suited, cigar-smoking wedge with Gerry leading the way. After a few minutes in the special-effects studio there was an enormous bang and the group emerged covered in dust with mangled cigars jutting out of some very surprised faces. Without another word they climbed back into the waiting limos and drove off. We never discovered if the 'accidental' explosion in special effects was revenge for Gerry's over-fussiness, but it was some years before the feature film was made.

Having moved out of the record label I watched with horror as Pye, with Benjy in charge, slowly destroyed it with the introduction of outside material, perhaps to prove that his initial comments were true. He also took over the running of the toy division. That was soon in trouble and was wound up, as indeed were the comics. I have never before or since seen so successful an empire so efficiently dismantled, and it is difficult to believe that it was not intentional. Benjy certainly had the ear and the support of Lord Grade, while Gerry was still anxious to get into feature films. I have since learned that Gerry Anderson now has no financial interest in *Thunderbirds*, which is a tragedy since they were entirely his creation. It must have hurt like hell when the series was recently revived on television and once again the toys began to sell and I was able to relaunch the records as a series of spoken-word cassettes.

Benjy seemed unaffected by the demise of the Anderson projects and went on to head up the Stoll Moss Theatre chain along with his duties as chairman of Pye and deputy to Lord Grade. I was to run into these two great characters again, but Benjy's impish style is best illustrated by the tale of how he launched the Golden Guinea series of low-price albums on television. This was a first in every respect, and all credit is due. However, Monty Presky, who was the production manager of Pye, told me of the time that Benjy had a lunch with the directors of Cunard Lines, who offered him a first-class return trip across the Atlantic in return for a picture of one of their liners appearing on a Golden Guinea sleeve. Monty was at a loss to figure out how to arrange this for his boss but eventually showed the series of sleeves to Benjy, who immediately enquired why an album entitled *Gypsy Camp Fire Music* should feature a picture of the *QE2* on the cover. 'Where are the gypsies?' he demanded to know. Monty pointed out that if one peered carefully into one of the portholes the gypsies could be seen enjoying tea. And that's how the album was released.

Perhaps the demise of the Century 21 empire is just another example of the creative elements being subject to the often ruthless activities of the business people. It would be pleasing to believe that they can work together in harmony, but the reality is that all too often the business side resents the creative process and will go to great and occasionally destructive lengths to demonstrate who, ultimately, wields the power. A recent biography of Gerry detailed a roller-coaster career in which, shortly after the worldwide successes, he was broke and working at home in an overcoat to save on heating bills. The Anderson magic has provided great entertainment for millions of kids, and without him I would never have been able to bring the original Lady Penelope and Parker puppets to my daughter Bee's fifth birthday party. That is an event that neither she nor I will ever forget.

Looking back, it now seems totally irresponsible to have put myself out of work yet again, particularly since Shurley had recently presented us with a new and beautiful daughter, but in those innocent days principles were still important. I returned to scuffling and hustling for a while, but with a new baby a larger house was required, and for that I needed a mortgage, which was obtainable only with a regular job and salary. Accordingly, I applied for and was appointed to the position of sales manager of a somewhat obscure company called Elektra Records. It was a move that changed my life.

POLITICS

Politics and politicians disenchant most of us. Back in the 1970s Shurley and I had an encounter with Prime Minister Harold Wilson at the BBC's Television Centre. We had just finished recording Top of the Pops with Clifford T. and entered a small lift, which we discovered to be occupied by Mr Wilson, somewhat the worse for drink and smoking a large cigar rather than his trademark pipe. Accompanied only by a female BBC employee and an aide, he had just completed a party political broadcast, and he managed, in the short journey to the ground floor, to address several offensive and suggestive remarks to Shurley. In an effort to avoid his embarrassing attentions we took evasive action on leaving the lift, but when Mr Wilson pursued us and continued trying to paw my wife I was forced to shoulder him aside. It was a most embarrassing and troubling experience, but our main concern was the vulnerability of the most powerful man in the country. He was leaving himself wide open to the attentions of blackmailers. I mentioned the incident to a colleague in the music business who was surprised by my surprise: he thought 'everybody knew' about Wilson and even gave me the name of the singer who was reputed to set up assignations for him. And you thought Mr Clinton had a problem.

Another time, visiting a friend at the Savoy, I passed an open door guarded by two huge bodyguards. Inside the room I glimpsed the back of a small man who was watching television with two athletic-looking gentlemen standing to the rear and each side of him. My friend told me that the occupant of the room was former American Vice-President Hubert Humphries and the bodyguards were armed and probably very dangerous. Later, as we left our room, the door was a little stiff and required a sharp pull, which made a loud report. Turning to walk along the corridor we were suddenly faced with one G-man on one knee pointing a huge revolver in our direction with another crouched by the stairwell waving an equally large gun. All this for a man who never made the top job! Later that day I travelled down in the hotel lift in company with Mr Humphries and his two minders. Upon reaching the ground floor the former Senator spotted an old friend and sped through the foyer with two heavily armed minders trotting in his wake. It didn't look like much of a life.

In a break between jobs I had time to be offended by the autocratic manner and language of building societies and formed a pressure group to try to make them more aware of the needs of their customers. It was successful enough to encourage the societies to plant 'moles' among our membership, and the group did, I believe, achieve some results. I was fortunate enough to get the support of Labour

MP Ken Weetch as chairman and found him to be a one of the brightest, most able people I have ever met. Ken arranged regular meetings in the House of Commons for our membership and, with no real knowledge of or interest in the financial world, would confidently address our meetings following just a very few minutes' briefing from me. Despite his considerable local support, he eventually lost his seat and began operating as a consultant to the housing business. Surprisingly, Ken never meant a great deal within the Labour Party, which meant either that the party was stuffed with geniuses or the leaders were too stupid to recognize his very considerable ability. You choose. At one of our meetings a coach party of pensioners arrived, each one of whom was warmly greeted by Tony Benn. I stood watching in admiration as Mr Benn keenly enquired about the health of the various named relatives. Perhaps that is what politics is really all about.

In a lighter vein, while working for Jonathan King in the mid-seventies, I became his campaign manager when he stood in a local election. We rented a room in the constituency, turning out and delivering handbills while Jonathan charmed the local residents. The campaign was, of course, unsuccessful but a lot of fun. One of the highlights was the appearance of Jonathan's friend Barry Humphries who, in the guise of Dame Edna Everage, turned up with his stunningly beautiful wife. We drove around the constituency for a while, making full use of the car's public address system, and eventually stopped at a local supermarket where Dame Edna accosted the customers on Jonathan's behalf. This was swiftly curtailed by an officious little store manager who ordered Dame Edna out. The fool should have let 'her' continue and phoned the local press. He could never have afforded to pay for that kind of publicity – but he preferred the power. And that, too, is probably what politics is all about.

These musings may not seem entirely relevant in the context of this book, but the fact is that politics and the quest for power will always play an important part in every career. There will always be the star or boss who tries to get into everyone's knickers regardless of the consequences; each organization will have a little Hitler prepared to cut off his nose in the pursuit of power, and every company or group includes the one who nearly made it to the top.

It may be that you, dear reader, have all of the ability and skills but find that for some reason your face doesn't fit. Perhaps you are lacking in what are euphemistically referred to as social skills but which are, in reality, an ability to kiss arse. Jonathan King always told me that I had a unique ability to 'get up people's noses'. He was probably right.

10. ELEKTRA

MUR

CS WITH LEVIATHAN

JUDY COLLINS

ELEKTRA RECORDS

Elektra Records' British branch in the mid-sixties was a small, reasonably successful folk label operating out of a couple of rooms in Soho over a basement where the great Blue Note jazz label was stored. With a total staff of four, comprised of a gentle Canadian managing director, who interviewed and hired me, his secretary and a somewhat unpredictable art director, we released albums by Judy Collins, Tom Paxton, Tom Rush, Phil Ochs, Spider John Koerner and the Paul Butterfield Blues Band. I had never heard of any of these artists prior to joining the company and was surprised to discover how popular they were with the folk cognoscenti.

We also distributed Blue Note and the Nonesuch classical label, both of which were imported from the USA in fairly limited quantities and sold directly to the major stores such as HMV in Oxford Street which would, astonishingly, order several hundred copies of the likes of Jimmy Smith and other big jazz artists.

Life at Elektra was fairly easy going, save for the fact that I detected a degree of animosity from Joe Boyd, who was at the time producing a new act called the Incredible String Band. Joe was a highly intelligent and cultured graduate of one of the great American universities and had been recently fired, with myself installed in his place. I had no idea of this at the time, and Joe appeared to be just another hippie hanging out with members of the fashionable 'underground' set. He went on to become a superb record producer, spending time with Warner Brothers films and producing several magnificent albums with Sandy Denny, Fairport Convention and dozens of important acts.

One of the most successful of Elektra's folk artists was Tom Paxton – probably best known for his haunting song 'Leaving London'. He could fill any venue without the benefit of a hit single, but his albums sold in substantial volume. He was popular with the rather arty television magazine shows such as *Late Night Line-Up* on BBC and was quite capable of giving a solo performance at the drop of a hat.

Television people really do believe they are special in some way, but it is always a shock to discover just how arrogant they can be. On one occasion Tom was recording a couple of songs for *Late Night Line-Up*, during which his performance was interrupted several times for technical reasons such as sound balance, lighting, camera position and so on. Tom bravely soldiered on, trying to retain some semblance of spontaneity through seven or eight takes and false starts until at last everything appeared to be in place and he commenced the master take. Halfway through this, an old chum of the director appeared and was greeted with shrill cries and much backslapping. Tom was ignored and had to decide whether to continue or take a gun to the ignorant shit. A somewhat subdued rendition was eventually filmed and shown, but it is not difficult to understand why artists turned to supplying videos that they could control.

On another occasion, following an appearance by Tom on *The Frost Show*, I was exposed to the full meaning of the expression 'cocktail-party eyes'. Tom and I were invited to a party celebrating some event in the great man's life, and when our host arrived, very late, of course, he swept into the room greeting and glad-handing the assembled celebrities without ever looking into anybody's eyes. David's eyes were permanently sweeping the room seeking out who was more important than whoever he was currently greeting. It was an eerie and rather ugly experience, but it does not appear to have adversely affected his career – in fact just the opposite. The Monty Python team got him just about right.

Mentioning the Pythons reminds me that we were once invited to see the group live on stage at the Drury Lane theatre one election night. The show was to be followed by a private backstage party attended by the group, and we eagerly anticipated an evening of wit and scorching satire as the results came in. In the event the Pythons were hilarious on stage but, in the tradition of great comics, after the show they were just a miserable bunch of sods with nothing to say to the guests or even to each other. At that time we shared the same accountant, so perhaps they, too, had a few problems in that area.

Some years later I recounted this tale to the new manager of the group, Dennis O'Brien, who was also George Harrison's partner in HandMade Films. Dennis went some way to restoring my admiration for the group by telling me of the time he took over their management. They had just cracked the US market, and the first film was doing great business with the inevitable result that their finances were in a bit of a mess and the Inland Revenue were making threatening noises. He called the team together and told them that he had set up a very important meeting with the inspectors, pointing out that it was imperative that they presented an appearance of sobriety and requesting that they all wore suits.

On the appointed day the various members arrived on time to meet their inquisitors and, at a prearranged signal, ripped off their coats to reveal themselves stark naked. According to Dennis, the inspectors were horrified and fled out of the office and down the street hotly pursued by naked Pythons hurling pillows. The explanation was that, as requested, they were wearing suits – albeit birthday suits. A lovely story, though I cannot swear to its authenticity.

Anyway, back to Elektra, where things began to change with the arrival of the first albums by Love, Tim Buckley and, of course, the Doors. While we were struggling to come to terms with what appeared to be a complete change of musical and business direction, the already legendary company founder and president, Jac Holzman, turned up in London and closed down the whole operation. This was my first encounter with the six-foot-four dynamic, articulate genius who was in the process of changing for ever the shape and sound of popular music. With the skill and dispassion of a surgeon, he fired everybody and virtually overnight closed a licensing deal with Polydor Records in which I was part of the package. He was gone within a day or so, and I took up my new position as Elektra label manager in Polydor in a state of some shock.

I imagine that the move had more to do with money than with personalities. The sudden American success of the Doors must have placed an enormous strain on Elektra's finances in terms of manufacturing and marketing costs, though Jac has always insisted that the strength of the Nonesuch classical collection sustained the company.

Sadly, the man who hired me, Don Johnson, never recovered from the abrupt termination and died shortly thereafter. His secretary, meanwhile, never forgave me for what she considered my act of betrayal, but the new situation left no time for introspection.

The music emanating from America was all-consuming and the Doors – despite the lack of conviction within Polydor – did eventually achieve a measure of success in Britain, more of which in the next chapter. Tim Buckley's *Goodbye and Hello* was heartbreakingly beautiful but probably three years too early for popular acceptance, despite a successful visit. David Ackles came close to it with his first album and the single 'The Road to Cairo', which can still give me goose bumps, but, even after a reception organized by Julie Driscoll and Giorgio Gomelsky and attended by Elton John, the Great British Public cocked a deaf 'un. (It is interesting to note that a couple of years after this Elton's huge American success came from opening for David at the Troubadour in Los Angeles.)

We finally cracked the British album charts with Love's *Forever Changes*, which was more successful in Britain than the USA. It is still considered by many to be one of the really great albums, to be ranked alongside *Sergeant Pepper*, and the single 'Alone Again Or' is regularly reissued with much radio exposure. The original album cut was considered by the Polydor people to be too long for a single, and I was persuaded to edit it down to around three minutes. This involved going into a studio with a sharp razor blade and editing out a complete section beginning and ending in the middle of a drumbeat. No problem with today's computer technology but a bit of a sweat then. I'm both proud and delighted that my edit is still the regular reissue.

Love is a tragic story of wasted talent. Arthur Lee was released from prison in late 2001, having served, as a third-time loser, five years of a twelve-year sentence for firearms offences; Bryan MacLean died in 1998; and an early member of the band reputedly had an accident with a pistol while on the drum stand and shot off a testicle. In the mid-sixties Love were considerably more popular than the Doors in their home town of Los Angeles, and they were Elektra's first rock act. In fact Love's 'My Little Red Book' became Elektra's first chart single, but Arthur refused to tour or do anything to consolidate the band's early success. Jac tells of weeks spent trying to persuade Arthur to come to New York for television exposure, succeeding eventually and depositing the reluctant teen idol in a hotel only to find him missing the following morning, leaving only a note saying that he hated big cities. Arthur did come to Britain some years later with a band he called Love, but by then the moment had passed. Another tale of what might have been.

Judy Collins was another somewhat reluctant chart artist. She made magnificent albums and could fill concert halls around the world with her clear, soaring voice accompanied only by her guitar-playing. However, when she first hit the singles charts in Britain with Joni Mitchell's 'Both Sides Now', backed by a full orchestra, Judy was unimpressed, having no desire to become a pop star. She steadfastly refused to undertake interviews or any form of promotion related to the single on the basis that it was irrelevant in the context of the state of the world. For instance, when I called her to set up a telephone interview with *Melody Maker* she did reluctantly agree, but on the condition that no mention was made of the record, which was, in her opinion, an irrelevance in the light of what was happening in Vietnam. (Try telling that to the average music hack.) That seems somewhat pompous now but was a reasonable reflection of prevailing attitudes among her peers.

Judy's biggest hit single was something of a surprise to her and to just about everybody – except yours truly. I first heard 'Amazing Grace' on a white-label test pressing of her album *Whales and Nightingales* in 1970, and I was immediately struck by the track, which was a traditional hymn recorded in a church and sung, for the most part, unaccompanied. I called Jac Holzman in New York and asked permission to release it as a single. Jac's response was that if this 'crazy limey' thought a hymn sung a cappella could be a hit I was welcome to try. Everybody at Polydor thought I had fallen off my trolley, as did David Platz at Essex Music, who published the B-side. Tony Blackburn, who was then presenting the *Breakfast Show* on Radio 1, proclaimed it a disaster and very publicly refused to play it, but – with a few plays on the John Peel and Wally Whyton shows – sales very slowly built into a Top Five hit and it ended up as the second-best-selling record over Christmas with over a quarter of a million copies shifted. Jac released it in America some weeks later with equal success.

'Amazing Grace' was, of course, a traditional hymn with no known composer to whom royalties were due. Judy could have claimed them as the interpreter and arranger, but that was not her style. Following the success of the record David Platz received a call from the bandleader of the Coldstream Guards requesting sheet music for the song. David obliged and thereby laid claim to the publishing rights to the new recording, which went on to sell over 7 million copies around the world; and all this despite the fact that David had been one of the many who scoffed at my original plan. I always felt that at least a Christmas card from him would have been nice, but he was probably too busy counting his royalties.

In Jac's splendid book *Follow the Music* he relates how he always knew that 'Amazing Grace' was a smash hit and was only beaten to the starting gate by the British release, which may be true but was certainly not apparent then. Whatever the truth, I'm sure he now believes it. It is, after all, in the nature of things to put one's own spin on events.

Judy is one of the great interpreters of other peoples compositions – her versions of Leonard Cohen and Bob Dylan songs are exquisite. She did once tell me that, in the really early days when she and Dylan were on the road and sleeping rough, she was trying to sleep in a barn while Mr Zimmerman was up in the loft struggling to write 'Mr Tambourine Man'. Judy heard the phrases so often while asleep that she found she could sing the song all the way through on awakening.

With two smash-hit singles and million-selling albums Judy was now a big star and was eventually persuaded to come back to Britain for some concerts and television shows. She was met at the airport by a posse of press people and photographers who waylaid her at the kerbside with the usual dumb questions and requests for photo opportunities. After about five minutes of this she spotted Johnny Cash in a similar situation about a hundred yards away. 'Oh, look,' she murmured to the assembled corps. 'There's Cash. Let's go see what he has to say', and with that she swept off to stand in the crowd around the great man.

Another time I collected Judy Blue Eyes from the airport only to discover that she had brought with her a bunch of superstars, including Joni Mitchell and James Taylor, who expected limos and five-star hotels to be laid on. It was an interesting glimpse into that strange, rarefied world where, among the dozen or so assorted stars, a number of the women were pregnant by guys who were with another partner – but nobody seemed bothered. To celebrate Judy's opening night I had booked a private room in a very grand hotel to accommodate about twenty people at midnight. On the spur of the moment she also invited Sandy Denny and her entire band and became both abusive and hysterical when no further places could be found for Sandy's roadies. We had a bit of a fight, and Shurley and I gave up our places and left the party to the embarrassment of the roadies, who probably only wanted the free drinks.

We met up again at Woodstock. Yes, I was there – and I hated it, as indeed did most of the acts at the time. I never got close to the stage or heard any music, and I spent most of the time watching old movies on television in the company of some very disgruntled artists.

The approach to Woodstock was like something out of a disaster movie. Since there were so many cars it was impossible to get near the site so, in true sixties fashion, the cars were left across the six lanes of the highway. Literally thousands of cars were abandoned just where they had stopped. It must have driven the cops crazy.

When Jac Holzman and I eventually made it to the hotel we learned that the crowds were so huge that it had become impossible to get anywhere near the performance area except by helicopter – the use of which was naturally reserved for the artists. This was an interesting start for me, as I had been engaged to report the event for Radio 1 and the *Melody Maker* – not easy from a mile away.

The hotel was the only one around and was, of course, madly overbooked, which resulted in several fistfights breaking out between the artists. When the rains came we heard tales of local people charging the fans $5 each for a bottle of milk or a loaf of bread. Since the audience did not have access to the helicopter they had no way of leaving the site for food and were thus subject to a bit of old-fashioned American opportunism. The scuttlebutt was that the original promoters of the event had taken all the ticket sale money and fled, leaving a couple of young promoters to try to pick up the pieces. It was a nightmare, with every artist and manager bitching and vowing vengeance upon the organizers.

Back at the hotel Jac and I gave up our rooms to those acts most in need, and I spent the first night watching an old Marlene Dietrich film while sharing a bedroom with Judy Collins, her current boyfriend – the then unknown actor Stacy Keach – her manager and about a dozen assorted musicians. It was not a comfortable night, and in the early hours I wandered outside to listen to the music wafting over the fields, almost drowned out by the sounds of the cicadas. Jac joined me, but we were unable to enjoy the moment on account of the truly dreadful smell emanating from God knows where. 'Smells like the Lord laid a fart,' said Jac. And that just about summed it up. The extraordinary thing was that years later when the movie came out all those artists who were bitching and fighting and swearing vengeance agreed that it was a truly spiritual event and one they would treasure. Wow, man. The PR machine rolls on.

Judy Collins had further hits, such as 'Send In the Clowns' in the mid-1970s, and those amazing eyes decorated a number of later hit albums, but disco rather swept away the folkies in the seventies, and though I occasionally see a Judy Collins concert billed I never quite get to it. I was recently informed that, with the advent of CDs, every one of Judy's albums has now achieved platinum status but that she is so unhappy with her current record label she is considering launching her own.

Getting back to Jac's book, another claim made in it is that he, among others, immediately recognized the potential of 'I Want to Make It with You' by Bread, which became a smash hit around the world. In fact I clearly recall Jac playing the album tape to me in Majorca and when I chose that track as a single release he was worried that US radio stations would not be happy with the suggestive nature of the title so that it would be better if it were released only in the UK. The real point is, of course, that Jac signed the band and released the album, for which he deserves all credit, as he does for his many other achievements.

Bread were a collection of very experienced and professional LA session men led by David Gates, who also wrote most of the hits. David came to England to promote the record just as John Fruin became managing director of Polydor Records, and discovered that the factory was out of commission and unable to supply the demand. In a rare instance of candour, John owned up to the deficiencies of the factory and promised to make good the situation. David, a particularly pleasant and agreeable man, accepted the apology with good grace and went on to have several more British hits. He now has a successful ranch in somewhere like Wyoming but still writes and records.

David's good grace was not matched by Jac's second-in-command Larry Harris. Larry was a short and short-tempered Jewish New York lawyer who acted as Jac's hatchet man on occasions. On one of his regular visits to England he stayed at the Playboy Club and suggested we meet there for, of all things, breakfast. Any night-club in the early light is a strange and faintly depressing sight, and the Playboy, with a few punters still at the tables, was all of that and more. The sexy Bunny Girls, with their deep cleavages and fish-net tights, were in attendance and serving breakfast as Larry went into considerable foul-mouthed detail about how he was going to 'ream those Polydor motherfuckers out and nail their livers to the wall'. He would pause occasionally to smile and gently address the waitress as she dangled her bosom over the scrambled eggs. 'Yes, darling, more coffee would be wonderful,' he gurgled in a voice dripping with lust before resuming his rantings. He had only a short spell with Elektra before joining Columbia Records where I'm sure his abilities and style were more appreciated. When I was fired by that company he sent me a kind note, which was appreciated.

Jac is a master in so many areas. He is a brilliant executive, a gifted producer, highly technical, an accomplished and economic writer – unlike this one – fiercely competitive, disarmingly honest, quick to praise or admonish and generous to a fault. He must have thought I was doing something right as, on a visit to London in 1971, he suggested that I return to working directly for him and casually mentioned that he would double my salary. I remember the time and place as if it were yesterday. Wouldn't you?

The new job entailed overseeing the British operation and travelling around

Europe seeking out the best potential licensees. In this capacity I would often run into Seymour Stein in various European cities where he was doing a similar job for Blue Horizon Records. Seymour went on to discover and record Madonna, found Sire Records and, at last intelligence, was running WEA Records in America. He remains a good friend.

The struggles with Polydor continued. They were committed to Atlantic Records and were finding their feet with local signings such as the Bee Gees, Hendrix and the Who but had difficulty with the eclectic range of Elektra. The many exquisite gatefold sleeves were considered too expensive to produce, and album sales were still secondary to single hits. The eponymous albums by Ars Nova and Earth Opera were excellent records in innovative sleeves without a single in sight. Tom Paxton and Tom Rush enjoyed healthy album sales with sold-out appearances but no hits, though Arthur Gorson, who managed Tom Rush, was convinced that 'No Regrets' would turn the tables. In the end it wasn't a hit for Tom, but the likes of the Walker Brothers and Midge Ure did chart with it later. He visited his friend Danny Secunda to play him the recording in his office some floors up in Soho and was disappointed in the quality of the available equipment. Danny agreed and, ripping the record player out of the wall, flung it out of the window where it fell three floors and crashed through a glass roof over the heads of a room full of seamstresses. Tom and Arthur were horrified, but Danny apparently failed to notice. It was the sixties, man.

On one of many visits to New York Jac suggested that I migrate there and assured me that I would be on an executive level comparable with Bill Harvey, who was Elektra's art director and responsible for all that fabulous and innovative sleeve design. Visiting Bill's home at White Plains, I was surprised to discover that he lived in a beautiful part of the country with lots of land and his own private lake. The house, on several floors with magnificent views and a fully equipped games room in the basement, made my little semi in Slough look slightly shabby in comparison. I was unable to take up the offer, as that would have meant leaving behind my three growing children who lived with their mother but with whom I was very close. Not for the first or last time, however, I was struck by the discrepancy between American and British salaries. It appeared that every young person in any worthwhile position was buying the latest Buick or Oldsmobile while I was having trouble keeping up the payments on a Mini. On a visit to Los Angeles Bill Harvey drove me out to Venice Beach where the handsome, bronzed youngsters frolicking in the sand and sneering at our suits made me feel old, grey and redundant. I was just thirty and, in the sixties, anybody over thirty was considered to be the enemy.

On that visit I was introduced to the Plaster Casters, who were a bunch of groupies that had achieved a degree of notoriety far beyond their appeal – their thing was to make plaster casts of pop stars' penises. I was also invited to a party at the house of Hollywood's most prominent television producer. It was a strange evening during which the hostess danced sexily with her female companion while the assembled males lusted on the sidelines, swam or played pool. I played chess with Mel Posner, Elektra's aggressive and gifted sales manager, until the hostess arranged for a projector screen to descend from the ceiling to show her in a clip from a television show in which she had appeared briefly with Tom Jones. Following this highlight a large black man, armed with a knife, invited us all to leave the house. We left at a pretty fast clip musing on the strangeness of Hollywood, where everything is an illusion.

Back in Britain, not everything went according to plan. I found and produced a group formerly known as the Mike Stuart Span, whom we renamed Leviathan. We released a couple of singles without any great success; but Jac was not pleased with the album and it never saw the light of day. One of the by-products of this adventure was a television film for BBC 2 following the group's emergence in which I claimed that in very short time young fans would be begging to know what the band wore in bed. The closing shot of the programme was a back view of one of the band members as he returned to his job on a building site. The programme has become something of a classic and is often repeated to the delight of my friends but not to me. I have a copy of the show but have yet to steel myself to watch it.

The 5000 Spirits or the Layers of the Onion by the Incredible String Band, produced by Joe Boyd, was another British album chart entry that failed in America; but the album that raised our expectations highest was *Accept No Substitute* by a bunch of Southern US musicians known as Delaney and Bonnie and Friends. It seemed that the entire music industry was breathless with anticipation, and Jac asked me to obtain quotes from various British musos to go on the British sleeve. Mick Jagger obliged by saying that it was the best album he had heard since falling out of his cradle, and both Eric Clapton and George Beatle agreed, even requesting to be allowed to play at the group's concerts. The Albert Hall concert was a sold-out triumph, but the album never quite clicked with the public and the group left Elektra for Atlantic where they fared no better. It is possible to be just too good.

The same cannot be said for either the Stooges or MC5, who also made Elektra albums before migrating to other labels. I loved the Stooges' album and was literally hypnotized by 'I Wanna Be Your Dog'. It is no surprise that Iggy Pop has gone on to such acclaim, but the raucous rantings of the Detroit-based MC5 left me stone cold as did the somewhat contrived David Peel. MC5's 'Kick Out the Jams' and Peel's 'Have a Marijuana' with his band the Lower East Side were bold and daring for the times but had little musical merit. Though I managed to get 'Apricot Brandy' by Rhinoceros used as the theme tune on a couple of Radio 1 shows, the public showed no interest in them or, in no particular order, Roxy, Paul Siebel, Clear Light, Carol Hall and a growing number of other releases.

It may have been that my responsibilities in Europe took my eye off the ball; or it may just have been a combination of looking after the interests of Elektra and its publishing subsidiary Nina Music plus my own companies Dandelion Records and Biscuit Music – the record label and its sister publishing company that I had set up with John Peel in 1969 (of which more later) – as well as having taken on the management of DJs John Peel and Pete Drummond along with a number of Dandelion acts that spread my limited abilities too thinly. Suffice to say, for much of this period I was fortunate to have the support of an extremely capable and self-effacing secretary Sylvia Kneller, but she eventually left to take up a career as a children's nanny in Sicily. So no change for her there, you might think. Sylvia's replacement appeared initially to be efficient and at the end of each day she would bring my letters, neatly typed and ready for me to sign. As time passed I became aware that many of these letters were unanswered. This was hardly surprising as I discovered that, for reasons known only to her, they all wound up jammed down the ladies' lavatory. I later learned that she tried to sell to newspapers the story that her subsequent dismissal was the result of a conspiracy between me, my 'brother' Paul McCartney and our 'father' George Martin. Sometimes the pressure can be too intense.

Jac tried to find a great British group and signed both Eclection and Renaissance. *Eclection* was produced by Ossie Byrne – who had achieved massive success with the Bee Gees – and featured musicians who went on to great things, and *Renaissance* was produced by Jac's old friend, the former Yardbird Paul Samwell-Smith. Perhaps if Jac had been around to supervise, the results may have been different. In fact one of the members of Eclection later joined the New Seekers, who gave Elektra one of its biggest-ever US hits with 'I'd Like to Teach the World to Sing' and, as we'll see later, another ex-Yardbird, Keith Relf of Renaissance, wound up producing Dandelion's first hit single.

During this period I was very proud to call Tim Buckley a friend. His first album, recorded when he was just nineteen, was a joy. Full of poetry and emotion, the songs were written by Tim with Larry Becket who was then building a reputation as a poet of merit. With the second album, *Goodbye and Hello*, Tim had matured into one of the truly great singer-songwriters, and today, many years after his tragic and early death, his songs live on through cover versions and movie soundtracks as well as a resurgence in interest in his own recordings.

He was a jolly if enigmatic character, devoted to his craft and with a vocal range that could stretch to four octaves. I once asked him in some trepidation the meaning of the lyrics of his classic 'Morning Glory' and was told that it was about a group of college kids 'beating up on a hobo'. Boy, you could have fooled me.

He first came to London in the late sixties for a few club dates accompanied by three musicians and his manager – and former Cuban Freedom Fighter – the legendary Herb Cohen. Because the flight arrived early and the hotel rooms were not yet ready, I invited the group back to my new little semi-detached in Slough where the garden had yet to be landscaped and was a sea of mud. Bored with the usual desultory post-flight conversation, Tim's eyes lit up at the sight of my two-year-old daughter Sam and, with a murmured 'I love kids', he disappeared with her into the back garden. They returned an hour or so later smiling broadly – the pair of them covered from head to foot in thick mud.

On that first visit he played the Speakeasy, seduced or was seduced by at least two of the girls in my office and recorded a session for the *John Peel Show* on Radio 1, which was produced by Bernie Andrews. Tim was a very intense performer and hated to waste time in a studio. Following a perfect first take Herb Cohen, who also managed the Mothers of Invention and other somewhat off-the-wall acts, turned to me and said, 'You know, I don't care much for this weird shit, but as shit goes that's pretty good shit', possibly unaware that the talkback mike was still open. Tim heard the comment and growled, 'Tell Herb to shut up and turn on the damn tape.' The resulting session was pure magic and was the main impetus behind why, twenty years later, I reissued the Peel Sessions on the Strange Fruit label label and managed to retrieve and release that session complete with Tim's comment.

Though Tim was never a commercial success, his reputation grew and, on a subsequent visit, he filled the Royal Festival Hall in London and gave a devastating performance that was released on CD a few years back to great acclaim. Here I should apologize on behalf of Pete Drummond, who appears on the disc as compère. Shurley and I managed Pete at the time and he was literally dragged out of the audience to introduce the show with no preparation when the billed compère failed to appear. At that time the British Musicians' Union had a reciprocal arrangement with their American counterparts to ensure work for their members by which all visiting American musos were bound to employ at least one local. In Tim's case we were fortunate to have the services of the great bassist Danny Thompson, who played on all the dates including the radio recordings and the one television show Tim completed on that tour.

Television exposure for cutting-edge artists such as Tim was next to impossible, so I was thrilled to receive a call from Stanley Dorfman offering a spot on the *Julie Felix Show* on BBC2. On the day, Tim arrived – at the usual bleak rehearsal room – in the company of Danny lugging his huge string bass. Without a word they unsheathed their instruments and launched into a mesmerizing and totally unrehearsed pastiche of jazz, folk and pure funk, which ran without pause for at least an hour. Stanley, Julie and I watched and listened in open-mouthed admiration as Timmy howled and wailed, shrieked and sobbed to his own guitar accompaniment driven on by the pounding bass lines provided by Danny.

It was an unique and unrepeatable experience made even more remarkable by the forbearance of the producer and the star of the television show who were expecting a three-minute single but who were sensitive enough to let it just happen. At the end of the performance Tim was soaked in sweat and drained. He put his guitar back in its case, donned his jacket, said, 'OK?' to Stanley, and the two musicians left dragging the instruments behind as they were too exhausted to lift them. An old cold former church hall in west London may still echo to that mystical event. No other words were exchanged, and Tim did appear on Julie's show with a three-minute number as requested.

Though looking and sounding like the archetypal hippie, Tim was very professional and had little truck with the time-wasting activities of so much of the music business. He told me once of spending months on the road and taking a short break to complete an album. Turning up at the Elektra Studio on time he was dismayed to find the sessions delayed while the producer and engineer set the right ambience for the recordings with a discreet display of soft candles 'and other bullshit'. When not working he kept fit by cycling on the beach – albeit with several cans of beer. But this was Los Angeles.

Tim left Elektra and made a couple of pretty dense and jazzy albums for Herb's own label, Straight Records. They were critically acclaimed but failed to build on the success of *Goodbye and Hello*. We stayed in touch, and the last time we met was at the

Troubadour in Los Angeles where Tim was sharing the bill with another act. He was obviously troubled and confided that he had taken to carrying a gun to defend himself 'against the LA cops'. It was a dramatic change from the engaging troubadour and bore all the signs of drug paranoia. I feared for him. Just a few weeks later he was dead; the victim, it appears, of an accidental overdose administered by a friend. Some friend.

The torch was eventually passed to his son Jeff who shared some of his father's gifts, though they barely knew each other. Jeff, too, died in tragic circumstances and at an appallingly early age. I never knew the son, but it just may be that Tim was a true child of the sixties and, like so many others, could never have become old. I do miss him.

Herb Cohen, his manager for many years, is a former coal miner and a very tough guy indeed. Whenever his colleagues complained of 'the pressure' or 'the work load' Herb would suggest a spell down the mines as an eye-opener, but even he, years later, could not prevent his eyes misting over when I asked for and received his permission to release Timmy's Peel Sessions – and you don't get a lot of that in the Industry of Human Happiness.

Herb is one of the great industry characters and continues to be a highly respected and successful manager. He was noted for always wearing the same style shirt to every occasion and apparently had them made in bulk. He was also the man for whom the mobile telephone was invented. Wherever he was he would head for the nearest phone and call his office with the number where he could be reached. This would happen twenty or thirty times a day. Mobiles must have changed his life. At any party Herb would be the guy in the corner hunched over a telephone.

At one party Herb displayed his experience and wisdom to my advantage. A loony who kept insisting, at considerable length and volume, that no modern guitar hero could compare with the likes of the jazz greats was dogging me. Clapton, Page, Hendrix, none of them could hold a candle to Charlie Christian with whom he had played as a saxophonist, apparently, on one occasion within the confines of a dustbin. In vain I sought escape and to my horror found myself seated next to this gentleman at dinner where he continued to regale me with tales of his life in jazz and his total disdain for the rock fraternity.

To my intense relief Herb appeared fresh from a telephone call and took up the challenge. He pointed out to our new friend that before getting into music manage-ment he had owned a restaurant, and whenever he had gone out to eat he had spent the whole time examining the condiments or the cutlery or the decor and had always been too busy to enjoy the meal. 'And that, my friend, is what you are doing with music.' It was a perfect and gentle put-down. It terminated a boring conversation and is a pretty good lesson in music appreciation.

Another Elektra lady was Carly Simon, who enjoyed a number of hits including, of course, 'You're So Vain', which became something of an anthem for the seventies and was rumoured to be written about Warren Beatty. Carly came to London to record and asked the record company to provide a furnished apartment for an indefinite period. One was found in Kensington – where else? – and, following her inspection and approval of it, I was somewhat nonplussed to receive a call from the owner enquiring in strident Kensington tones if Ms Simon had 'a touch of the tar brush'. Summoning up as much icy politeness as I could muster, I responded that I had not paid a great deal of attention to the singer's pigmentation but felt that, as the daughter of one half of the mighty publishing conglomerate Simon and Schuster, it was reasonable to assume that the lady was properly housebroken.

Carly was a very effusive and over-the-top person. A chum of mine told me that he had attended a James Taylor concert with her in New York where she was so taken by the performance that on meeting the man backstage after the show she enthused about the concert, praised his voice, his hair, his smile and on and on until James became overwhelmed and, trying to be gallant, looked her up and down and said, 'Gee, Carly, you've got great tits.' They later married, but I wouldn't recommend it as a chat-up line.

Phil Ochs, the highly respected and very political balladeer, came to London shortly after I joined Elektra. He, too, had a substantial following, particularly among the left wing of the folk movement, and a small reception was arranged at the office to allow the critics and reviewers to meet him. The gathering consisted of many duffel-coated and bearded leftie writers for little magazines – and then there were the men. The questions were deep and concerned with communism, capitalism, socialism, feminism and a whole slew of 'isms' that kept the party bubbling along like a wake. When one very intense young lady quoted a line from Karl Marx, Phil borrowed some lipstick and wrote it out in three-foot-high letters along our newly decorated office walls where it remained until we vacated the premises. He deserved a better fate than suicide by hanging.

Spider John Koerner was another travelling troubadour of the early days of Elektra. He arrived at Heathrow carrying only a guitar case and, when I enquired about the rest of his luggage, opened the case to reveal, in addition to his guitar, a toothbrush, a razor and a change of underpants. That was it for a three-month visit. Spider John's best selling album was called *Blues, Rags and Hollers*, and he was a favourite of John Lennon.

The great Fred Neil made a couple of albums for Elektra before disappearing to Florida to serenade the dolphins. I never met him but remain enthralled by that fabulous voice. Tim Buckley told me that he and Frank Zappa contributed a proportion of their earnings to support Fred in his lean times because they so much admired him. It is a strange turn of fate that both Tim and Frank are gone while Fred remains in semi-seclusion somewhere among the dolphins.

I was never a fan of the Mothers of Invention, but Frank had the most piercingly intelligent eyes I have ever seen and a very thoughtful manner. It all kind of fell into place when Herb Cohen, who was also their manager, pointed out to me that the Mothers were essentially a jazz band but, without the off-the-wall appearance and antics, who would listen? I hope that doesn't shatter too many illusions.

The enigmatic Nico made an album for Elektra, but we never met. She would occasionally call and suggest a meeting – usually in a coffee shop. She never showed up and, months later, would phone again to apologize, because 'Fellini asked me to fly to Rome to discuss a film part' – which may just have been true.

The late sixties were a heady, breathless, exciting time when we truly believed that music could make the difference. In our rather naïve way we had hope that the world could become a better place with peace and love to spare. Honest, guv! The era came to a fairly abrupt end for me in 1970 when Elektra was sold to the Kinney Corporation, which had acquired Warner Brothers and Atlantic Records from a base that included car parks and shoe stores.

Around this time the Stones' Decca contract was about to expire, and naturally everyone wanted to sign them, but the two front runners were Ahmet Ertegun of Atlantic and Clive Davis of American Columbia. In an effort to ingratiate himself with the band Ahmet spent several weeks hanging out with them to show just how cool he and his company could be. At his age, or at just about any age, the Stones' lifestyle could at best be described as taxing, but Ahmet persevered and after a few weeks believed that he and Mick had found some common ground. Finally exhausted, he asked Mick when he could expect a decision about which label he would choose. 'Right after I've talked to Clive' was the somewhat ambivalent reply.

Mick Jagger carefully cultivated his image as an anti-Establishment rebel, yet he is one of the brightest and most intelligent men you could meet. When Decca were unable to find enough quantity of a particular board required to manufacture one of the Stones albums Mick spent several days telephoning suppliers around the world and found what was needed in Eastern Europe. Rock and roll, eh?

The Stones did, of course, sign with Atlantic in the end, and the first release was the smash hit 'Brown Sugar' off the *Sticky Fingers* album, with the Andy Warhol-designed cover featuring a zip. (Perhaps Mick was getting some of his own back for the problems with the Decca cover, because manufacturing that sleeve was a nightmare.) Before the release, however, Ahmet wanted to show off to the world his new acquisition and threw a huge party at the exclusive Yacht Club in Nice to which I was briefed to invite representatives from the world's press, radio and television.

Mick had recently married the ravishing, if slightly boyish, Bianca, and for that reason alone the media interest was enormous with invitations strictly limited. On the night, all of the Stones were there – though Keith was perhaps there more in spirit. He looked really sick. I have never seen anybody before or since with such a ghastly pallor. It truly looked as though he had died and been buried – honestly, he was a deep shade of green. It's terrific to see him now looking so much fitter, but on that night, in the midst of all the action, Mick was constantly attentive to Keith's every need. The purpose of the party was, of course, to publicize the new alliance of Atlantic and the Stones, and the best route was through a photo of the band with Bianca and Ahmet, which would be published around the world. Getting everyone together for that shot was, to say the least, difficult, but towards the end of a long evening it was arranged. The fly in that particular celebrity ointment was the sudden appearance in the centre of the group of Eddie Barclay, who was not only the owner of Barclay Records, a rival company, but who had also had a long relationship with the lovely Bianca.

Ignoring the howls of protest, Mr Barclay refused to move, and it looked for some time as though Ahmet's moment of triumph would be ruined. Without a word, and from a sitting position, Mick picked up the portly Barclay, who weighed at least twice as much as him, carried him to the edge of the encircling journalists, deposited him in their midst, patted him on the head and said, 'Now be a good boy, Eddie.' A potentially sticky situation was avoided with good humour, tact and a remarkable show of sheer strength.

The photographers were having a ball, but one German guy was so persistent that a print-out of his pictures would have made a stop-motion film. Jagger accommodated him for at least a couple of hours during which he was snapped from every conceivable angle. Eventually Mick called a halt and asked the guy to stop and let him enjoy the party. His request was ignored and the snapper continued flashing bulbs just inches away from his face. Mick politely asked him again to stop, with the suggestion that surely he now had enough pictures for a book. When the idiot refused he got the full contents of Mick's glass in his face and lens. I never checked, but I have an idea which picture appeared in the German press.

We subsequently went to see the Stones at the Roundhouse, a converted railway shed in north London, but found the act to be boring, predictable and much too obviously choreographed. The Roundhouse was never one of our favourite venues and when a warm yellow liquid, which we hoped was orangeade, began to trickle down upon us from the gallery above we left before it got worse.

In the sixties I used occasionally to visit Jagger in his London office where he held court in a peacock chair, and was there one time when Janis Joplin showed up. I had seen Janis with Big Brother and the Holding Company at an early gig in Los Angeles. She and they had been sensational, with Janis downing her usual bottle of Southern Comfort on stage, but Janis remembered it only as 'a Mafia gig' at which all of their equipment had been stolen. In Mick's office she looked awful, bundled up in a white fur coat and with a complexion that resembled a relief map of the moon. As we conversed she leaned over me with one foot on the arm of my chair and gazed fairly intently into my eyes. 'Look out,' said Mick, laughing at my obvious discomfort with a teacup balanced precariously in my shaky hand. 'Janis wants to ball.' With a raking and contemptuous look at my wilting ego Janis growled, 'I'm not that fucking desperate', and the moment passed.

As part of the Elektra deal I joined the new organization, which was initially known in Britain as Kinney and subsequently became WEA Records. Ian Ralfini ran the new set-up with a very talented staff of dedicated people. The first few months were promising, and I was encouraged to bring Dandelion into the fold, which I did, and we enjoyed our first ever Top Twenty record. Derek Taylor joined the company from Apple and immediately positioned his desk behind a large fishing net through which he would peer and regale people with his dry humour. Alice Cooper dropped in one day unannounced. Since he was almost unknown in Britain at that time the receptionist was somewhat confused by this tough-looking bearded guy with a girl's name. I would like to reveal details of a scintillating conversation, but Alice had a couple of six-packs of Miller's with him and was suffering from jet lag. He drank them and fell fast asleep with his head on my desk until his manager arrived and carted him away. Frank Zappa fixed me with those piercingly intelligent eyes before he, too, fell fast asleep.

The Family and the Faces were Warner's biggest local acts, but the company was always looking for new British talent. One day, while Ian Ralfini and his cohorts were off canvassing in America, Jeff Dexter walked into the office. Jeff was then a DJ at one of the underground clubs and was managing a band called America. He came in with an acetate of one of the group's songs and its producer Ian Samwell. Since I was not very busy and merely deputizing for the absent MD I listened to the acetate, loved it and devised a grand marketing campaign, which thrilled Jeff and Ian and was very successful. The acetate was 'Horse With No Name'. Later I listened to the whole album and found it a bit weak, but that didn't stop it from becoming a smash hit both here and in the States, but I've often wondered what might have happened if circumstances had been different. Jeff was delighted to be managing a hit group but had the management taken away from him shortly after taking them across the pond. That's rock and roll.

The business of music will always be a lottery with comparable prizes and disappointments. Adam Faith was busy producing Leo Sayer at this time but, despite the support and interest initially shown by the company, every track he produced was rejected by the Ralfini team. Legend has it that, with advances and studio costs in excess of £100,000 but no working relationship with the executives, Adam asked to be released from the contract and was immediately given a handwritten release allowing him to keep the master tapes. He promptly flew off to the USA and sold the tapes to WEA there, who were unaware that they had already paid for them. He then licensed the masters to Chrysalis in the UK. Of course, Leo Sayer became an international superstar, so everybody was happy – with the possible exception of the accountants at WEA after they discovered that they had paid twice and the London team who had seriously blown it. The story may be apocryphal, but I wouldn't put it past any of the principals.

With three (four with Dandelion) fiercely independent labels to juggle, Ian chose to try to amalgamate them into one unit, which was a political mistake. All four labels had built substantial reputations in different areas and I fought the homogenization, which earned me the reward of being demoted to export manager. Jac was busy establishing himself with the WEA group in Los Angeles and offered little support. It was a difficult time and, as the group established offices in France and Germany, Ian spent most of his time and energy polishing apples with the bosses in Los Angeles in competition with his French and German counterparts. The combined costs of their air fares alone were enough to launch several new acts and created a competitive and political situation completely at odds with the musical ethos of the times.

I decided to leave, but not before most of the company had descended on Hamburg, where I made a second reluctant visit to Club Salambo, which had formerly been the German home of the Beatles. As I discovered on my first visit – when I had been taken on a whirlwind tour of Hamburg's red-light district by a local journalist – the club featured rather perfunctory live sex on stage to the accompaniment of a prerecorded soundtrack. This was considered to be 'entertainment' for visiting businessmen. On this occasion one of our party fell deeply in love with one of the performers and, despite being married at the time, disappeared with her for several days. I deduced that something was amiss when, following the performance, in which the young lady had performed most of the popular sex acts with a variety of partners of different colours and genders, I innocently enquired of her if anything actually turned her on. My smitten colleague soundly admonished me – for my insensitivity.

On another night in Hamburg I spent time with the great Tony Joe White, who is currently enjoying something of an overdue revival. Tony wrote 'Polk Salad Annie' and 'Rainy Night in Georgia', among many others, and was a great fan of Elvis. Imagine his delight when he learned that his hero had recorded one of his songs and was about to première it in Las Vegas. He told me how he had sat in the audience drinking rather more than he should in nervous anticipation until he could no longer hold his water. Dashing to the men's room he was in full flow when he heard Elvis announce his song and suggest that the composer take a bow. Stepping out into the crowded lounge in a full spotlight he took a bow with all of his, as it were, talent on display. Tony claims that his wife never forgave him.

Life in the record business is never truly dull, but life at WEA came as close as I ever wish it to be and so, with considerable sadness and the gift of a toy motor cycle from Jac, I reluctantly took my leave. It had been an exhilarating, joyful and instructive period, but it was time to move on. Elektra continued to enjoy great times with hits by the Cars, Carly Simon and Harry Chapin, for whom Jac returned to the studio in the role of producer. Not long before Harry's tragic death Shurley and I spent time with him and his wife Sandy. They were going through a bad patch at the time and we were delighted to be credited with saving their marriage. Jac signed a number of established British acts and truly hit the jackpot with the New Seekers and Queen but was unable to do much for our Dandelion acts.

Jac Holzman and Elektra Records were an inspirational force with which I was proud to be associated. It was also a great learning experience. We continued to be friends with Jac and have enjoyed his hospitality and generosity on several occasions. In life there are far too few genuine heroes or mentors, and I am fortunate to have met more than my share. Not everybody can be multi-talented or skilled but Jac was once kind enough to tell me that what I did best I did best of all. Faint praise, you might feel, but it serves as good advice for the ambitious: find what you do best and aim to do that to the best of your ability.

CS WITH ROBBIE KRIEGER AND JIM MORRISON OF . . .

11. THE
DOORS

Jac Holzman

THE DOORS

Sadly, it fell to me to inform Bill Siddons, the Doors' manager, of the presumed death of Jim Morrison in July 1971. In fact, even though thousands of fans make the annual pilgrimage to a tombstone in Paris, I have never been convinced that Jim died in the place and in the manner generally accepted. The facts don't appear to hold up, and it may just be that the Lizard King is alive and fat and laughing at us all.

Before the event he had questioned a number of friends, myself included, as to whether we felt that he had yet reached the status whereby in death he would become a legend. We, of course, rushed to assure him that it was much too soon – but events have proved us wrong.

I first heard the first Doors album in the form of a white-label test pressing from America a few months after joining Elektra. It was both electric and electrifying and only the label's second venture into what became known as 'West Coast rock', the first of which had been *Love* by Love. *The Doors* was magnificent in terms of performance, content and production. It was also immediately apparent that it would be very difficult to sell to a British public and particularly to British radio. The only national radio station playing pop music was the BBC Light programme, which was extremely limited in the amount of records it was allowed to play and heavily reliant on the happy sound of a two-and-a-half-minute pop single.

Elektra Records at that stage was rather less than the sophisticated marketing and promotional organization through which to launch a major world-class act, but we nevertheless released the album and set about trying to get radio plays, press reviews and, it was to be hoped, a degree of acceptance with the leading taste-makers, such as the Beatles, who then were in the process of recording *Sergeant Pepper*.

At this remove it is difficult to even recall just how revolutionary *The Doors* really was, but there was no doubt that we were entering new musical territory and meeting a lot of opinionated opposition. Most of the initial reviews were mystified or hostile, but a minor breakthrough was a tiny mention in one of the music papers that Ringo had suggested that the Doors were 'one of the more interesting bands to emerge in America'. Sales were non-existent, and there was nobody on pre-Peel national radio in Britain even to give it a listen.

A single was needed, and it occurred to me that an edited version of 'Light My Fire' might provide the breakthrough, at least in terms of radio exposure. Working from home with primitive equipment I completed a rough edit, bringing the piece down to about three and a half minutes but leaving the soaring instrumental middle section intact. I sent the edit with some trepidation to the boss in the USA. Jac Holzman called back to say that the notion of an edit was approved but that the task had been given to the producer of the album, Paul Rothschild, who was approaching the project from another direction.

Eventually Paul's edit arrived, and I was horrified to discover that virtually the entire organ and guitar 'bridge' had been removed. Nevertheless we released the new version and began to pick up a few plays on the pirate station Radio London, which was broadcasting somewhere out in the North Sea and becoming increasingly popular with a young audience that was being ignored, or at best patronized, by the BBC.

'Light My Fire' eventually charted at the lower end in Britain but took the USA by storm, where it dramatically shot to number one and took the album with it – no doubt helped by the stunning publicity shots of Jim stripped to the waist and looking suitably enigmatic.

Elektra was the hot new label and probably severely stretched financially. A million albums have to be manufactured, distributed and paid for before any money comes back, and these costs, along with recording, promotion and advances to a newly successful act, can, you may be surprised to learn, bring down a company without adequate financial resources. Add to this the fact that most of the big retail chains in America only pay their accounts when they need to order more product and it becomes apparent why so many successful small labels end up in the hands of well-funded multinationals or the Mafia. It also illustrates the importance of the follow-up single or album, since all too many times the label without a second hit may never be paid in full for the first and still be stuck with all of the costs.

All this explains why Jac Holzman arrived out of the blue and informed us that he was closing down the UK operation. During the move to Polydor 'Light My Fire' flickered and died, but interest in the band was growing, at least among the new hippie movement which now had a voice in the new underground papers, the two most influential being *Oz* and *International Times*, or *IT* as it was known. John Peel was introducing the Brits to West Coast rock via his magical *Perfumed Garden* show on Radio London and *Sergeant Pepper* was top of the charts. It was probably the most exciting and hopeful time for anyone under thirty and truly a golden age for those lucky enough to be in the music business. We released 'Alabama Song' as a follow-up single without success, but it helped maintain momentum for the band, who were now superstars in America where Jim was already becoming an icon as well as an iconoclast.

The Roundhouse was the only sizeable venue willing to book this new underground music in London and the Doors, who had just released *Strange Days* as their second album, agreed to appear there for two nights at the start of a short European tour. The new single in the States was 'Hello, I Love You', which bore rather too strong a resemblance to the Kinks' 'All Day and All of the Night' – not that surprising since Jim in particular was a great fan of theirs. It was, nevertheless, another huge American hit and, on the strength of that, I was able to get the band on to *Top of the Pops*, which was the only meaningful television exposure available and pretty much guaranteed a hit if the record had what it took. I also entered into negotiations with Granada TV to film the tour and the performances for a hitherto unheard of one-hour show devoted to the band. Not even the Beatles or the Stones had yet been accorded that level of exposure.

Here I supply a footnote to remind younger readers that most of the music world and virtually all of the established record companies hated this new music and hoped that it was a passing fad which would go away as quickly as it had arrived. As detailed elsewhere in this book (see the chapter on mavericks), Polydor were not convinced of the long-term potential of the Doors, and every penny of promotional support had to be gouged out with much kicking and screaming. Jefferson Airplane were due to support us at the Roundhouse, and their record company refused even to advertise their album in the underground press, who left blank pages in their publications where an advertisement had been expected. Strange days indeed.

In the teeth of much opposition I was able to arrange a number of record-shop window displays in the West End, around the Roundhouse and along the route from Heathrow – which, it turned out, impressed the band no end. The main task, however, was to find a dramatic and innovative venue from which to introduce the band to the media, and here again it was my old chum John Peel who came to the rescue. At John's suggestion I got in touch with the Institute of Contemporary Arts in the Mall, which was showing an exhibition of Cybernetic Serendipity at that time – no, I didn't know what it was either, but it sounded right – and they agreed to let us host the reception amid the robots and strange exhibits. Invitations were sent to the music media which responded very favourably.

The Doors arrived red-eyed on an overnight flight from Los Angeles and were met by the Granada team who stuck cameras and microphones in their faces and asked them to identify themselves as they stepped off the plane. Perhaps not the best possible way to enter a country for the first time, but the lads were polite and good-humoured and, even in those trying circumstances, their characters emerged. Ray was quiet and studious, Robbie was so shy that he appeared stoned and inarticulate, John Densmore was slick and looking for aggravation, while Jim was enigmatic and almost unbelievably beautiful. Bill Siddons, a former road manager now hired as a salaried manager, accompanied them. The band were shrewd enough even then to realize that they would always take the important decisions rather than pay a percentage of their now enormous earnings to a management team.

As the limos transported the group into London the camera crew recorded their first impressions, and I was delighted to see how thrilled they were with the window displays along the route. (It is worth noting, for any aspiring entrepreneurs, the value of window displays, which are one of the most cost-effective promotional items. I've yet to meet an artist who wasn't bowled over by the sight of his or her face dominating a window.)

After a few hours rest the 'freaks' were collected from their hotel with some difficulty, as they had never heard British telephones ring and their wake-up calls had them believing that the rooms were infested with grasshoppers. They were driven down the Mall past Buckingham Palace to the ICA, where a surprisingly hostile press was waiting to pounce. Quite why they were so hostile I have never understood. The setting was superb, with an abundant supply of food and drink amid great modern art and artefacts, highlighted by a squadron of mobile robots moving silently among guests, but hostile they were and none more so than that the music press.

Perhaps they were intimidated by the band's reputation or by the surroundings or, more likely, by the group's obvious intelligence. With the exception of the underground publications, the press was actively anti and tried to trip the various members into making stupid statements. The most obnoxious was the girl from the *New Musical Express* who now has a column in a national newspaper. Jim was the obvious target and refused to be badgered into instant responses to daft questions such as 'How do you feel about God?' and 'Tell us the meaning of life as you see it?' Honest. Instead, he gave a slow, well-considered answer to every damn fool question, which infuriated the press even more while the cameras popped and whirred. Perhaps it was his courtesy or the evidence of his very considerable physical presence that upset them so. Who knows? At the time, all too many members of the British press were, with a few honourable exceptions (they know who they are), nasty, lazy, greedy, uninformed and too fond of the bottle. Ray had brought his new young Japanese-American wife and she was both horrified and mystified. I was just ashamed.

The next day was given over to a sound check at the Roundhouse and to recording *Top of the Pops*, where the band posed for a picture with my secretary Sylvia and me in the scruffy dressing-room. Again, the band were professional, turning up on time and enduring without complaint the endless false starts and general hanging around without which television appears to be unable to function. Following the television performance, which in those days was recorded live on Wednesday for transmission on Thursday in time for the weekend rush to the record stores, the visitors had a night off and may well have sampled some of London's legendary nightlife.

On the day of the sell-out show at the Roundhouse I collected the band for a sound check in the afternoon before they went off for an early dinner. Unfortunately the Granada producer must have mentioned to them at some point that they would be required to open the show rather than close it. This was to avoid the possibility of his crew being required to work beyond midnight, when 'golden time' – that is, double wages – would apply and for which he had no budget. The Doors had naturally expected to close the show as headliners and were not about to be seen as a support to Jefferson Airplane on their first European tour.

When the time came to start the show the Doors were nowhere to be found and the Airplane were not ready to perform, since the television team had told them that they would close the show for the opening night. While Peely played records to an increasingly restive audience the minutes ticked by with no sign of the group. I then had a call from John Densmore who would not say where the band was but demanded to know whether they would be closing the show. When I tried to explain the problems and the importance of the television coverage he hung up. Over the next hour or so I received several such calls, each one with the same simple question and each time terminated by the dialling tone when I tried to explain the situation or enquire about the whereabouts of the band. I later learned that they were simply circling the venue in a limo and, in those pre-mobile phone days, dropping off every few minutes to make the calls. The audience were very pissed off and slow handclapping, the television people were desperate, I was frantic and John Peel was outraged at being left alone to amuse an increasingly mutinous mob who had no idea of the problem.

The manager of the Airplane thought all this was hilarious. Despite the fact that RCA had done little to support Jefferson's appearance it now looked likely that they would be seen to headline over the mighty Doors. Eventually Densmore stayed on the line long enough to allow me to explain the situation and to point out that the eventual audience for the television documentary would far exceed and outweigh the immediate consideration. They arrived and were quickly announced, but I now cannot recall whether they opened or closed the show.

The Roundhouse was a dark and rather dangerous place, but it was full to capacity and I could find nowhere to stand that would give me a view of the proceedings that I had spent so much time and energy arranging. The only visible spot was up in a dis-used balcony closed off to the public on safety grounds and guarded by a typically obdurate jobsworth. My appeals, threats and offers of bribes fell on deaf ears until, just as the show was about to start, Jac arrived and with his usual authority and economy said to the guardian, 'This is my band. I intend to see them. If you don't get out of my way I'll cancel the show and you will have to explain your actions to a few thousand murderous fans. You've got five seconds starting now. Four, three . . .' We went upstairs. It is a line that I have subsequently tried on several occasions without success. A question of natural authority I guess.

The Doors were in fact only OK. The group was terrific, but Jim's performance appeared, to me at least, to be overly studied and theatrical – probably as a result of play-ing to stadium audiences where everything needed to be on a larger scale. They were nevertheless very well received, with a number of encores, and the whole performance was captured on film for television. 'Hello, I Love You', which may be the lamest single the band ever recorded, became their biggest-selling UK hit. Does that tell you something?

The next stop for the band was Amsterdam, where Jim, to all intents and purposes, died – and I don't mean just professionally. He apparently ate a huge chunk of hash washed down with a bottle of brandy and lapsed into a coma with all signs of life gone. Fortunately he was rushed to hospital where a stomach pump saved his life – but you have to wonder what the long-term effects were.

I met up with him again in New York where he was attending a sales conference with sales people and distributors all eager to hear and order the next album. He was in fine form, laughing and shaking hands with the commercial representatives. He even found time to try to pull Shurley, who just smiled her enigmatic smile. I recall Jim cracking up when one of the enthusiastic salesmen referred it as 'their third straight platinum album', and I pointed out that, in my opinion, they had yet to make even the first straight album. The sales meetings across the USA were a huge success with orders pouring in, but I wonder how many of today's pampered rock stars would make the effort to get to know the folks that work to make them rich. At that time Jim looked his best. He was fit, tanned, relaxed and very good company.

The second and last time the Doors came to Britain to perform was at the Isle of Wight Festival in 1970, which was probably the most star-studded event ever staged on – or, in this case, off – our shores. By this time he had become fat, bearded and some-what subdued and paranoid owing to his escapades in Miami, where he had been accused of exposing himself during a concert. If found guilty he faced a stretch on a chain gang, which would induce a degree of paranoia in just about anybody. I later learned that the incident in question came about as a result of the commercial usage of

'Light My Fire' in a television commercial for Buick cars. Apparently the song was leased to television without Jim's approval while he was away on holiday and he was outraged but unable to reverse the decision. The commercial appeared as 'Come on, Buick, light my fire' and, on that fateful night in Miami, Jim had left the stage in uproar and apparently said to the rest of the group, 'Now let's see if Buick still want to use my song.' The ploy worked but at great personal and professional cost.

If the Doors' Isle of Wight performance was mechanical and perfunctory, the event itself was magnificent in terms of music though somewhat marred by hordes of crazies demanding to be let into the site for nothing and trying to tear down the fences. Why? Do hairdressers and plumbers give their services for nothing? They would laugh at the suggestion. But these people believed that promoters, artists, musicians, suppliers of sound equipment and tents and the rest live in another world where they are not expected to eat or support their families.

Despite everything, it was indeed a star-studded event with acts of the highest calibre being introduced as 'and now from Hollywood . . .' – you know the routine. At a low point in the early hours, when everybody was sated and barely awake, the compère Jeff Dexter announced, 'Here's a nice little band from Shepherds Bush . . . The 'Oooh.' They were pure dynamite. The sound washed over the island and on the surrounding hills dozens of campfires sprang into life to complement the brilliant searchlights that were panning the audience from the stage. Daltry was at his dramatic best, and Townsend will never know just how good he was. The fans came alive as possibly never before, and for an hour or more I was just delighted to be alive and a small part of a great business.

By this time Jim was a published author and poet, who wanted nothing more than a period of quiet reflection and obscurity to enable him to concentrate on writing, with a view to becoming a respected literary figure. With a string of platinum albums behind him, he wanted to conquer new areas and, hidden by his bushy beard, he was able to walk around Paris, Amsterdam or London unrecognized. In the USA he carried his notoriety on his back, and it was around this time that he began to question his legendary status in the event of an early death. When he was in London he would often drop into my office unannounced for a chat about anything but music or business.

Penny Valentine was a popular columnist and feature writer for *Disc and Music Echo*, with offices close to mine in New Oxford Street. She called me one morning to say that she had picked up a rumour that Jim had died in Paris as a result of a massive heart attack and could I check it out? I immediately called the US Embassy in Paris, which had no reports of any such occurrence and assured me that any hospital or physician treating any US citizen would be bound by law to report any fatality. Somewhat relieved, I called Penny, who told me that her source was reliable and gave me other leads to pursue, which I did without any further confirmation. Certainly at that time there were no official reports of the death of any young American male in Paris. I did nevertheless feel obliged to call Bill Siddons, who was still managing the band in Los Angeles and who, owing to the time difference, was asleep in bed. He took the news very calmly and promised to get back to me, and I felt reassured that the rumour was just that.

Less than forty-eight hours later I read in a national newspaper, which had been printed twelve hours earlier and no doubt written some hours before that, an interview with Billy to the effect that he had been to Paris, identified Jim's body and returned to make a press announcement. Bear in mind that I had in fact awakened him with the news, following which he would have had to book a twelve-hour flight to Paris, find the hospital, make the burial arrangements and then make the twelve-hour return flight to arrange and attend the press call all within thirty hours – I remain somewhat sceptical.

The more likely scenario is that Jim decided to vanish and made arrangements to cover his tracks. I sure hope so. As the years pass, with no sign or word from the Lizard King, it does seem increasingly likely that he is no longer around. Were he still alive I'm sure he would have broken cover with the release of the Oliver Stone film, which was a grotesque caricature of the band and the people around them. Jim may well have had a dark side. It has been said that he was an 'Irish drunk', but I never saw it. I am reminded of the story that at a party in Hollywood he grabbed Janis Joplin's ponytail as she passed, causing her to collapse backwards. Janis, it would appear, bided her time and, at the end of the evening, as Jim was getting into his limo, smashed a full bottle of brandy over his head. Jim is reported to have said, 'Thank you, Janis', before speeding off into the night covered in blood.

I was fortunate to consider him a friend and saw only a sensitive, charming and highly intelligent young man. Can you imagine the monster portrayed in the movie coming with me to Windsor Castle and hanging around to catch a glimpse of the Queen? Obviously movies have to be sold – and nothing sells better than sex, drugs and rock and roll. One is bound to wonder about other Oliver Stone biopix when Jim has been portrayed as a drug-crazed moron and elegant, sophisticated business people like Jac Holzman and Paul Rothschild are depicted as foul-mouthed hustlers.

Tragically Paul died in 1995, and it is a great loss to the music community. The many gold and platinum singles and albums he produced sound as fresh and contemporary now as they did quarter of a century ago. Oddly, they can now be heard frequently on British radio, which virtually ignored them first time around. With Jim gone, the Doors tried to reform with different singers, but the magic had gone. They even tried recording with Kevin Coyne, whom I was managing at the time. Kevin rarely talks about the experience, but it was clear that much more than six thousand miles separates Los Angeles from Derbyshire.

Naturally the appalling movie created a huge wave of interest in the band, and their work became much more successful in Britain – twenty years too late. Thousands of new fans make an annual pilgrimage to Jim's grave at Père Lachaise Cemetery in Paris, and I understand that the twenty-fifth anniversary of Jim's reported death drew such crowds that the French government has been forced to declare it a national monument. The Lizard King would have found that very amusing – and possibly does.

MAVERICKS

One of the many and great joys of working in the music industry is that it offers a welcome – and an opportunity to flourish – to so many maverick characters who might be stifled into conformity and snuffed out of existence in another environment. Artists are, of course, expected, if not required, to be nonconformists for as long as it takes to attract attention, but maverick executives are an unexpected joy. I realized recently that I may fall into this category when a former colleague mentioned his surprise that his first sight of this writer was upon entering the WEA boardroom and discovering me conducting a meeting while standing on my head. I do recall a period when it was generally accepted that standing on one's head increased the flow of oxygen to the brain – or maybe I was bored.

Another former colleague told me of the dismay among the other rather more conventional directors when I arrived on the first day at Pye on a large motor cycle dressed in black leathers. To me it was simply a sensible way to negotiate London traffic, but I guess none of us recognizes our own eccentricities.

When I was at Vogue Records the man in charge of releases was an unpredictable jazz buff. Upon hearing the first tapes of the great saxophonist John Coltrane, he rushed out into the street and accosted passing old ladies to whom he hummed the intricate phrasings of the solos and demanded to know if they agreed that this was sublime evidence of the man's genius. He was not stoned at the time. This was back in the late fifties, and it is interesting to recall that a photo of the great blues artist Big Bill Broonzy placed in the window of our Chelsea offices drew so many complaints from residents that it had to be removed on pain of losing the lease. Perhaps things have moved on in the intervening forty years.

I first met Frank Fenter when Elektra was transferred to the Polydor offices, where Frank was to Atlantic Records what I was to Elektra. Frank was born and raised in South Africa and, either because of or despite his background, he was passionate about black music in general and Aretha in particular. He occupied a huge office opposite mine and played host to an extraordinary collection of visitors and guests, all of whom made liberal use of his well-stocked bar and record player.

Many of the faces were familiar either as artists, disc jockeys, pluggers, managers or producers, but a con-stant presence was Tommy, a short, dapper, close-mouthed American who occupied a permanent position in the corner where he read and reread the trade papers and racing forms. Very occasionally Tommy would make or receive a telephone call, following which he would disappear for a couple of hours before returning, without comment, to his position in the corner. I never saw him in conversation with Frank, to whom he was, to all intents and purposes, a part of the furniture. I never even found out what Tommy did. He was unfailingly polite but uncommunicative. When my curiosity could stand it no longer I asked Frank who he was and was told, 'Oh, he's just a guy.' So that cleared that up.

When the Doors were planning their first UK visit it was my job to promote them, the tour and, of course, the records. Since Elektra was licensed to Polydor, who were responsible for expenditure, I could only prepare marketing plans and budgets for the approval or otherwise of Alan Bates, Polydor's marketing manager. Alan had a rather inflated opinion of his duties and worked behind a permanently closed door with a red light outside indicating that he was not to be disturbed. Less than ideal circumstances for the exchange of ideas.

The Doors were already very successful in America, and in Britain they were scheduled to top the bill at the Roundhouse and appear on *Top of the Pops* to promote the new single 'Hello, I Love You'. They were an important act by any standards and should have been treated accordingly, but every plan and budget I submitted was rejected as too costly. I begged, threatened, cajoled, screamed and even resigned as the ultimate sanction but nothing worked. As the tour dates approached I became ever more disillusioned and depressed. The man in charge of the money was another jazz buff who believed that psyche-delia was just a passing phase and that the Doors were 'too American' to

be accepted in Britain, in which case they were not worth more than a token effort.

Frank Fenter saw my despair and, upon being told the reasons, grabbed me by the arm and marched me up to Alan's office on the fifth floor where the illuminated 'Do Not Disturb' sign was a semi-permanent fixture. Kicking open the closed door, Frank marched across the room to where Alan sat in deep telephone conversation behind an impressive desk. Without any preamble Frank threw the desk and its occupant over on their backs where they landed with a mighty crash. Gazing down upon the terrified executive he suggested in a strong South African accent that my marketing plans for the Doors were well thought out, entirely reasonable and should be accepted and acted on in full. Failing that, further violence might occur. From his position on the floor, partially obscured by desk debris, Alan squeaked his approval and we left. During this encounter I had been silent and open-mouthed but back in my office I thanked Frank for his support and enquired why he had chosen to act so precipitously on my behalf. 'If we let the bastards do that to the Doors they just might try to do it to Aretha' was his response.

The tour went ahead, as I've detailed elsewhere, but it would appear that over at RCA Jefferson Airplane had no such champion in the company. They, too, were on the bill at the Roundhouse and were touring the UK for the first time, but promotion was almost invisible. The obvious place to promote 'underground' acts was in the 'underground' publications such as *Oz* and *IT*, in which I had taken full-page advertisements for the Doors, and the publications had expected at least as much from RCA. In protest at not receiving any such support from the record company both publications left the pages opposite the Doors' adverts blank.

Usually the manager of an act will take up the cudgels with the record company, and unfortunately very few acts prosper without some spirited fighting on their behalf, but when the act is from overseas it is up to the local label manager to fight for attention. Many don't bother, which may be why your particular fave has yet to come through.

Frank Fenter later left England to work for the Allman Brothers' label based in Macon, Georgia. One of his first visitors was his beloved Aretha who, with her husband, stayed overnight in Frank's new home. The very next day Frank had a visit from the local chief of police advising him that overnight stays by 'people of colour' were not encouraged; no matter that the lady in question is one of the greatest artists who ever lived. I saw Frank once again some years later in Cannes, where it was all too apparent that life in the Deep South had led to an increase in his already hefty intake of alcohol. He died shortly after and is much missed.

Tony Stratton-Smith was an ex-journalist who turned to music and made a huge contribution to the success of Genesis. He was always late for appointments, and I only recently learned that this was deliberate, as he had been due to fly back with the doomed 'Busby Babes' Manchester United flight but missed the plane because of a hangover, which almost certainly saved his life. He vowed thereafter never to be on time and never was.

'Strat', as he was known, founded Charisma Records, and for many years supported Genesis and their massive tours without ever seeing the success and profits that the band eventually achieved following the sale of the company to Virgin. His original assistant, who became general manager of the label, is a most talented and respected person called Gail Colson, who went on to manage Peter Gabriel and Morrissey among others.

Strat considered the music business to be an amusing hobby. He was in love with the world of horse racing, and any meetings to discuss various aspects of an act's career were constantly interrupted by a succession of calls from or to his trainer, jockey, vet or just about anybody willing to talk horses. Even with a Top Ten record like Clifford T. Ward's 'Gaye' it was rarely possible to hold his attention and Cliff, who believed that his career was the most important aspect of everybody's life, found this very hard to accept.

Strat did, however, achieve considerable success with his hobby and a major hit with Gary Shearstone's 'I Get a Kick Out of You', though Genesis was his priority. An amusing and engaging man, he eventually sold the company to Virgin who, as seems inevitable with anything associated with Richard Branson, reaped the full rewards of his faith in Genesis with a barrowload of platinum albums and singles throughout the world. Strat meanwhile devoted his time to the track and lived long enough to see his faith justified.

Richard Branson qualifies as a maverick even though he is now a fully paid-up member of the Establishment. I am astonished by how he retains his image as a friendly and successful entrepreneur, being recently voted the man most Brits would trust with their money. My own view is somewhat different. Richard has never claimed to be 'into music', and his early days as a retailer were, to say the least, precarious. It has been written elsewhere that his main reason for opening so many stores was to benefit from the availability of cash flow, inasmuch as it was possible to obtain records from manufacturers on credit and collect the cash over the counters before the bills became due.

Our paths first crossed when I was closing down Dandelion and seeking alternative record deals for the artists still under contract. Having built a good reputation through the record shops, Richard was about to launch Virgin Records, which promised to be a quirky, underground and artist-orientated label. It seemed a likely home for one of my favourite artists, Kevin Coyne, who was as quirky and underground as it got. A meeting was arranged, and I arrived at Branson's barge in Little Venice to find a line of hopeful art students all eager to see their work on album covers. They each received a few seconds of the great man's time and a cursory glance. Hardly the image I had anticipated, but a deal was agreed, which at least gave Kevin the opportunity to continue to record.

Richard's other signings were Hatfield and the North and Mike Oldfield. At the same time I made a deal with MCA Records for Bridget St John to cut a single. Some weeks later Bridget was ready to record and studio time was booked at Chipping Norton Studios in Oxfordshire. On the way to the studio Bridget suggested that we stop by Branson's Manor Studios where a friend of hers had agreed to interrupt his recordings to play bass on her session. This we did, but before proceeding to Chipping Norton with us the bassist played us some of the material he was working on. It was truly awful; so bad that we had great difficulty in keeping straight faces. To compound matters, on arrival at our studio we discovered that the bassist was too 'out of it' to play, and he was sent back to the Manor in a taxi. We managed to finish a lovely little single that was released on MCA and sold about three hundred copies. The bass player was Mike Oldfield. The suite he was recording and which we found so amusing was *Tubular Bells*. Peel played it all the way through on his show and it went on to sell zillions. Ah, well.

When Kevin eventually started recording at Manor Studios we would occasionally visit and be astonished by the weird scenes there. These included two horse-sized dogs who each filled a five-seater settee and a horde of hippie girls dressed very quaintly and trying to look busy while stoned out of their minds. They were like scenes from a bad Fellini movie and more depressing than risible.

When Kevin's first Virgin record was completed Richard Branson called me seeking advice on marketing in general and chart expertise in particular, as I had something of a reputation in these areas. Since Kevin was likely to benefit from any help I could provide, I spent several hours at Virgin with Richard and his staff, taking them through the mechanics of chart manipulation and providing them with the essential information.

Some years later, when Richard was about to launch the 'Now That's What I Call Music' series of compilation albums, he offered the job of chief executive to my partner in another business in which I had become involved. Though the salary and perks offered were attractive, my partner refused the offer, since he was a solicitor with very little knowledge of or interest in music. He did, however, suggest that the job might be right up my street. I duly telephoned Richard whose response was 'What have you ever done in the music business?' Rather taken aback, I reminded him that I had been a director of three major record companies with a string of smash hits, launched my own record label and managed a number of successful acts. 'Yes – but lately?' was his unnecessarily spiteful reply. I could not bring myself to remind him of the hours of free advice I had provided and gently replaced the receiver vowing never again to do free favours: the recipients always resent it. Thanks, Richard. I'll never fly in one of your planes or buy one of your insurance policies, and you will never know nor care.

Closer to home, my son Chet, who with his sister Bee runs the very successful Beechwood Music group of companies, can be somewhat unpredictable. Their business entails licensing in hit tracks from other companies to be included on carefully crafted compilation album releases and, all financial considerations aside, it is crucial that they maintain good business and personal relationships with representatives of the major labels. To this end Bee invited the licensing manager of one of the most important companies to lunch in the exclusive restaurant at Shepperton Studios where Beechwood had offices. The lunch went well but was perhaps too long or too liquid, for when Bee returned to the by now almost empty restaurant after making a few calls she discovered her brother and his guest locked in fierce physical combat. With coats off they were sprawled across the table trying to put each other's lights out. Bee describes the scene as something out of a Wild West movie, with blood and broken crockery littering the floor and a horrified staff too intimidated to intervene. At last Chet appeared to come to his senses and withdrew but, just as his sister began to approach and apologize to her important guest, the door was flung open and Chet hurled himself across the room, dragging his opponent to the floor where they began once more to beat the crap out of each other. I have no idea how the confrontation began or even ended, but the two combatants are now good friends and have an even better business relationship. I dare not ask.

With the emergence of so many lawyers and accountants in positions of power in the industry over the past few years, there is most likely less room for the unconventional within the corporations. In management and among artists it remains essential – but a degree of talent helps the rest of us to accept it.

The world of broadcasting is, of course, full of mavericks. No doubt you have your own favourites, among whom may well be the late Kenny Everett, but I would have to include Pete Drummond and Johnnie Walker. Less so now perhaps, but then maturity does tend to smooth out the edges.

Like John Peel, Pete got his early radio experience in the USA before joining the pirate ship Radio London. When the government closed that operation down I was able to get Pete accepted at Radio 1, initially as co-presenter of *Top Gear* with John and eventually with a series of his own shows. Pete also presented the early series of the *Old Grey Whistle Test* on BBC television but was quickly replaced owing to his inability to be nice to the right people. We were careful to apprise him of the power of one of the female assistants and to warn him to be wary, so the first thing he did was to comment at some length on the lady's bosom, or lack of it, so that gig was fairly short lived. At Radio 1 he refused to be jolly and vivacious on air, preferring to let the music dominate, which was then a form of heresy among the producers who were looking for 'personality' presenters. Pete has one of the great radio voices and now makes a career of trails and voice-overs. It is close to impossible to listen to radio or watch television for an evening without hearing Pete, which probably suits him, as he has no need to develop relationships with producers – or their assistants.

Johnnie Walker was a star on the other great pirate ship Radio Caroline. When the government closed down all the pirate radio ships Caroline soldiered on for a couple of years against mighty opposition, and Johnnie stayed with the sinking ship to the end. This did little to endear him to the Establishment in general or Radio 1 in particular. With the end of Caroline, Johnnie was keen to continue his career as broadcaster but filled in time driving a lorry. Several agencies tried to introduce him to Radio 1 without success, and when we met he was close to desperate. Perhaps the timing was right, because, like John and Pete before, I was able to secure him a contract with the station. Here, you have to be reminded that the BBC was the only game in town. There were no commercial or local stations. Probably because he wanted to make up for the 'lost' years Johnnie sought more aggressive representation, though we remained friends.

At this time FM radio was breaking new ground in the USA and Johnnie felt that was where his future lay. He felt confined by the strictures of the Radio 1 playlist and, despite our assurances that disc jockeys were fairly low down the pecking order over there, he resigned from the Beeb and set off for America. When he returned, somewhat chastened, Radio 1 welcomed him back and now, despite the odd well-publicized problem, he presents a great show on Radio 2 where his earlier love of soul music is in evidence.

12. JOHN PEEL

JOHN PEEL

Now, to backtrack a little, I think it might be an idea to give a little space here to the man who was my partner in Dandelion Records and Biscuit Music during the Elektra and WEA years – and whose career is still skilfully influenced by Shurley. Dr John Robert Parker Ravenscroft, BA, MA, OBE, left school with four O-levels and became an icon. Son of a very well-to-do cotton broker and educated at Shrewsbury, one of the top public schools, where beatings and buggery were the norm, he survived National Service and resolutely avoided any opportunity to become 'officer material' fearing that might distance him from his new-found colleagues.

Following his short and unremarkable military career, John was shipped off to the USA to learn the cotton business. There he struggled as a computer programmer before moving on to sell storm insurance to farmers, which gave him a view of Middle America and an opportunity to fall in love with fast American cars.

When the Beatles captured the world, John telephoned a local radio station in Texas to correct something he had heard and his English accent got him invited on to the airwaves as an authority on Mersey Mania. In fact, John described his accent at the time as resembling that of a junior member of the Royal Family, but the strength of the English invasion was such that he became a minor celebrity in his own right.

Even back at public school he had sought favour among his schoolmates by organizing 'recitals' of gramophone records and was easily able to graduate to playing records on the radio. As for any young man, the formative years were something of a blur. With his new celebrity John found himself mobbed at public appearances and made the most of his status at the start of the Swinging Sixties in the land of the free. He was even welcomed on Indian reservations, where he entertained with his eclectic collection of records, though on one occasion the heady combination of music and hard liquor resulted in a severe beating from a group of Native Americans. On the next reservation appearance he hired a couple of braves as bodyguards and watched in dismay as, fuelled by liquor, the two of them set about everybody else.

As a journalist he shook the hand of President Kennedy on that fateful day in Dallas and was present when Lee Harvey Oswald – the alleged assassin – was brought in and subsequently gunned down in prison. Hosting his own radio show in California, John lived the hippie life and voiced opinions that generated the occasional death threat – this *was* the time of John Wayne and *The Green Berets*. On one occasion a caller detailed all of John's movements on a particular day and ended the conversation with a reminder that a bullet from a well-aimed rifle with telescopic sights could have taken him out at any time. Truly the land of the free.

In California John met and married a young American girl called Shirley. So young, in fact, that crossing a state line with her – even as a wife – was considered a criminal offence. She had misled John about her age, which was discovered only at the ceremony. With the death threats and the prospect of prosecution John decided to return to the UK, where he managed to get a job as a disc jockey on the pirate station Radio London. There he was renamed John Peel and allowed the freedom of the air-waves after midnight in the belief that nobody was listening at that hour.

The Perfumed Garden was unique in British radio. It still is. John would play complete albums by the emerging American West Coast groups who were completely unknown in Britain. Between records he would talk about the colours of the rainbow, the shapes of the clouds and the delights of nature; all rather embarrassing now, but then inno-vative, exciting and arresting. To listen to *The Perfumed Garden* offered membership of a small, elite club of which John Peel was the spiritual, if self-effacing, leader. That may sound far-fetched in these hard-nosed materialistic times, but the new music emerg-ing from Radio London after midnight actually brought people together in an all-too-brief spirit of love and peace. It may never happen again, but those who were part of it treasure the memories.

I first met John when, as general manager of Elektra Records, I was promoting this new music and in particular *The 5000 Spirits or the Layers of the Onion* by the Incredible String Band. The title of the album probably says more about the period than anything I could write, and John was the only person on radio in the whole of Europe who was prepared to give it a listen. In fact he loved it and played both sides of the album on his first show upon returning to the ship. I further discovered that he was familiar with, and enjoyed, most of the recordings in the Elektra catalogue including Love, the Paul Butterfield Blues Band, Spider John, Phil Ochs, Judy Collins and more. So began a friendship and professional association that has lasted the best part of forty years. Our musical tastes have diverged over the decades, but he remains the most interesting and innovative presenter of music in the world.

At that time John was living with his young American wife in a small flat in Fulham, which he referred to as 'the unfashionable end of the King's Road'. I visited them and found Shirley ironing while John listened to music. Something was said – I don't recall what – and she suddenly flung the hot iron at John, which just missed his head and buried itself in the flimsy wall. She then pursued him down the road and around the block, both barefoot, with John trying to offer explanations over his shoulder and Shirley, in the absence of more flat irons, hurling abuse.

Since John was spending most of his time on board ship and only home for a few days this seemed an odd way to pass the time they had together but – different strokes . . . Over the next few weeks I developed a considerable antipathy to Shirley, who represented just about all of the very worst aspects of a type of American woman. To this day I have great difficulty in warming to that assertive but ill-mannered and essentially insecure type. Fortunately they divorced, but Shirley returned to haunt him in various ways before she died.

The Labour government, being unable to control or tax the pirate radio ships, decided to outlaw them on the dubious basis that they were cluttering up the airwaves to the detriment of the emergency services. What lies! I imagine that the hundreds of commercial stations currently in operation are cluttering up the same airwaves, but the franchise fees and taxes they pay make it acceptable. Johnnie Walker and Radio Caroline struggled on for months, but Radio London caved in and went off the air to the strains of the final chord of the Beatles' 'A Day in the Life'. It was a very moving ceremony – particularly for the participants, who were now, thanks to Harold Wilson, out of work.

As a sop to Britain's youth, whose world leadership in music and fashion earned the country billions in exports, the BBC created Radio 1 from the remnants of the pirate stations that the government had destroyed. In its early years it was exactly what one would expect from an essentially middle-aged, middle-class establishment and never approached the buccaneering spirit of the age.

Still controlled to a large extent by the Musicians' Union, the station was severely limited in the number of records it could play, and the gaps between the records were filled by 'cover' versions of hits played by various house orchestras, who had little or no understanding of current music trends. Peel recalls a version of a Hendrix guitar solo sounding for all the world as if the soloist had hurled his instrument down a flight of concrete steps in order to obtain the right sound.

Radio 1 valiantly signed up most of the ex-pirate disc jockeys to short-term contracts. All except John, who was considering various alternative employment opportunities such as working at London Zoo. I respected and liked John as a professional and as a rebel and without his presence there was little chance of any radio exposure for Elektra Records, so I suggested to him that I approach Radio 1 on his behalf. He agreed and in September 1967, with just days to go before the station was launched, I began a series of negotiations trying to convince the management that John was neither a junkie nor a threat to the Establishment.

I was fortunate in having made friends with Bernie Andrews, who was then producing the extremely popular *Saturday Club* on the BBC's Light Programme and was himself possibly the only rebel in the organization. He liked John's style of presentation, and together we managed to convince the management to have Peel on board, albeit only as a co-presenter with Tommy Vance or Pete Drummond on alternate Sundays on a programme to be called *Top Gear*. The agreement was signed with minutes to spare as all the new presenters lined up outside Broadcasting House for the official launch photograph. John was reluctant to appear and can be seen sitting apart from the main group and gazing somewhat disconsolately in another direction. The extraordinary thing is that thirty years on he is the only one of the group still broadcasting on the station.

The original brief for *Top Gear* was to 'look over their horizons of pop' – and scheduled for the first show was an interview with Lulu backstage at the London Palladium! John worked well with both Pete and Tommy but never sounded happy as co-pilot. His approach to radio is very personal and relies upon creating a one-to-one atmosphere with the listener, which is impossible under those conditions. Eventually, with many misgivings and reservations, the management gave *Top Gear* exclusively over to John and Bernie Andrews, who had been given the job of producer.

Bernie was an anachronism. A talented single man with a complicated personal life, he rebelled constantly against the strictures of working within a huge organization, fought constantly with the management but was lost without its authority. He lived in Shepherd's Market, London's most exclusive red-light area, where he welcomed frequent visitors such as the Beatles and Bowie. According to Bernie, Paul stopped visiting when the resident mina bird addressed him as Ringo.

Despite his antipathy towards the organization, or possibly because of it, Bernie had spent a long time auditioning hopeful new acts and fondly recalled the surge of excitement when a callow, nervous young Tom Jones first roared into an audition session. With this background and an uncanny ability to identify the birthsigns of complete strangers Bernie was the ideal producer to encourage the stream of new talent drawn to *Top Gear*. Each new act was expected to perform four songs in an audition session, which was then reviewed by an internal panel of experts. On many occasions Bernie circumvented the panel and their views by broadcasting the original audition session, which for dozens of new acts was an instant move towards stardom.

I remember David Bowie aimlessly wandering the corridors of Broadcasting House, when he was still known as David Jones, before the audition panel rejected his efforts as being 'too much like Anthony Newley'. On another occasion I followed Fleetwood Mac along those same corridors with their arses literally hanging out of their jeans, all soaking wet, having pushed their van the last half-mile to the studio. Marc Bolan was a fixture. He would sit in the corner of my office composing semi-literate notes to my young daughter Sam, on to which he would paste coloured stars. John took him everywhere and would split his fees from college and disco gigs with Marc and his partner Steve after driving them there and back. It got to the point that promoters would try to engage John for a night on the basis that he didn't bring 'Larry the Lamb'. This was when Marc was half of the two-piece known as Tyrannosaurus Rex. As soon as he hit big as the electric T. Rex those same promoters were offering thousands for a show but not before the head of Radio 1 had sent Peel and Bernie a memo requesting no further exposure for the act that 'would never become popular'.

I always thought of Marc as an engaging hustler and was not really surprised when, years later in the company of Bridget St John, I encountered a drunken Marc at BBC Television Centre. He introduced Bridget dismissively to his companion Harry Nilsson as 'you know – one of those Peel protégées'. The little shit. Still, since they are no longer with us I suppose I should not speak ill of the dead. Probably by that time Marc had made himself forget how much his career owed to John's support. Very few artists acknowledge any of the help they receive, though all too many are quick to apportion blame when it all goes south.

Despite his enormous popularity and influence John was paid a pittance for his weekly programme and made his living expenses from appearing at clubs and colleges where he played records through indifferent sound systems. He has a collection of posters advertising these events, where he headlined over (in very small letters) acts such as Pink Floyd. He was, and remains, popular in Europe where he appeared at clubs and festivals. How many other broadcasters, I wonder, have weekly radio shows in English in Germany, Finland and Holland – and on the BBC World Service? On one occasion I made a rare visit to one of his university gigs in, as far as I can recall, Reading, where he arrived straight from Holland in great pain from a kidney stone, which he managed to pass in the toilet just before going on. He then offered up the stone to the assembled students as a spot prize, to their obvious delight. Shurley and I left before the unique prize was won and often wondered if it became a cherished possession. On another occasion John told the audience that Mr Peel could not appear that night and that he would deputize for him. The audience booed him off the stage and demanded its money back. So much for celebrity.

Eventually we managed to secure a further series of late night shows on Radio 1, in which John interviewed various guests, which at that time was not one of his strengths. When interviewing the late actor and satirist John Wells he incurred the wrath of Prime Minister Harold Wilson during a discussion about South Africa. Complaints from Number 10 were registered and the Director of Public Prosecutions demanded a transcript of the conversation. It was front-page news for couple of days, during which we prayed that something important and newsworthy might happen – Miss World losing an earring, for example – to get John out of the headlines. In the event, the transcript demonstrated that John's contributions to the subversive discussion were his usual series of 'ers' and 'ums'. That was close to thirty years ago, and the politicians are still at it.

There were the usual management shuffles at the BBC, and the new controller of Radios 1 and 2 invited me to lunch for no reason that I could discover. Over soup he asked me my opinion of Jimmy Young, who was then still one of the mainstays of Radio 1. I responded that I was unable to offer a reasoned opinion since whenever I heard him I became nauseous. At that precise moment Mr Young appeared over my shoulder and greeted us warmly. Was I set up? He must have heard my thoughtless comment, but he was as charming as ever. I've nothing against the man: he is a very accomplished professional with years of success as a singer and broadcaster – but those recipes! He went on to Radio 2 and, very properly, remained, in his late seventies, one of their enduring stars until he hung up his headphones in 2002.

That controller went and was replaced by an ex-squadron leader, who was about as close to Britain's youth as Castro was to Kennedy. In the never-ending quest to get more programmes I discussed with John the possibility of approaching the new man with a suggestion that Radio 1 record selected groups live in concert with Peely intro-ducing them. John decided that we should approach the controller together, which we did by special appointment. The controller of the nation's only pop radio station listened carefully to our suggestion and responded with 'Yes, but can these pop chaps play for longer than three minutes?' Having spent the previous evening at the Royal Albert Hall listening to what seemed like several hours of the Incredible String Band in concert we assured him that that they could indeed – and *In Concert* was born.

I happened to be in that chap's office when the first copies came in of the Beatles' single 'The Ballad of John and Yoko', which featured the refrain 'Christ, you know it ain't easy'. Panic ensued and the executive excused himself, listened to the offending lyrics and issued a decree that the station would play only the B-side.

Bernie Andrews, as John's producer, felt increasingly unable to cope with the strictures of the organization and, since the programme was regularly winning awards in the music press, was under the impression that his views carried weight with the management. They didn't, and in a crushing blow he was removed from *Top Gear* and handed the task of compiling a programme that called for no more than a turntable and a stopwatch. He was devastated and expected John to leave the programme in protest – but what would that have achieved? The BBC appeared to be completely unaware of John's importance and influence with young listeners and would barely have noticed had he left. Bernie struggled on for a while, becoming increasingly morose and difficult, but eventually was forced into early retirement, which was a tragedy for someone who had given so much and had so much more to offer.

John's new producer was a very different character. John Walters, or 'Petals' as he became known, was a former musician. A big man with an extraordinary sense of humour laced with Geordie directness – though originally from Nottingham, he had gone to university in Newcastle and been in Newcastle band the Alan Price Set – he had previously produced the Jimmy Saville shows. And Peel and Saville could hardly have been more different in style. It is worth noting here that Sir Jim was very kind to John on his first *Top of the Pops* appearance. In rehearsals John mentioned that he had first seen one of the scheduled groups when he had been working in California, and Jimmy suggested that John omit that piece of information on the basis that most of the audience had never ventured further than Morecambe. A decent gesture to help a television novice.

Without apparently trying, John Walters had a considerable influence on the Peel shows, and they worked together in acrimonious harmony for the next two decades. They were one of the great comedic double acts, and time spent in their company left you doubled up with laughter and wishing you had taken notes or made recordings. Together they promoted punk and booked all manner of groups who went on to become international stars. Among these sessions were recordings by the Police, who provided a brilliant set for the programme, but neither of the two Johns recalled it with pleasure. During this period John called and asked us to send a few hundred pounds to a band in Ireland who needed it to make a demo. The tapes eventually arrived and, out of curiosity, I played them before sending them on to Peel. I was not impressed, but WEA were thrilled, and the Undertones remain one of John's very favourite bands.

Apart from the odd *Top of the Pops* appearance John had a regular journalistic spot on a BBC television show called *How It Is*. This was produced by Tony Palmer, who virtually invented those distorting camera-phasing techniques that became so popular when rock bands performed on television, and made a famous recording of Cream in concert just before they broke up. Neither John nor Tony was ever happy with the 'pieces to camera' that John did for the programme. Palmer always wanted a political comment upon the events of the week without ever getting 'too political', a balancing act of which John soon tired. It was there at the studio, however, that he first met Sheila, or 'the Pig' as he affectionately dubbed her on account of her laugh.

One of the smartest things JP ever did was to marry Sheila, who is a very cheery and down-to-earth Yorkshire lady. They wed, in Liverpool FC colours, of course, and the reception was held in a beautiful old building in Regent's Park attended by Woggle, John's sheepdog, a host of stars and BBC personnel and with Rod Stewart as honoured guest. Rod was not yet into his American superstar mode. He was still one of the lads and one of John's favourite people. A well-remembered clip from *Top of the Pops* shows our man complete with very long hair pretending to play the mandolin while the Faces kicked footballs about. Twenty-five years on and John and Sheila are as happy together as, well, pigs in clover.

We made a pilot arts programme hosted by JP with a view to doing a series for Johnny Hamp of Granada. It was very much of its time, with a dog scampering about, poets and authors sitting cross-legged on cushions and appearances by Marc Bolan and Blodwyn Pig. In truth, it was a bit twee and was never shown, let alone considered for a series. That, however, is the kind of television show that John enjoys. He gets several invitations every week to appear as a celebrity on this or that chat show but resists them all. His theory is that most Radio 1 disc jockeys see their programmes merely as stepping-stones to hosting a televised panel game. Channel 4 issued a standing invitation to John to come along with ideas for a show of his own and, after several meetings and serious negotiations with the Head of Music at BBC 2, Shurley was given the green light for John to have total artistic control over any new series he was prepared to host for that channel. Other agents with a different client might well have stopped off and ordered a new Rolls on the way back to the office, but we knew better and were not really surprised when our client failed to attend even a discussion.

John is happiest in a darkened studio chatting informally to his audience and introducing to them the records and sessions that excite him. That and a bit of writing are his total ambition. He generally does not encourage visitors to the studio, but on one occasion a group of friends turned up, one of whom was wearing several bangles, which jangled during John's radio introductions. John Walters complained and asked the young lady either to remove them or leave the studio, which, Peel felt, was somewhat hard. Some weeks later John informed his producer that sadly she had, in fact, taken her own life, to which Petals responded, 'So she jangled off this mortal coil?' John was not amused, but the story goes some way to defining the relationship.

With a large family to support he does need to supplement his income with the occasional voice-over or commercial, but in these areas his highly developed sense of ethics costs him hundreds of thousands of pounds annually. In the early days of his career I received a call from the agency representing a major bank requesting two or three minutes of speech from John. It was to appear on the B-side of a promotional record specially recorded by the Faces to be given away to new customers. The Faces had insisted that John narrate the piece, which gave us huge leverage. Taking a deep breath I quoted a fee that was more than John was then earning in the year. There was a sharp intake of breath from the agency and much sucking of teeth, but eventually they agreed to it. In some excitement I called our man and he, too, was delighted until I told him the name of the bank, which then had a strong South African connection. Needless to say, he refused.

One commercial he did accept was for a lawn treatment, which sounded fairly innocuous and right-on. After it appeared several listeners wrote saying that the product contained Agent Orange, the chemical which had caused so much devastation in Vietnam. It was not, in fact, true but caused John so much aggravation that now, when asked to quote a fee for a commercial, we first establish that the product in question contains no animal products, is not promoting smoking, does not exploit Third World countries and finally, if in doubt, we request a chemical analysis. It would be fair to say that this does occasionally try the patience of some of the busiest commercial agencies. Most recently we have had the problem of genetically modified foods, which are now added to the proscribed list, as are the retail chains who stock them. The odd television commercial has nevertheless enabled the current 'Peel Acres' in Suffolk to be expanded from an old thatch-covered witch's cottage to something more suitable for a growing family.

John Walters left the BBC and, up to his death in 2001, made a pretty good living from the occasional radio or television appearance and taking up a number of the commercials that JP refused. He had, as a former professional musician, that rare ability to put aside his own musical tastes or judgement and go along with new styles. How else could the two Johns have booked and broadcast so many artists and groups who didn't obviously display any evidence of talent or ability? Who else could have booked the Frantic Elevators for a session? They were astonishingly awful, yet the lead singer has achieved well-deserved international stardom in Simply Red. Who else could have booked the Slits or the early Banshees? The punk phenomenon was a free-for-all, but somehow the two Johns singled out a great many hit-makers.

Life will never be quite the same without John Walters. As befitting a man with a unique attitude to life, at his request his funeral was a riot of music and laughter, which was a fair reflection of a remarkable personality. Those who knew him will never forget him. By an extraordinary coincidence, John Peel, in his weekly column in the *Radio Times*, wrote a piece saluting his old friend, which was published the same week that Petals died. It had been written three weeks before, with no indication or premonition of the tragedy.

Peel himself has discovered and brought hundreds of new groups to the attention of the public. He found many bands through his own appearances at colleges and universities, where part of the deal was for the venue to book the best local bands to appear in support. If he was really impressed with an act John all too often gave the group his entire fee – occasionally leaving himself with insufficient money to get home. Try explaining that to the taxman.

One of the very big groups, which split up into two equally successful acts, did several gigs and sessions with John. This eventually brought them to the attention of a major record company who offered their fairly unsophisticated manager a blank cheque. The manager telephoned me for advice and, under the circumstances, I suggested he asked for a truly outrageous figure as an advance with a substantial royalty. Some time later he telephoned to thank me for the advice. He had apparently obtained everything he wanted and the group went on to massive international success – but not before they sent us the bill for drinks and refreshments for the roadies on that last gig they did with JP.

The sessions came about through an agreement with the Musicians' Union to continue to offer employment to musicians. They were never meant to be more than that, and it is only as a result of Peel's innovative approach that the sessions gained credibility. In fact John Walters went on record as saying that Peel is the single most influential person in popular music over the past thirty years. He may well be right, but I'm reminded that when Walters first moved to London he glued up the curtains in his new flat, never having heard of curtain rings. How could this man be taken seriously?

The other part of the agreement with the Musicians' Union required that the recordings be destroyed after six months – again with a view to providing continuing employment for their members. That, coupled with the BBC's need for economy, has ensured that most of the early session tapes were wiped. Bernie Andrews kept some copies but could never find them, John Walters kept copies of most of the punk sessions, and Jeff Griffin, who produced most of the *In Concert* series, retained copies of the best. Jeff is possibly the most experienced and able concert-recording producer in the world but took very early retirement as part of the new lean and hungry Corporation. What a waste.

Anybody interested in the sessions could do worse than look out for Ken Garner's book *In Session Tonight*, which lists almost six thousand sessions, including every one broadcast on the various Peel shows. It is virtually impossible to overstate the importance of Radio 1 session recordings. The quality of the recordings, which were completed in just a few hours, was often superb. Frankie Goes to Hollywood recorded two complete Peel sessions before being signed to ZTT. Two of their biggest hits were written on the train to London to do the sessions, yet when they came to record the album a complete day was taken up with recording a splash in a swimming pool! Needless to say, despite Peel's extraordinary influence on their career, the Frankies were one of the first to refuse permission for their sessions to be released on my own label Strange Fruit, which I started in the 1980s. Gee, thanks, guys.

Some day John may well write his own autobiography. If it happens it will no doubt be an amusing and self-deprecating view of a remarkable life. Much has been written about him and, with the exception of a bitchy piece by that cow in the *Guardian*, most of it is true. What you see and hear is very much what you get. Over the years he has written extensively for a variety of publications from *Oz* and *IT* through all of the music papers to *The Times* and the *Radio Times*. If these articles could be collated into a book it would provide a fascinating overview of the world of pop and rock over the past three decades – though John might well be a touch embarrassed by the early clouds and flowers period.

At one point in John's career, when relations with the Corporation were at very low ebb and showing every indication of an early termination, I arranged a series of shows on Radio Luxembourg just to demonstrate to the Beeb his continuing popularity. I shall long remember the look on the face of the Radio Lux top man when John, instead of calling his show something snazzy along the lines of the *JP Rock 'n' Roll Extravaganza*, insisted on calling it *Stenhousemuir 2, Cowdenbeath 2*. Ah, that ceaseless quest for fame and popularity.

Over the last few years he has broadened out into mainstream broadcasting and his *Home Truths* on Radio 4 is collecting as many awards as his music shows. John Walters was also famously quoted as saying something along the lines of, 'If Peel ever reaches puberty we are all in trouble.' Peel reached puberty some time ago but somehow manages to retain the excitement of a kid when hearing something he likes. Perhaps uniquely among his colleagues he buys a lot of the records he plays and has been known on a number of occasions to buy several copies of a record he favours to distribute among those colleagues. Occasionally a journalist will complain that John continually reinvents himself, but I think that is called evolution and it happens to all but a rather sad few. He remains besotted with music and is the only person I know who can watch an exciting football match on television while listening to and timing a pile of records.

Peel has compèred more music festivals than anybody else in Britain – or maybe anywhere else for that matter. He did the Reading Festival for years and still does Glastonbury – and refuses to be paid for it in the belief that the profits all go to charity. In vain his friends point out that it is a commercial operation, with only a small percentage going to charity, and that he is the only one giving his services free. He just calls me a fascist, which I fear is becoming increasingly close to true. In 2000 highlights from the Glastonbury Festival were shown on American television with all of John's contributions deleted and replaced by zany shots of a groovy chick introducing the bands that might be popular over there. Peel thought that was most amusing.

A long time ago, 1967 to be precise, I was at one of the first big festivals in Britain, the 'Festival of the Flower Children' at Woburn Abbey, which was compèred by both my DJ clients, Peel and Pete Drummond. At one point, in the early hours, John ceremoniously burned an early copy of that day's *News of the World*, which had featured an unpleasant story about Brian Epstein. They never forgave him and for years afterwards tried to nail him with a story. Woburn was how a music festival should be. The music and the night were spectacular and the audience was there for the music and the vibes. I will never forget the eerie sound of the *Zodiac Cosmic Sounds* album floating over the assembled peaceful and peace-loving gathering. By contrast, at the Alexandra Palace Festival the same year, which was also hosted by Peel and Pete, the shysters cottoned on to the scam and whether anybody got paid was a lottery. All this was, of course, the early days of the hippie movement and some time before the emergence of the 'weekend hippies' who were looking for a bit of free love, nudity and soft drugs.

My favourite broadcaster is not without the odd fault: he is over-sensitive to ill-informed criticism, can be grumpy and is somewhat fanatical about written English. On receipt of an ill-tempered letter from a famous woman television presenter complaining about something he had said John returned it without comment but with all grammatical and punctuation errors underlined in red. He also has a romanticized view of the working classes, which he sees as 'salt of the earth' despite all evidence to the contrary. He is nevertheless a thoroughly decent, kind and honest man who loves his family, his job, his music and his growing collection of decrepit cars. Along with millions of listeners, my life has been enriched by his presence – but for heaven's sake don't tell him that. He would be deeply embarrassed.

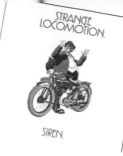

STRANGE
LOCOMOTION.

SIREN.

DAVID BEDFORD
NURSES SONG WITH ELEPHANTS

ask me no q

bridget st jo

Bridget St John

Thank you for...

Stack waddy

BUGGER OFF!

KEVIN COYNE

MIKE
HART
BLEEDS

Basher, Chalky, Pongo and me.

VICTORY FOR THE ALLIES

Mike Hart
and comrades.

13. FINE
AND DANDY

BEAT
ON
THE DRUM

bradar

STACK

THE
OCCASIONAL WORD

THE · YEAR · OF · THE
GREAT · LEAP
SIDEWAYS

the way we live.

Polydor
Medicine

FINE AND DANDY

Looking back from these self-obsessed times it seems barely conceivable that we started Dandelion Records for purely altruistic reasons. But that's what we did between 1969 and 1972 – and, given our time all over again . . . er, don't you believe it! We called the label and its sister publishing company Dandelion and Biscuit after John's two hamsters, and the company logo was designed for us by a real-life pixie living on Dartmoor. No, I'm not stoned now and wasn't then. It was a sixties thing.

By 1967 things were going pretty well for a lot of people, and both John Peel and I were enjoying a decent living from the music business. Neither of us was getting rich but we were each fairly successful at what we did. Me with a few hits and a high profile via the Elektra label, while John was becoming something of a guru to the industry with his talent for finding and promoting new acts.

With his growing reputation as a taste-maker John would receive – as he still does – literally thousands of demo tapes every year from young hopefuls, and he was becoming increasingly frustrated by his inability to do more than offer a session to just one or two each week. Whether record companies picked any of them up was completely out of his hands. At the same time he continued to be deluged by what he considered to be crap releases from the major labels.

Having had some experience at promoting new and innovative acts at Elektra, all of which John had supported, I suggested to him that we might start a record label of our own based loosely on the artistic aspirations of Elektra with John in charge of finding talent and Shurley sharing all the other duties with me. We all felt that this would be an opportunity to put back a little something and were prepared to work for nothing in the expectation that some years down the line we may achieve something worth while.

John agreed in principle and on the strict understanding that he was to have no financial involvement or participation since he feared that to do so might influence his artistic judgement and restrict his ability to play the records on his radio shows. This last was crucial since it was pretty obvious that any acts that John liked were unlikely to be played by his colleagues. Somewhat miraculously, the mandarins at the Beeb agreed to allow him to go ahead, and I began to organize contracts and distribution.

The contracts were easy. They were simply standard affairs bought 'off the shelf' from Harbottle and Lewis – who are one of the leading music law firms – photocopied and with the names added as we went on. We decided that a fair division of royalties was an even split between artist and company, with the company share going towards further recordings. There was never any question of advances beyond recording costs, on the basis that any artist who was in a position to demand an advance did not need any help from us. The recording costs were to be debited against any future royalties, as is standard practice in the industry. I am always astonished when artists blithely spend months in a studio, building up astronomical costs, and are then both surprised and bitter to learn that no royalties are forthcoming even after considerable success. Do they think that the studio costs are paid by a fairy godmother? Many US labels charge all marketing and promotion costs, including air travel, hotels and pluggers' time, to the royalty account, which can often leave even a million-seller in debt – or 'unrecouped', as it is known. On the plus side it will always be easy for any million-selling act to get a substantial advance from the company, but that's what it will be, an advance or loan against future royalties.

Though we would have preferred to proceed without contracts, on the understanding that artists were free to leave whenever they chose, I discovered soon enough that it would be impossible to obtain distribution and finance without long-term agreements with the acts. Nobody was prepared to put money and effort behind any artist who, with a degree of success, could go off and sign with another company. First lesson.

Purely on account of John's reputation, Elektra were quick to agree a deal for North America that gave us half the required finance and at least a shot at the American market. In hindsight I should have demanded guaranteed releases but was still then in the 'blue-eyed' phase. Scouting the British companies was another matter. There was a degree of interest but very little money on offer. Very British. Though Peely had helped Decca and EMI earn millions from acts they never knew they had, he was still regarded as a dangerous hippie and certainly not as a potential business partner.

Eventually I got some interest from CBS, who were at least prepared to meet us at John's mews flat close to Regent's Park in London and discuss our needs. On the day of the meeting about half a dozen CBS executives arrived in suits and ties eager to discuss details. They sat cross-legged on the floor in the absence of any furniture, and a lively discussion ensued, during which John fell fast – and noisily – asleep.

I tried valiantly to retain everybody's interest with diminishing success, pointing out that John was 'not into business, man', but things were somewhat enlivened by the sudden appearance of quite a famous young lady of the time clad only in a very short string vest. Rubbing her eyes blearily she wandered into the middle of our little circle and began to search for a lost earring, bent over double and slowly circling as she peered keenly into the carpet. We had a deal at last. Not a great deal by any standards but a bit of money and a hundred hours of studio time against a royalty of 10 per cent for Britain and half of that for overseas. For that we had to deliver half-a-dozen albums and singles each year.

The first act John chose was Bridget St John, who was a very nice middle-class folk singer-songwriter. John 'produced' her first album, which is to say that he was there at most of the sessions and made the occasional suggestion. This was not laziness. We had decided early on that we would only record acts that needed minimal production. Bridget had a following on the folk circuit and eventually asked us to manage her, to which Shurley and I happily agreed and undertook the job for a few years. Of passing interest is the fact that during this time Bridget was often booked out by the Ellis-Wright agency and all too often was required to spend a whole day in their offices waiting for them to receive money to enable them to pay her fee of £75 for a gig.

Chris Wright and Terry Ellis, two ex-students' union bookers, had started the

Ellis-Wright agency on a shoestring after leaving university. Terry and Chris went on to discover Jethro Tull and Ten Years After, which became the foundation stones of Chrysalis Records, making the two lads multimillionaires and owners of racehorses and football clubs. To give an example of the way they operated, Jethro Tull were originally booked into a club for £100 and were so sensational that they were immediately booked to return the following night for ten times the amount. That is sheer public demand unprompted by hype or marketing skill. I was with Jac Holzman when Chris Wright played him an acetate of the first TYA album with a view to leasing it to Elektra for America. Jac demanded to be allowed to remix it, but Chris refused, released it himself and the rest, as they say, is history. The two parties went on to have a succession of hit acts such as Leo Sayer, Blondie and scores more.

Another early 'Dandy' act was Coyne-Clague, a five-piece group from Derbyshire. They left a demo tape for John but omitted to include an address or telephone number. JP was so impressed with the tape that he posted notes on lamp-posts around London asking anybody who knew them to get in touch. I'm not making this up, though John refuses to remember it. We did make contact and John loved their album, as indeed did Jac Holzman, but I was not too keen. Despite that, the singer Kevin Coyne later became one of my heroes. Some years after this I was proud to produce Kevin's first solo album, which still gives me goose bumps. It was profoundly influenced by Kevin's time spent as a psychiatric nurse in a drug rehabilitation centre, where he was once chased around the ward in the dead of night by a patient wielding an axe. Kevin is now based in Germany, where he has become an influential figure in the arts world, still doing concerts as well as painting and getting books published. This followed a long period of depression and alcoholism, from which he has now recovered at the cost of his youth and marriage. I found him very easy to work with – if a little scratchy at times – but felt great sadness for his wife and children, who put up with his socialist principles, which included his once insisting that they live in a rented Brixton slum where they were regularly abused and burgled.

Beau was the pseudonym of a gifted folk singer from Yorkshire who worked by day for the Halifax Building Society and who was then a committed communist. He wrote and recorded the single '1917 Revolution', which became a Top Ten hit in, of all places, Israel. We never saw any royalties for that. Beau was a joy to produce. He would arrive perfectly rehearsed and dressed – as were all folkies – in dramatic black pants and sweater, eat only apples and cheese and be finished in time to catch the train home. He was and still is a Dylan disciple and has recently published the definitive discography of his bootleg recordings.

John also recorded Principal Edwards Magic Theatre, whom he had seen doing dance and mime at one his university gigs in the West Country. I hated them and thought they were the most pretentious act I had ever come across, but our policy was to agree to disagree on artistic matters, and John had a pretty impressive track record to date. Around this time John fell ill with jaundice and was bedridden – owing in no small part, I'm convinced, to the almost permanent presence of several of the dozen or more members of PEMT at his one-bedroom flat, who devoured any available food so that he never really ate properly.

When Melanie visited England to promote her latest hit she hotfooted it round to 'Peel Acres' in Park Mews along with her fast-talking manager Artie Ripp. Ever polite but hollow-eyed and pale of pallor, Peely was treated to a very up close and personal rendition of 'I've Got a Brand New Pair of Roller-Skates' while he was suspended in his bed about three feet below the ceiling accompanied by cries of encouragement from the aptly named Mr Ripp.

A friend of John's happened to be there at the time and admired Artie's expensive Leica camera, which Artie immediately handed to him as a gift in that spirit of generosity so prevalent among Americans and Arabs. The friend, Pete Sanders, went on to become a wealthy and successful photographer, starting with pictures of his pal Marc Bolan and the photo on the cover of this book of John on his bike, me on my moped and Pete Drummond in his beaten-up Ford. This was a pisstake of a recently published picture of Tom Jones, Engelbert Humperdinck and their manager in their Rollers with personalized plates.

Both of us were busy earning a living elsewhere, so things moved rather slowly, but eventually we were ready with our first releases and CBS decided to launch the label with a press party. Because it was the sixties – and we were the first 'hippie' label – it was decided to have a macrobiotic party and serve only macrobiotic food – and, of course, dandelion wine. What a blunder: the food was diabolical. I hope not to offend anyone who regularly eats macrobiotic, but how is it possible to make strawberry shortcake taste like old cardboard? If the food was bad the absence of regular booze was a disaster. Never separate a music journalist from a healthy supply of liquor. Insult them if you must, harangue them, starve them but always keep them lubricated. (Some years later, as a director of CBS, I arranged a press reception for Art Garfunkel at the Savoy where the invited music journalists got systematically and paralytically pissed, shouted over the guest of honour and noisily fell over. They still managed to write fulsome articles drawn exclusively from the press releases provided.) What few column inches Dandelion received were both scathing and scornful. The music was barely mentioned and we were labelled 'precious and earnest'.

We had struck a publishing deal for our publishing arm, Biscuit Music, with the CBS affiliate April Music, which was then run by Derek Green, who I recall as being very trendy in his leather trousers. Within just a few weeks he wanted out of the deal and the return of the modest advance that we had agreed. He went on to run A&M Records with great success and now has his own indie label. He was probably right to panic, but over the years Biscuit would have returned his investment tenfold.

The poor response to the launch rather took the wind out of the CBS sails and they never gave us any worthwhile support despite our chart success in Israel. We nevertheless struggled on, and John discovered Medicine Head, who were then employed as gravediggers somewhere in the Midlands. Together they produced a raw but beautiful album called *Old Bottles, New Medicine*. It received a few nice reviews but was only ever played on John's radio shows and sold poorly – which was true of all of our first releases. Oddly enough, those early Dandelion singles are now considered great rarities and change hands at high prices, which is rather at odds with the CBS accounting system, which reported them to have all sold in minus quantities.

One of my favourites from this time was Mike Hart, who wrote the achingly beautiful 'Almost Liverpool 8', which appeared on his first Dandy album. Like so many of our acts, Mike drank too much and spent a lot of time dossing or staying with friends. He also had a penchant for the telephone and would call at unsociable hours to discuss his career at somebody else's expense. On one occasion he called Shurley around midnight from a friend's phone in Edinburgh and, falling fast asleep in mid-sentence, began to snore. No shouts or whistles could awaken him, so Shurl replaced the receiver and went off to bed. When no calls had come in by noon the next day she checked the phone and there was Mike still snoring at about a pound a minute. *Mike Hart Bleeds* was his first Dandelion album. It contained some magical moments and was dedicated to a lost and unrequited love. As an indication of the strength of feeling involved, Mike covered the album artwork with his own blood and defaced the photo of the girl on the cover. Years later Bridget St John confided to me that Mike had never actually met the girl in question but had fancied her from afar.

John was close to the editors of both *Oz* and *IT* and often contributed articles. One day early on in Dandelion's history he was called by the Australian editor of *Oz*, Richard Neville, who alerted him to a great new Aussie group in town called Python Lee Jackson. The band had been moderately successful in Australia but, like so many others, they were now trying to conquer the world from a base in Swinging London and finding it very hard. John duly went along to the Arts Lab to check them out and was most impressed. The lead guitarist had apparently played solos of such length and blistering intensity that his fingers bled. Bleeding hands being the name of the game, I felt obliged to track them down to a squat in Notting Hill Gate and offered them a chance to record.

We booked a few hours in the R.G. Jones studio in Morden, south London, which was a cheap mono rehearsal studio. The results were magnificent, so I lost no time in booking a whole day in CBS's high-tech studios in London's Bond Street. Again the band were brilliant but, as the day wore on, they became increasingly the worse for drink until we had to cancel the rest of the session with nothing usable recorded. Figuring that it was just a case of nerves from the pressure of recording in a top-flight studio, I rebooked them into R.G. Jones where again they excelled. (God, I wish I had kept those mono demos.)

Believing that the group had now overcome their nervousness, I again booked a day in the CBS studios, where the band showed up on time, sober and with a new manager whose real job was selling secondhand cars. The session progressed well with Mick Liber on guitar particularly outstanding. The trouble began when the backing tracks were completed and a break was called for refreshments. An hour in the local pub was enough to leave most of the band, and the lead singer/keyboard player in particular, paralytic. Try as we might, we were unable to get anything like a lead vocal. The singer kept sliding gracefully to the floor before he could open his mouth. The situation became desperate, with expensive studio time ticking away and no resolution in sight.

At this point the manager suggested that he knew a good singer who had just left the Jeff Beck Group and was between jobs. For the standard £15 session fee he just might be available to come in immediately and sing the three songs for which we had by now completed backing tracks. Following a telephone call, a cab was dispatched while various members of the group walked the singer around the block to sober him up and keep him away from the studio while a stranger sang the songs he had written.

Eventually this very jolly young man arrived, whom Peel identified as Rod Stewart. He listened to the playback once, scanned the lyrics and sang all three songs perfectly with surprising feel and apparent sympathy for the complex and fairly obscure words. We were delighted, and the band's manager asked Rod if, rather than have a session fee, he might prefer something for his car. Rod mentioned that he did indeed need a new differential for his old banger and arranged to visit the manager's yard the next morning to pick up £15 worth worth of nuts and bolts in full payment. John had by now left, and we spent the remainder of the night mixing the three tracks to highlight both the vocals and Mick's brilliant guitar.

Unquestionably the strongest song was 'In a Broken Dream', and I at least was convinced that we had our first smash hit. Unfortunately our distributors did not agree. CBS thought the tracks were old-fashioned and amateur, while Jac Holzman said that blues records were dead. We nevertheless persevered with trying to place the record and eventually, having exhausted all possibilities with major labels, we licensed it to Miki Dallon at Young Blood Records. Miki was on a roll at the time with two or three recent big hits. He remixed our masters, rather badly I thought, and released 'In a Broken Dream' through EMI where it sold three hundred copies and died. It was by now over a year since we had finished the recording, but we still had faith and prevailed on Miki to release the record again, whereupon it sold 202 copies and died again.

When Miki's deal with EMI terminated he came to an arrangement through a third party for his label to be distributed by CBS. I had by this time pretty much given up on Dandelion and had joined CBS in charge of marketing. To my delight, Rod had by now become famous, and Miki rereleased 'In a Broken Dream' for a third time still under the name of Python Lee Jackson and without mentioning Rod's name. This time it soared into the charts, reached number two and sold over a quarter of a million copies. Same record that had died twice. The band was thrilled and asked me if I would advance them sufficient money to fly back to Australia for an extended holiday. With over a quarter of a million sales registered I was happy to oblige, since I knew that the two or three thousand needed would be more than covered by the royalties due to us as the original producer and owner of the hit. Oh yeah?

Unfortunately – again – when the royalties became due we discovered that the 'third party' through whom Miki had done the CBS deal had in fact buggered off back to the Caribbean with all the bread. Miki was badly hurt, since 'In a Broken Dream' was only one of three huge hits for which he was never paid, and we were in the possibly unique position of having lost money, by virtue of recording costs and flights, on a quarter-of-a-million-seller. It took almost twenty years to recover our outlay, and that only came about when Miki Dallon sold his rights to the master tape to another company which managed to persuade Rod to include the track on one of his greatest hits albums. At last even Rod had a share in the success.

An amusing sidebar is that when Miki and his partner were touting the record

With big sister Joan

Did all evacuees look like this?
In Reading during the war

'Helping' Dad lay pipes

First sports jacket: the Southern Comfort years with friend Derek

Marty Wilde introducing Broderick
(left) and Chet (top of head) Selwood
to the delights of a misspent youth

CS and son Brod (bottom right)
hyping the charts with 1961
Eurovision runners-up, the Allisons

CS with Monty Presky of Pye and Keith Shackleton of Century 21, modelling suits and ties with Aqua Marina from *Stingray*

Elektra band Leviathan filming a television special

Meeting Judy Collins and a posse of friends at Heathrow

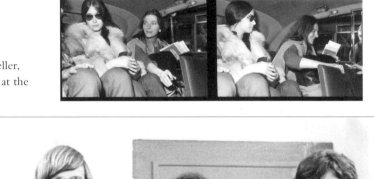

CS and secretary Sylvia Kneller, with a famous Elektra band at the *Top of the Pops* studios

Billboard April '70

onal News Reports

The beginning of the
Dandelion years

OUTSIDE THE PARADISO, Amsterdam, where they gathered for the launching in Holland of John Peel's Dandelion label are, left to right, Beau, John Fiddler of Medicine Head, Bridget St. John; Pete Hope-Evans (Medicine Head); Ko Kooijman (Dutch CBS, publicity); John Peel, Derek Johns (CBS, London); Leo Moolenijzer (CBS, Holland, public relations); Jacques Barrs, an Amsterdam record retailer, and Derek Witt of CBS, London.

DJ Peel's Dandelion debut set

DISC JOCKEY John Peel launches his own Dandelion label next month. The label is being released in America via Elektra but CBS has captured British release rights to the label under a deal set by Clive Selwood, Peel's manager, who is also Elektra's British representative in this country.

The label will be introduced under its own logo in this country in the middle of next month with a possible release of three singles by the Principal Edwards Magic Theatre, a Yorkshire writer called Beau, and Brigitte St. John. All three singles have been produced by Peel.

Selwood told RR last week that all income brought into the Dandelion account would be split among the artists signed to the label to assist in the recording and promotion of future talent. CBS will mount a major promotion campaign which Keith Howell, the company's press officer, said would be "very provocative".

RECORD RETAILER 15/6/69

ASK ME NO QUESTIONS
BRIDGET ST. JOHN

SIDE ONE

The original Dandelion label,
designed by a pixie on Dartmoor
(note the hamster)

Some of the (un)usual suspects

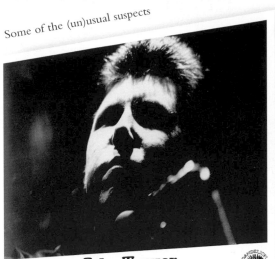

John Trevor

Bridget St. John

Principal Edwards Magic Theatre

Burning Red Ivanhoe

Kevin Coyne

Above: CS and Clifford T. Ward outside
Polydor's London offices, launching Clifford's
first album

Below: Clifford T.'s notes for a meeting with CS,
in which he promises to write more songs

Right: Tragically, time ran out for Clifford in
2001

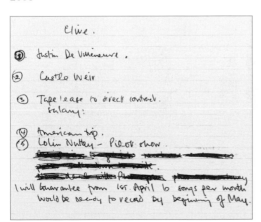

Brickies by day; rock gods by night: JP's favourite group (note the different label used on later Dandy albums)

33⅓ STEREO
2310-231
℗ 1972
DANDELION RECORDS

1.F.D. & H.2.Carlin M.3.Jewel M.
4.Kags M.5.Biscuit/Warner
Bros.6.Kassner

BUGGER OFF

1. ROSALYN (Duncan - Farley) 2. WILLIE THE PIMP (Frank Zappa) 3. I'M YOUR HOOCHIE COOCHIE MAN (Willie Dixon) 4. IT'S ALL OVER NOW (B. & S. Womack) 5. SEVERAL YARDS (Foxtrot) (Knall-Banham-Stott-Groom) 6. YOU REALLY GOT ME (R. Davies)

STACKWADDY

Produced by Eddie Lee Beppeaux and Kevin Spotte

MARKETED BY POLYDOR

ALL RIGHTS OF THE MANUFACTURER AND OF THE OWNER OF THE RECORDED WORK RESERVED · UNAUTHORISED PUBLIC PERFORMANCE BROADCASTING AND COPYING OF THIS RECORD PROHIBITED

MADE IN GREAT BRITAIN

John Fiddler (left) and Peter Hope-Evans of Medicine Head, after giving up their day jobs

Keith Relf (left) flew the Yardbirds' nest to produce Medicine Head's first hit. He and John Davies (centre) replaced Peter on the *Dark Side of the Moon* album.

Jim Milne and Steve Clayton of Tractor (aka The Way We Live)

The sartorially elegant busker Lol Coxhill

GENE VINCENT

He's back & he's proud of his brand new recording

BE BOP A LULA '69

Arriving Great Britain November 5 for Top of the Pops Television on November 13 and a National tour

'Grease me some of that that teenage . . .'
A release fraught with danger

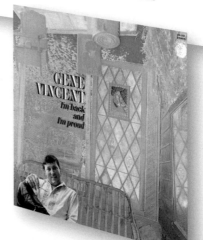

Above: Johnnie Walker and friend with Ian Ralfini of WEA and Mr and Mrs Selwood at yet another WEA party

Left: The two Samanthas – Drummond (Pete's daughter, left) and Selwood – discussing Japanese culture at the Yamasukis' launch party with CS and Shurley

Left to right: Svelte and hirsute Danny Loggins with CBS sales director Jack Florey, Terry the CBS accountant and CS

Into the lion's den: (left to right) Maurice 'Obie' Oberstein, Danny Loggins, CS and Dick Asher, all of CBS

CS and Obie make love to the camera, while Art Garfunkel and Stuart Grundy of Radio 1 compare perms

Chart-topper David Essex (left) and England football captain Gerry Francis (right) flanking two fat businessmen

CS with Greg Edwardes, DJ and promotion man

Bazza, the 'Walrus of Love', is on the left

Melba Moore and the Pye team

The Real Thing smiling through the
Black Umbrella débâcle

Right: Marty Machat (second left) and Freddy Haayen, MD of Polydor (raised fist), encouraging Shurl and CS to sign the contract for the creation of Sarabee; and (above) the Sarabee logo

Above right: Band of Joy, the best band to have never quite made it: (left to right) Frankie, Kevyn, Johnno, Michael and Paul

Above: Johnno and Kevyn

Right: The Wailing Cocks; Andde Leek is second from right

THE ALBUM THAT TOOK 25 YEARS TO CREATE

ONE AND ONLY
36 CLASSIC TRACKS ON 2 CDs or 2 CASSETTES

DIRE STRAITS • ELTON JOHN • U2 • SIMPLE MINDS • POLICE
IRON MAIDEN • ERASURE • UB40 • DEPECHE MODE • JOE COCKER
STATUS QUO • MOODY BLUES • CULTURE CLUB • FREE • EMF
T. REX • THE MOVE • JIMI HENDRIX • TRAFFIC • ELVIS COSTELLO
O.M.D. • SOFT CELL • MADNESS • JETHRO TULL • YARDBIRDS
THE SPECIALS • GARY NUMAN • THE SMITHS • FAIRPORT CONVENTION
ARTHUR BROWN • BAUHAUS • JOY DIVISION • TEN YEARS AFTER
CAPTAIN SENSIBLE • MANFRED MANN • CHICKEN SHACK

Specially compiled for
25 YEARS OF RADIO 1

OVER 2 HOURS OF MUSIC FROM THE
ORIGINAL ARTISTS INCLUDING 22
PREVIOUSLY UNRELEASED RECORDINGS

36 CLASSIC TRACKS ON 2 CDs FOR £19.99 or 2 CASSETTES for £10.99
AVAILABLE FROM ALL GOOD RECORD

OR IF IN DIFFICULTY, BY MAIL-ORDER DIRECT FROM: BAND OF JOY MUSIC LTD, SARABEE,
RIDGWAY, PYEFORD, WOKING, SURREY GU22 8PW AND TAKE ADVANTAGE OF THE
SELECT £2.00 DISCOUNT (Discount for mail-order in the UK only) Please make cheques/postal
orders payable to: Band Of Joy Music Ltd.

£2 DISCOUNT!!! YESSIRREE BUB!!!
NAME:
ADDRESS:

TICK A BOX CD □ £17.99

JIMI HENDRIX LIVE & UNRELEASED THE RADIO SHOW

Above: Every musician on every track hunted down and contract negotiated

Strange Fruit: one of the most successful indie labels anywhere ever

Strange Fruit
Strange Fruit Records
By arrangement with BBC Records and Tapes

Side 2

45 rpm Stereo
Made in U.K.
THE PEEL SESSION

SFPS080 - 2

℗ BBC
BBC Enterprises Ltd.
© Strange Fruit Records

All rights reserved by the Producer and the Owner of the recorded
works reserved. All unauthorised copying,
public performance, broadcasting,
hiring or rental of
this recording
prohibited.

Above: Band of Joy Music's best-selling release (top) and the second-best-selling, a limited edition collectors' item

Above: CS's daughter Bee at the Strange Fruit launch, with a very young Andy Kershaw (left) and Steve Mason, Pinnacle MD (beard)

Right: CS's youngest daughter Sam at the same do

John Peel on his bike, Pete Drummond on his Zodiac and CS on his hog. This picture was taken to send up a well-known photo of the time in which Tom Jones, Englebert Humperdinck and their manager show off their Rollers.

CS and Peel, not happy that the only place the photographer could get the 'right light' was in the gents at the BBC

The late lamented Pres with friend in the twenty-first century

around America they tried to sell it to Mercury Records, who at that time were top of the charts with Rod's 'Maggie May'. After a couple of listens the groovy A & R man vouchsafed that the vocal sound was familiar. One more listen and he stopped the playback with an imperious gesture. 'Got it,' he pronounced with a smile. 'It's Johnny Ray.'

Rod and I met socially here and there and, while Rod was always affable, I don't think he ever forgave us for paying him a few quid in car parts for a silver disc. He is, however, a master of his craft, and I can think of nobody else who could have produced such a remarkable performance without any rehearsal or foreknowledge.

Anyway, as time went by most of the people at CBS with whom we had first reached agreement had moved on to other companies, and their successors simply did not know what to make of us. It was around this time that Elektra Records were sold to the group that became WEA, and I had moved with the company to the new offices. Pretty much the first priority of any American company opening a British office is to find and promote local talent. Dandelion Records, or more specifically Peel, must have looked like an easy route to new acts for WEA managing director Ian Ralfini, who made us an offer that we and CBS found difficult to refuse.

The release from CBS was very painful, as we had sold next to nothing and were required to repay all the advance money. The folks at WEA knew how badly we had fared and adjusted the advance accordingly, but they were a classy company and we were hopeful that we would get the kind of marketing support that would bring us some success.

Anyone not familiar with the ways of the music business may be surprised to learn that, absolutely regardless of the flattery, money and assurances that you are wanted for what you are or do before the deal is struck, every attempt will be made to change you into whatever is currently popular or successful as soon as the contract ink is dry. So it was with Warners, who initially signed us for our rugged independence but quickly decided that what they really wanted was a minor-league hits factory.

The launch at least was done with style. A new and beautiful label was designed and the first releases through WEA were presented in magnificent presentation boxes that included artists' biographies along with bits and pieces like flowers and bags of dandelion tea. In fact, just a few years ago we were contacted by the Victoria and Albert Museum to ask if we had one of the original boxes that they could put on display. We had and it was.

Warners also provided a batch of expensively produced posters of Bridget and Medicine Head for display in stores, and it began to look as if we were rolling. John had no ambitions for the label beyond it becoming an outlet for new and, in his opinion, interesting artists, but quite properly WEA were anxious for us to have a few hits to justify their faith and expenditure, which placed me pretty much in the firing line. In an attempt to provide us with at least a presence in the charts, Ian Ralfini asked if we would allow a Japanese hit that he had picked up, 'Yamasuki' by the Yamasukis, to be released on Dandy. It was pretty deadly, but in a spirit of cooperation we agreed, which gave Warners an excuse for another party. They were very good at parties. A Japanese restaurant was chosen, and the entertainment was provided by a troupe of Japanese sword jugglers. They came close to giving us some unwelcome headlines when, after the sake had been flowing for some time, one of them lost his grip on a huge cutlass, which skittered across the restaurant, narrowly avoiding beheading a large section of the media. Despite being an early example of a single in a picture bag and picking up a few radio plays the record was not a hit, though I understand there is now a considerable demand for it as a collectors' item.

As I mentioned earlier, I had enormous trouble relating to Principal Edwards Magic Theatre and tried to avoid any meetings or discussions with them as, perhaps unwittingly, they did my head in and I was unable to function following any contact with any one of them. For their second album they managed to engage the services of Nick Mason of Pink Floyd as producer. The production manager at Warners at that time was a rather self-regarding man named Lionel Rose and, when Nick arrived one day unannounced to inform us that the test pressing of the album was satisfactory, he was dressed in jeans, T-shirt and sneakers. The members of Pink Floyd were never the most recognizable, and Lionel had no idea who he was talking to, so he decided to patronize this scruffy-looking individual.

'Well, you say it's all right,' he said, 'but how do I know that's true? I mean what did you play it on?'

Nicky looked crestfallen. 'I've got this old Dansette,' he replied without cracking a smile. 'The head jumps a bit, but I balance a couple of pennies on it and that seems to do the trick.'

'Bloody useless,' snarled Lionel. 'Just leave it with me and I'll deal with it later.'

Without a word Nicky left and almost immediately Lionel went off to lunch muttering about 'bloody amateurs'. He returned just a few minutes later red-faced and confused.

'Who was that bloke?' he demanded. 'I've just seen him outside getting into a Ferrari with more hi-fi equipment in it than I've got in this office.' I've always admired Mr Mason for not pulling rank and would like to think that it was a lesson in manners for a rather pompous individual. The album never sold anywhere near enough to cover its cost, however.

The Occasional Word Ensemble was a bunch of poets cast along the lines of the Scaffold. I was once quoted in some journal or other as saying that 'one of them was institutionalized, but it could have been all of them', which, twenty-five years later, still seems a reasonable assessment. Their Dandy album was an odd mix of poems, songs, sketches and rather awful jokes. Some of them smoked herbal fags, and I recall Rik Sanders telling me of the time that he and another member of the group went for a walk while a bit out of it. In fact they were so stoned that when they were attacked by a group of skinheads they just stood there wrapped in duffel coats like Michelin Men while the blows rained in. It was shortly after our album was released that one of the leading players, Pete Roche, became convinced that God had instructed him to eat only an apple a day (no more and no less) until Liverpool Football Club won by a particular score. Pete soon began wasting away at an alarming rate. He was eventually persuaded to seek treatment, and a year later I saw him on a train, complete with brief-case and *Daily Telegraph*, apparently on his way to the City. Shame.

Fortunately, in 1972 John Fiddler of Medicine Head struck up a friendship with Keith Relf, who had been a leading light in the Yardbirds and who knew a thing or two about hits. I had known Keith from his days with Renaissance, which he had led briefly with his sister Jane on vocals, when they had made an album for Elektra. Keith was a shy, introverted man who spoke quietly and was the antithesis of a rock star. He was, however, very talented and produced our first hit, 'Pictures In the Sky', which took Medicine Head – and Dandelion – into the Top Twenty. At last.

With a hit as credentials WEA were keen to show us off to their American and European partners, so they organized a party, at which some of the acts agreed to play. Another disaster. John was and still is a fan of possibly the first ever punk band, Stackwaddy from Manchester. They were punks before the genre was invented. We had released one single from them during our time at CBS and lived in dread of the late-night calls whenever their van broke down and left them stranded on the motorway. They were, to say the least, untutored but had an energy and dynamism that Peely admired. In retrospect, they were perhaps the least suitable of our acts to inflict on the assembled manicured executives.

Coming straight to the party from the building sites they worked on by day, still in work clothes and covered in mud, they set about the free food and drink with abandon; so much so that by the time they were due to play they were close to legless, and after just one number the singer stopped to take a pee on the side of the stage. There was an audible gasp from the assembled executives and their wives who made their excuses and left. Stackwaddy may have sealed our fate with WEA. They certainly sealed their own fate later that night when, lost on the way to another gig, they stopped to ask a policeman the way, and the driver, who was still pissed, threw up all over the copper's boots, which brought them yet another of many nights in the pokey. (Incidentally, one member of the band was at one time hiding from two wives, the army, the police, the gas board, the electricity board, social security and several children.)

Their second album for us was called *Bugger Off* in recognition of their response to Peel's attempts at production. Over the next few months they managed to blow up several vans, starved, made another album that horrified the trendies, chased women, drank a lot and eventually disbanded. They were a decade ahead of punk and left us a legacy of such great compositions as 'Several Yards (Foxtrot)' and 'Meat Pies 'Ave Come But Band's Not Here Yet'. I heard recently that they had re-formed – but, I hope, not reformed.

In an attempt to broaden our audience Peely also contacted a number of acts from outside Britain who were keen on getting into our market, and we released albums from the Danish band Burnin Red Ivanhoe and Holland's Super-Sister. Neither of them sold, despite John having them stickered as 'Common-Market Toe Tappers' complete with a scantily clad woman.

I had high hopes for a single by Bill Oddie of the Goodies singing 'On Ilkla Moor Baht'At' to the tune of the Beatles' 'With a Little Help From My Friends' with the original Joe Cocker arrangement and musicians, including the great Sue and Sunny, who were the best backing singers in the country. Like so many of our releases it is now probably a collectors' item, and I have even mislaid the master tape. It was a brilliant session with John's wife Sheila brought in as 'technical consultant', but nobody got the joke. Recently it was played on Radio 4, which was probably only its second airing in thirty years. It still sounded terrific. The B-side was another spoof on the then current craze for mysticism. It was called 'Harry Krishna', produced by Sue and Sunny, with the credits listing Peel on tape reels and additional vocals by 'Petals Khan', aka John Walters. All this might seem like the kind of behaviour you'd expect from a bunch of kids let loose in an expensive sweet shop, but a little of that kind of lunacy would not go amiss in today's po-faced market.

Lol Coxhill was, and still is, a street musician. He is also one of the vainest men I have ever met in a lifetime of hanging out with people whose livelihood depends on them having a high degree of self-belief. He is an odd-looking cove, with a completely bald head atop a stout frame, and on his last visit to my home took some delight in detailing the total cost of his wardrobe as less than fifty pence through canny purchases at jumble sales. He plays a saxophone and, in true Dandelion fashion, John agreed to finance and release a self-produced double album of his work, *The Ear of the Beholder*, with contributions from some of his friends, such as David Bedford and Kevin Ayers.

WEA were pretty horrified and I found it hard to justify the release, but I was able to license the album to Ampex Records in America where it began to pick up ecstatic reviews and very encouraging sales. Ampex were a major player in the tape market and were just trying to break into the record business. I guess they didn't try hard enough, because they closed down the record division and wound it up without paying us a penny in royalties. Another one bites the dust. Later I persuaded Lol and David Bedford to record for me what I hoped would become the worst record ever recorded. It featured Lol singing (!) his own composition 'Pretty Little Girl' on one side and a medley of 'Sonny Boy' and 'Oh, Mein Papa' on the reverse. It was staggeringly awful, and I was sure that it would be recognized as the ultimate piece of kitsch and become a novelty hit. Nobody reviewed or played it, and yet again I have mislaid the master.

In deference to Jac Holzman, who insisted that Americans would never get their tongues around the name Coyne-Clague, they changed themselves into Siren and released a rocking album called *Strange Locomotion* through WEA. Jac was thrilled with it and placed major ads in *Rolling Stone* and other music journals to no response. By now Bridget's reputation was growing, and her second album also came out through WEA to encouraging reviews and reasonable sales. Medicine Head, with Keith Relf at the controls and adding guitar, released *Heavy on the Drum*, which would have sold better had it included the hit single 'Slip and Slide', but time and interest were running out at WEA. I was forced to fight for even modest marketing efforts, which was rather difficult as I was also an employee.

In fact life at WEA became increasingly difficult as the heads of the British and German companies and the head of the Atlantic division in the UK vied with each other for the attention of the American bosses and the ultimate prize. Perhaps I should have become more involved, but office politics was never high on my list of priorities, and it was at this point that I found myself demoted to export manager with a sick label and no support from Elektra in America where Jac was having his own problems in the WEA hierarchy. I felt it was time yet again to pack up and move on.

While I was pondering the possibilities and thinking about a distribution move for Dandy, I received a demo tape from an act which purported to be a couple of lads from Rochdale. It was not very well recorded but featured a singer and guitarist of sublime talent. Shurl and I were fairly certain that it was the product of one of the many 'super-groups' of the time and had been sent to us as a gag in the expectation that we would pass and be left with egg on our faces. Peely agreed. It did not seem possible that these were the efforts of a couple of unknowns, but a call to the enclosed telephone number confirmed the few details that we had. Shurl and I sped up to Rochdale and there we met The Way We Live, who were indeed a couple of teenagers that had recorded a complete album in the attic of and under the direction of a pal who had a job at the Beeb. The band was essentially Jim Milne on vocals and a number of guitars aided by Steve Clayton on drums and percussion. Jim had a job as a trainee schoolteacher, and Steve spent his time painting and writing poetry.

With the approval of their parents we signed them up and, after providing some better recording equipment, awaited a masterpiece. It duly arrived and was released under the title *A Candle for Judith*. Some of the reviews were raves, but there was no obvious single to draw radio exposure and the sales were negligible, though I was able to get them a short television series in the education area. Another case of 'don't give up the day job'.

In the absence of any exciting offers elsewhere I decided to take Dandelion to Polydor, who showed some enthusiasm and had the benefit of a fully functioning European set-up. They swiftly arranged a European tour to promote the label. The tour consisted of Bridget, Medicine Head, Beau, Kevin Coyne and myself – all crowded into a minibus along with roadies and a few Polydor people – thrashing across Germany, Belgium and Holland to play in clubs such as the Paradiso in Amsterdam. It was memorable in that Bridget struck up a relationship and wrote 'The Road Was Lonely', which she performed on television the first night we got back to Britain. Her boyfriend of some years heard the performance and immediately called up to break it off. Perhaps it was in code, since I was there when she wrote it and never suspected a thing.

David Bedford is an extremely talented serious musician. He is, however, not very commercially inclined, so it was with some trepidation that I booked studio time for him at John's request. They had agreed to complete an album of David's work that would include the girls from the very smart school where he taught: they would sing and twirl plastic pipes. Oh joy! Since David was the only professional musician we had yet recorded John felt that we should leave him to get on with it without any input from us or supervision. The studio's and musicians' bills were substantial but not excessive for what we assumed would be a major work, and on completion I was delighted to collect the copy master tapes to take home and review in comfort. That evening I carefully wound the tape on to our trusty Revox, but after a few bars was disappointed to realize that the tape was running backwards. This was a not unusual occurrence with large studio tapes. but these were usually clearly marked 'Tails Out' if they needed to be rewound. Imagine our consternation when, after the recordings were rewound, they sounded, to our ears, exactly the same. Again I reversed the tape and again I was horrified, but Peely was sanguine and assured me that it was indeed a Work of Art. He was mightily amused by the vowel sounds of the girl singers and intrigued by the twirling. After several more plays I began to make some sense of it and enjoyed the Kevin Ayers contribution, but Polydor thought we had gone mad – and they had a point.

Mike Hart presented us with his epic pisstake on old British war movies that he had recorded in Edinburgh with Viv Stanshall and friends. It was called *Basher, Chalky, Pongo and Me*, which was the best part of it.

John suggested The Way We Live change their name to Tractor. We thought things might also be improved by moving to a proper studio and visited Strawberry Studios in Manchester, where we listened to a track recorded by the owners entitled 'Neanderthal Man' as a demo of their sound and fell about laughing at their incompetence. That record, of course, went to number one and the group became 10CC, with whom I worked with considerable success some years later at UK Records. The Tractor album was eventually released but suffered the same fate as the first. They were very talented but would have improved considerably with public appearances to sharpen them up. However, they were unable to reproduce their sound live.

Clifford T. Ward made an appearance at this time and was, in my opinion, our potential saviour in commercial terms. John was not at all impressed, but again we agreed to disagree. Cliff was working as a schoolteacher in Solihull and was notable for his very long fair hair, which was unusual in that profession at the time. Ken Wright, who also played drums in Cliff's band and had a day job as an accountant at the BBC, managed him. Ken was a very droll guy who put up with a lot of Cliff's foibles and went on to become one of the BBC's chief accountants. Cliff had recorded before for another company and was contracted to Island Music for publishing. As I intended to spend a lot of time and money recording Cliff, I suggested to Lionel Conway at Island that we come to some arrangement with regard to publishing income. He offered to sell me his rights for £1,000, but I refused in the belief that this was excessive since he had only ever advanced Cliff £100. What a fool I was. His song writing has earned tens of thousands over the years with covers being done by the likes of Ringo and Cliff Richard. Ringo's management demanded a piece, of course – and got it. Polydor shared my faith in Cliff and went to bat for us with a big campaign that included posters on the sides of London buses, but despite substantial airplay on the two singles from the first album sales were derisory and Polydor began to lose heart.

Medicine Head meanwhile were going through changes. I had managed them in the lean period, but with success they attracted attention from others and decided to make new arrangements. This was acceptable in principle and in fact. The only problem was that a new management team would inevitably try to hit up the record company for money. They always do, and this lot was no exception. This made for a difficult situation since, just at the point that the band were about to make some money, not only was I being asked to give up management but more money was being demanded from my own company. The next thing they requested was the return of the publishing catalogue. This I refused, since I didn't trust them to look after it.

John Fiddler and Peter Hope-Evans were truly gentle souls when we first met.

John was very spiritual, and Peter was shy and enigmatic. He simply never spoke except in whispered asides to 'Fiddler John'. Even at the height of their success, when girls would throw themselves at the pair, Peter would shyly turn away – though I believe a few got through. With success John became remote and much harder, while Peter became increasingly disenchanted and eventually left to take up a career writing for radio. I believe he now teaches. Keith Relf joined the band as a full-time member, and Medicine Head continued to have a few hits through Polydor. Tragically, Keith was electrocuted at his home. He was a talented man who seemed quite unable to cope with the trappings of success. Medicine Head lumbered on for a couple of years before John Fiddler joined the British Lions, another band that never realized their potential.

In the end Polydor informed us that they no longer wanted anything to do with Dandelion, except they wanted to keep Medicine Head. It was no great surprise.

Even Kevin Coyne's solo album, which ranks alongside my edit of Love's 'Alone Again Or' as one of my proudest achievements, could not save us. Having failed with three different distributors I had had enough, and we had come close enough to success to send alarm signals to Peely. He is really only interested in the new, and without his input the label was worthless. In a fairly short time we had found some talented and interesting acts, spent a large amount of time, effort and money, driven a few record people crazy and made some kind of statement. In the process we – or at least John – had also recorded an album with Shakin' Stevens, whose manager subsequently took our recordings off to another company. We 'discovered' Roxy Music, who, after an initial encouraging meeting with me, became the subject of a full-page feature in the *Melody Maker*. This started a bidding war that was won by Island Records, which had deeper pockets than Dandy and could afford advances and the kinds of marketing campaigns we never could and so gave the band a better shot at hitting the big time. And we made what was eventually a smash hit record with Rod Stewart and a group of crazy Aussies. We decided it was time to call it a day.

In hindsight, perhaps the apparent failure of Dandy could have been avoided if I had fought harder and spent more time and money on those acts with commercial potential. It was and increasingly is a very tough business with little regard for altruism, despite the machinations and efforts of the PR departments. We, however, never considered it to be a failure and are happy that our efforts contributed in some degree to a changing attitude from record companies towards their artists and laid the groundwork for the emergence of the indie record industry.

On the plus side is the fact that, had we been more successful, John would have pursued his plans to record Rancid Cyril and his Mighty Balloons and even possibly assembled enough Girls Named Sharon to produce the hundred-piece choir he envisaged. You were at least spared that.

14. GENE
VINCENT

GENE VINCENT

One of the more memorable episodes of the Dandelion years involved one of the great pioneers of rock and roll, Gene Vincent. By the late sixties Vincent was a sad and lonely figure, driven by drink and having spent many years coping with the pain of a partially severed leg. His smash hit, 'Be-Bop-A-Lula', had topped the charts around the world in the mid-fifties and is even now included on every worthwhile compilation of fifties' hits.

Our paths crossed on a number of occasions, the first of which was at London's Finsbury Park Empire in 1960 when, already past his prime, he was sharing top billing with Eddie Cochran. Eddie was a revelation, one of the most dynamic performers I have ever seen. He opened his act with curtains closed over the opening bars of Ray Charles's 'What'd I Say'. As the curtains opened, there was Eddie with his back to the audience, and on the first words, 'Hey, Mama', he spun around to face the audience, wearing black shades and standing legs apart with his guitar spitting fire. Old hat now but dangerously exciting and innovative then.

I was enthralled and took my companion backstage to meet him; he was polite, friendly and gallant. Gene, with whom he shared a dressing-room, was morose, tending to fat and drunk. It was nevertheless an enjoyable encounter made even more so when Don and Phil Everly dropped in to show off their 'quick draw' skills and challenge Eddie to a Western-style shoot-out.

When it was time to leave I suggested that, rather than take a train back from Bristol the following night, where they were due to play another concert, they might want to rent a car and enjoy the scenic drive. I've never truly forgiven myself for that advice since, as the world knows, Gene, Eddie and his girlfriend Sharon were involved in a horrific car accident on 17 April 1960. Eddie died and both Sharon and Gene were badly injured.

When next I saw Gene it was in California in 1969. Flower power was in full flow, and that night in Los Angeles was like a microcosm of the rock-and-roll lifestyle. Dandelion Records was up and running, and John had heard that Gene, one of his early heroes, was out of contract and looking for a record deal. As I was already visiting Los Angeles on Elektra business I arranged to meet Gene in Hollywood.

Shurley and I were staying at the glamorous but decidedly dated Hollywood Roosevelt hotel, where the movie stars of the twenties and thirties had trysted amid the palm trees and cabanas surrounding the pool. The decor of our suite reflected that period, and it did not take a great deal of imagination to conjure up pictures of Garbo and Valentino reclining on the damask-covered chaise-longue.

Gene arrived on time and limped into the room looking old, fat and in pretty poor shape. A very tall, slim young-looking man, whom Gene introduced as 'my producer, Kim Fowley', accompanied him. Kim – who later informed me that he had become a millionaire at eighteen from writing and producing a string of hits – strode across the room with outstretched hand and said, 'Hey, grease me some of that teenage dogshit', which still ranks high on my list of innovative greetings, though I've never quite found an opportunity to use it myself. We discussed the album, agreed terms with both Gene and Kim and went on to consider the album cover, which Gene felt should feature a picture of him 'next to my star'. It came to light that Gene's name had been enshrined in true Hollywood fashion on the sidewalk just outside the hotel in bronze with his own star alongside those of that select band of showbiz greats similarly honoured. As a good ole Southern boy Gene would not address us by our first names but insisted on the formal 'sir' and 'ma'am' despite being senior to us in age and achievement. It was a cruel moment when, as he was leaving, he asked shamefacedly for a token advance of $50 to pay the back rent on the garage where he was living under the threat of eviction.

All of these discussions were continually interrupted by completely incomprehensible interjections from Mr Fowley, but eventually Shurley and I reeled off into a balmy LA night. To clear our heads, we went for a drive into the fabled Hollywood Hills listening on the car radio to a local rock station that was interrupted with the first news of the horrible Manson Family murders. Hollywood in microcosm.

Following the Dandelion policy of allowing the artists total freedom to record what and how they chose without interference or supervision, Gene and Kim commenced recording at Elektra's brilliant new state-of-the-art studio. Meanwhile Shurley and I returned to our little semi-detached in Slough where we continued with our various activities. These now included looking after the recordings of Elektra and its publishing arm Nina Music, running and administering Dandelion with all of the studio booking, royalty accounting, legal work, artist negotiations and so on, setting up and administering the Biscuit Music catalogue, along with managing Peel, Pete Drummond, Johnnie Walker and three of the Dandelion acts.

Since I was also required to spend a fair part of most weeks travelling Europe on Elektra business, leaving Shurl to cope with our small child, perhaps it would have been wiser to have brought in some help.

First reports from LA were that the album was progressing well. Kim had found some superb musicians, and the recordings were attracting such diverse celebrity visitors as the Doors, the Everlys and members of Steppenwolf, all of whom were delighted to see the legendary old rocker back in the saddle. Then began a series of frustrating and lengthy late-night telephone calls. Usually they came in at about 3 a.m. and often lasted an hour or more. They would begin, 'Mizz Selwood, ma'am. Ah hate to trouble you, but ah jist cain't work with Kim Fowley.'

Shurley would express regret, pointing out that it had been Gene himself who had presented Kim as a *fait accompli* but nevertheless offering to dispense with him as a producer.

'Ah wish you wouldn't do that, ma'am' would be the reply, in that slightly eerie metallic sound that accompanied transatlantic calls in those days. We would then suggest that perhaps Kim should stay on as producer in the hope that it would work out.

This elicited the response 'OK. But ah cain't work with him.'

One of us would then suggest that we remove Kim as producer but state that the decision was ours rather than Gene's to avoid any personal difficulty.

'Ah wish you wouldn't do that', would be the baffling transatlantic response. With mounting desperation we would, night after sleepless night, offer various solutions to the problem, only to be met with the same response. Many of our suggestions were met with total silence save for the singing of the telephone wires, then, after several silent minutes, a disembodied voice would say, 'Ah'm still heah and nobody's talking to me.'

After a time we received a three-page cable from Gene, thanking us for our kindness and bidding us a sad farewell, since he was now resident in the Cedars of Lebanon Hospital with only hours to live. In a state of some agitation we rang Gene's home to discover him alive and with no recollection of the cable.

Eccentricity in the music industry is so commonplace as to be almost mandatory, but it still comes as a shock to discover that the person in whom you have invested a great deal of time and just about all of your money is in fact clinically mad.

Somehow the album was eventually completed and John Lennon, via Peel, offered to supply one of his drawings to go on the cover. Sadly he withdrew the offer after hearing a test pressing of the album, which did not fill us with confidence. I then got a call from one of the most feared and notorious operators in the business. In a voice heavy with menace Don Arden, who had a reputation to strike fear into the bravest soul, informed me that he had 'Gene Vincent Craddock' under an exclusive contract covering all aspects of entertainment for the next hundred or so years and that, by recording Gene, we had incurred his displeasure. I was stunned. 'Do you want to discuss it?' enquired Don, and in a faltering voice I agreed to meet him the following day.

Now Don had a reputation at that time for using any means whatsoever to get what he wanted including, it was rumoured, physical damage of the terminal variety. Books have been written and newspaper articles have appeared suggesting that he was not a man with whom to cross swords or even words. The most popular tale is of my caller dangling a very famous person out of a fourth-floor window by his ankles until he got what he wanted. I always believed the story to be apocryphal until I talked to the man who was holding the other leg!

Needless to say I was terrified and urgently relayed the bad tidings to John, who suggested that we simply give the finished album to Mr Arden and be done with it. When I pointed out that the album had already cost us our entire recording budget and more for the next few years, John very properly pointed out that no amount of money was worth risking a life for.

Still in a blue funk, I apprised Shurley of the situation and she expressed surprise at Don's fearsome reputation. Shurley had known him in his early days as a band singer when she was a dancer and had always found him to be polite and courteous. 'Give him my regards,' she said, remembering card schools on trains to and from various theatrical dates around the country.

Came the day and I was ushered into the man's plush offices where he sat at a huge desk flanked by two obvious heavies. Before I could say a word the telephone rang and Don listened for a moment before snarling 'Sue the bastard' and banging down the receiver. The phone rang again immediately and the performance was repeated, but this time with the message 'Break his legs.' I figured that this was a little bit of showbiz, designed to put the fear of God into any visitor and that the calls were in all probability from his bored receptionist acting upon instructions. But the fact that he had bothered to set it all up was, at the very least, an indication of his seriousness.

'Now, what's this little problem all about?' he said eventually in his best sarf-London accent, settling back and drawing upon his cigar while the two heavies glared at me.

'Er, well, um, I understand you have Gene Vincent under exclusive contract,' I quavered.

'That's right. And you've gone and made an album with him without my permission' was the implacable response. Summoning up the last shred of courage I asked if I could in fact see the said contract, whereupon Don opened a desk drawer, peered keenly into and said, 'There it is', before slamming the drawer shut. The two heavies continued to scowl at nothing in particular – me being the nothing in view.

'Right then. That's enough pissing about. What do you suggest we do about it?' he barked.

'Before we get into that,' I trilled (not easy with no breath in your body), 'Shurley sends her regards.'

'Shurley who?' he said, glancing at the two sentinels who were now, at least in my imagination, beginning to salivate. I mentioned Shurley's maiden name and reminded him of the card schools. His face cleared.

'She was a very nice girl. What's your connection?' When I told him that I was married to that very nice girl Don arose from his desk, placed an arm around my flinching shoulder and walked me to the door. 'Give your wife my best regards, and if the album sells well you owe me a drink.' And that was that.

Over the years I became quite friendly with Don and his son David and, in fact, one of the heavies. I found them to be helpful and great company. But what might have been without a little help from that very nice girl with whom I share everything?

With a little prompting from Adrian Owlet, Gene's most devoted British fan, Gene decided to come to Europe to promote the album. Normally this would be welcome news but our experiences to date made us a shade apprehensive. Peel, of course, refused even to meet the man, having discovered all too often that his early heroes usually failed to live up to their reputations. Gene was, nevertheless, still something of an icon to the biker fraternity, for whom black leather and long greasy hair were then – as they still are in some circles – symbols of macho virility. I hit upon the idea of having Gene met at the airport by a posse of bikers, who would then give him a motor-cycle escort into London. A few calls to various chapters around the country confirmed that there would indeed be a massive turn-out of hairy bikers – enough to stop the traffic to and from Heathrow. Sensing that this could become one of the publicity stunts of the year, I passed the information to the news desks of BBC, ITV and every national newspaper, who all agreed to cover the event. The prospect of London being brought to a standstill by hundreds of leather-clad, tattooed Hell's Angels on two wheels made even those world-weary editors sit up.

I then placed a full-page advertisement in the *Record Mirror* with a picture of the album cover, which featured a photograph of Gene taken by top rock photographer

Ed Caraef. A huge mistake and something of a cautionary tale for would-be marketing people.

On the day, Gene duly arrived, dead drunk, and rolled off the plane to be greeted by hordes of newsmen, press photographers and television cameras – but not one single biker. A true non-event. Having made the trip out to Heathrow the assembled scribes did in fact interview a rather bemused Gene and managed to ignore Peter Noone of Herman's Hermits, who, at that time, was one of the hottest acts in the world. Peter joined the throng around Gene for a few minutes before walking quietly to his waiting limo. After depositing our man in a Bayswater hotel with strict instructions to lay off the booze, I called a couple of the biker chapters to enquire whether perhaps they had got the day wrong. No. The unanimous response was that the album cover picture of Gene had convinced them that their hero had 'gone psychedelic' – a hippie, in fact – and was no longer one of them. The marketing lesson is never to overlook the detail.

While I was back at the office Gene somehow made his way out to Adrian Owlet's parents' house in Walton-on-Thames, where he proceeded to clear, in one afternoon, the accumulated liquor collection of twenty-five years of weddings and christenings. We later learned that on the transatlantic leg of the flight Gene had discovered Tom Jones and his party travelling first class, attached himself to them, bored them all senseless and drunk himself into a stupor at their expense. He had also, God knows how, managed to spend a few days in France and Germany where he had a big, loyal following. There he had performed a few club dates and made off with all the money – including all of the fees and commissions due to the agents and promoters.

I was, happily, not involved with the subsequent UK tour. That was arranged by Don Arden's office. There was also a television documentary, which was broadcast some time in the 1990s for, I believe, the first time. I was horrified to see myself on film trying not to become involved in the madness.

A side benefit of the tour was that I became friendly with the tour manager, Henry Henroyd, who had toured with the great rock-and-roll stars of the fifties, playing one-night stands at theatres and cinemas across Europe. Henry is a fund of hilarious stories about the glory days of rock tours and in particular the famous rocker who ostentatiously carried a Bible wherever he went. His rather special edition contained a listing of known gay men in every part of the country, to be sure that he was never short of a partner. This was, of course, when homosexuality was a dark secret rather than a marketing device. This particular rocker, who is still working and appearing in movies, refused to fly on the basis that if God had wanted him to fly He would have given him wings.

Apparently our Mr Vincent had a drink problem even in those days and had a specially designed walking stick that could be filled with Southern Comfort without the knowledge of his minders. Henry would pay off the roadies to ensure that Gene was given only Coca-Cola before appearances, but Gene would pay them more to prise off the caps and half fill the bottles with brandy. The trick, apparently, in those halcyon days was to keep Gene vertical on stage while Henry legged it around to the box office to collect the takings. Many were the nights when a totally plastered Vincent would be carried out to the centre of the stage with the curtains closed and be propped up with the mike stand shoved up his black leather jacket for just long enough to get through one number until Henry had collected the dosh and started the van. Ah. The glamour.

Gene was at one time married to an English woman called Margie who, having been married to or closely associated with such other rock eccentrics as the Shadows' Jet Harris and Terry Dene, could be described as unfortunate in her choice of men. In his drunken paranoia, Gene believed her to be promiscuous, causing Henry and others constantly to defend themselves against accusations of infidelity.

On one notable visit to Paris, Henry was awakened by a knock on the door at 3 a.m. to discover an apologetic waiter with Gene in a hammerlock, explaining that Monsieur Vincent believed his wife to be in Monsieur Henroyd's room and would not retire until the truth had been established. With Gene bent double in a vicelike grip, the pair peered into cupboards and under the bed to the somewhat muffled accompaniment of, 'Ah know she's in here, Henry.'

On another occasion, as Henry was paying the bill at the exclusive and imposing George V hotel, Gene appeared at the top of the very grand marble staircase and shouted, 'Henry. You've been fucking Margie. She's had more pricks in her than a fucking porcupine.' With horrified matrons fleeing the scene, the cashier was so dumbfounded that he distractedly handed all of the money back to a delighted Henry who pocketed it and sped off, with Gene slithering crazily down the staircase dragging his bad leg. Margie, it would appear, was no shrinking violet and occasionally engaged her husband in fisticuffs that, according to Henry, on at least one occasion resulted in Gene breaking his other leg and finishing the tour on crutches.

Following our tour Gene returned to the USA and made another album for someone else. We never recovered our costs on the album, and I never heard from Gene again, though we were saddened to hear of his death some years later. He truly was a one of a kind. I hope. Thank God I never got to work with Jerry Lee.

One last footnote. One day, as I was leaving the WEA office, I spied Kim Fowley and, attempting to sidle past without attracting his attention, fell noisily down a flight of steps breaking a finger. I'd do it again if necessary. I was, however, shocked to read of Kim's tragically early death in a car accident, as reported in a lengthy obituary in *Rolling Stone*. I was even more shocked to get a call from Kim a year or so later from Sweden. He had apparently loaned his car and documentation to a young kid, who had crashed and died, causing the authorities to believe that it had been Kim in the car. It appeared to have suited Kim at that time for the world to believe him dead, and he just never bothered to get around to setting the record straight. Well, you don't, do you?

EXECUTIVES

Executives in the music industry are often no less hungry for fame and fortune than the stars they help to create. None more so than Clive Davis, the head of Arista Records, who only recently was reported to have received several million dollars as an inducement to renew his employment agreement.

I first met Clive and his rather solemn wife in Majorca at an industry conference – er, lig? – over dinner with Elektra's founder and president Jac Holzman. Jac was at that time right at the cutting edge of the rock and psychedelic explosion. Clive had quite recently taken over as head of Columbia Records and, having been to Monterey and seen the possibilities of the emerging music, recognized the opportunity to carve a personal niche in musical history. It was an odd evening, in which we somehow found ourselves seated at a table on a raised platform overlooking the very crowded room. Since it was an industry event, the room was full of music people, many of whom worked for Columbia and seized this rare opportunity to introduce themselves to the boss. There followed a procession of strange faces literally looking up to us and being greeted with a semi-royal nod or wave and an occasional word.

To his credit, Clive did recognize a surprising number of managers and salesmen and addressed them by name, which almost caused them to faint with pleasure before being dismissed. I drew the conclusion that Mr Davis was a pompous, self-regarding rather cold fish and I was happy in the belief that our paths were unlikely to cross again.

Cut to a few years later, while I was at CBS Records in the UK, which was the British arm of Columbia. An important part of my duties was to chair a weekly meeting of sales, promotion and marketing people, at which we discussed and reported on the various releases before deciding priorities and strategy. The meetings were deliberately informal and designed to encourage the team to express opinions and beliefs that they may not have shared in a more formal atmosphere. It was my occasional habit to conduct these meetings while standing on my head in the corner of the board room, since this did in fact assist creative thought and was a clear signal to the team that any formality was unacceptable. It is not easy to stand on ceremony when the boss is standing on his head. Try it.

Imagine my surprise one week when everybody wore suits and the managing director, his deputy and a dozen or so accountants and lawyers attended my informal meeting. I learned that Clive Davis was in town and planning to visit the office and my meeting. Sure enough, the doors were flung open and Clive entered at the head of a small wedge of assistants and acolytes. With the sole exception of yours truly everybody present leaped to their feet and began to clap and cheer enthusiastically. When the commotion died down Clive gave a short but gracious speech, at the conclusion of which several staff members ripped open their shirts to reveal 'Clive Davis Appreciation Society' T-shirts! My first exposure to American corporate bollox and quite sickening.

Immediately after Clive's departure I was cornered by the managing director and informed in no uncertain terms that employees who wished to retain their positions were expected, nay required, to stand up and applaud when the president of the company arrived. I pointed out that if that truly were the requirement I would be happy to seek employment in pastures new. A bit churlish on reflection but the first of many such altercations.

Not long after that Clive was summarily fired and escorted from his office with barely enough time to clear his desk. The word was that he was offered up as a sacrificial lamb to the Nixon administration, which was threatening to take away Columbia's radio and television licences over their coverage of Watergate. Corporate life can be a minefield.

Following his dismissal, Clive went into a period of seclusion, during which he wrote an eponymously titled book explaining in some detail how he had personally changed the course of music history. How we laughed. He eventually re-emerged as 'consultant' to the newly formed Arista Records, which he was creating from the bones of a previously highly successful company called Bell Records. Bell, under the leadership of Larry Uttal, had enjoyed a string of hits by essentially singles acts such as David Cassidy, David Soul and the Bay City Rollers.

Larry had by then left the company to form Private Stock Records. Still with me?

At this time I was running Jonathan King's UK label and doing pretty well, so it came as no great surprise to receive a call from a former Bell executive now working for Clive suggesting that I fly to the USA to discuss setting up a British division of Arista. I did not want the job, but after a chat with Jonathan we agreed that Clive was probably too important to refuse without at least hearing his offer.

Arista provided the first-class air fare, and I duly set off for the Big Apple convinced that nothing that Mr Davis could offer me could compensate for the horror of working for him again. I made this clear over lunch, even going so far as to tell Clive that he was too demanding and, in my experience, pushed too hard. The intermediary at the table with us was at great pains to correct my impression of the great man. 'You don't know Clive like we do,' he gushed. 'Why, Clive doesn't push too hard. He's a joy to work for.'

This statement evinced one of the more chilling demonstrations of executive ego. Clive, who until then had been grazing abstractedly, carefully placed his utensils on a plate, half turned to our companion and, with a predatory smile, said, 'Perhaps you are unaware that over at Columbia I broke people's health', and resumed eating.

On the walk back to the offices on Broadway, in an effort to extricate myself from an increasingly pressurized situation, I suggested that, in any event, as a new company Arista might not be willing to afford my services. Taking a deep breath I inflated my then salary by 400 per cent, only to be told that the money would present no problem and I could expect the use of a company Rolls-Royce as part of the package. Back at the office Clive removed his jacket, smoothed it out and placed it on a hanger, which he then put in a cupboard. He then returned to his desk and enquired if I would like some chewing gum. Receiving a negative response, he returned to the closet, removed the jacket, extracted a packet of gum, removed one stick, replaced the pack and repeated the earlier performance. Silly details, I know, but all the time I was asking myself if I could possibly work for this man.

Towards the end of a long day I agreed at least to think over the proposal and gave Clive a number where I could be reached for a final discussion. Though my mind was made up, a small voice was asking if I did not owe it to my family to take the offer, if only for a year or so. Of course, Clive did not ring at the agreed time. He's much too grand for that. But I had anticipated his style and, though I was in fact at the designated place until ten minutes past the appointed time, I told the secretary to say that I had left for another meeting where I would be for another hour. Then began a silly series of calls, each one arriving just five minutes late, until I wound up at Jonathan's New York apartment where I began the lengthy process of locking up prior to my departure. Sure enough, as the last tumbler fell the telephone rang, but by then I was outside and on my way to the airport. At Kennedy the

plane was on time and, as I settled back into the first-class seat, which had, of course, been booked by Arista, a stewardess informed me that there was a call for me from a Mr Davis and, yes, they were prepared to hold the flight. Now that's clout! I told her to say that the flight had already left, and we took off for a 'red-eye' flight back to Blighty.

On arrival at Heathrow at about 8 a.m. the next day Shurley met me with the news that somehow Clive had contacted Jac Holzman on a canal holiday in Holland to ask him to ask me to call him immediately on my arrival. By then it was an easy decision. There is simply not enough money in the world to compensate for that kind of arrogant long arm reaching out over the Atlantic to dominate your life. The job was finally offered to an old colleague who lasted a year or so then retired from the music business to run an off-licence – presumably a broken man.

Clive's success and longevity in the business is ample proof that he is indeed one of the truly great music executives. He's just not as great as he appears to think he is. But then nobody could be.

A positive bonus of the trip was that I got to meet the president of Columbia Pictures, who were funding Arista. As a lifelong fan of the movie business, it was a particular thrill to sit in 'the front office' high above Broadway where, in the heyday of the movies, the deals were done. Alan Hirschfield was a kind and gracious man. When I mentioned that I had been seeking a biography of the first head of Columbia Pictures, without success since it was out of print, he kindly went to his bookcase and presented me with his own copy. As a biography of one great movie mogul given to me by another it remains one of my proudest possessions. Sadly, Alan, too, was the victim of corporate hooliganism, and his book *Indecent Exposure* is a riveting read.

Another executive with delusions of grandeur was Gerry Oord, a Dutchman who had formerly been head of EMI Records; when I met him he was managing director of RCA Records in London. Gerry was planning to retire and called me with the offer of a lunch, at which he suggested that I take over the job as his successor. I thought he was mad. He made extravagant claims, including one that he had discovered the Beatles, and told me so often that he was the greatest record executive in the world that eventually I started counting. He repeated this statement a further eleven times before I became too bored and embarrassed to continue. I declined his kind offer and later learned that shortly after his arrival at RCA he had initiated a regime of executive meetings commencing at 7 a.m. every day on the basis that an early start would give the company a head start over the competition. Most people in the industry can barely breathe at that hour and are rarely fully functional before ten o'clock. What Gerry failed to mention was that one of the perks of the job was the provision of a penthouse apartment immediately above the Mayfair offices to which he could retire for a snooze following the dawn pep talks.

The former incumbent at RCA had been Ken Glancy, a short, tough but quietly spoken American who was never seen without a cigar. Ken was both well liked and respected as boss of RCA and in his earlier capacity as managing director of CBS Records. When Gerry Oord left RCA, John Howes, whom I had known in various capacities over the years, replaced him. John had always struck me as a regular guy but when I visited him in his new job I was astonished to discover that he had undergone a personality transplant. He had become Ken Glancy complete with Ken's American accent, his large cigar and even Ken's Groucho Marx walk.

We exchanged pleasantries, and I congratulated him on his new appointment, omitting to mention that I had refused the job. John went on to explain that he felt that his exalted new status was due in no small part to the close and influential relationship that he enjoyed with Tony De Fries, who managed RCA's biggest-selling act, David Bowie. This made sense, as Mr De Fries was a strong and forceful character, known in some parts as Tony Deep Freeze owing to the chilling demands he was known to make on behalf of his clients. At that precise moment the phone rang, and John delightedly informed me that this was indeed Deep Freeze calling from New York and I was welcome to stay and witness the subtle negotiating skills and diplomacy that he was about to display. I, of course, heard only half of the conversation, which, as far as I could tell, consisted of John making a series of minor requests, all of which were abruptly refused. This was followed by a discussion about transporting a large party of journalists to New York to see and write about Bowie's next concert. John thought that the journos should travel economy class and be accommodated at a modest hotel. Deep Freeze insisted on first class all the way and refused to participate in the cost. Having gained everything he wanted and committed RCA to huge costs, Mr De Fries then, amazingly, refused permission for any of the scribes to meet Mr Bowie either individually or as a group. 'See what I mean?' said John at the end of the conversation. I withdrew quietly musing yet again on the awesome powers that stars exercise over their record labels, the executive capacity for self-delusion, and grateful that yet again I had passed up another golden career move.

There are – or were – a number of highly talented record executives in Britain, which may go some way to explaining the spectacular international achievements of the British music industry. One of the least known but most influential is a gentle soul called Roland Rennie. He was the first managing director of Polydor Records when the German giant opened its first tiny London office. Top executives are known by and large by the stature of the acts they sign, and Roland's track record is second to none.

Very few acts are discovered by any one person. It is almost always the culmination of a lot of effort and investment by a group of people, among whom are talent scouts, managers, agents, A & R staff, publicists and any number of hangers-on and believers. If reasonable sums of money are initially involved, the act will be watched over a period and numerous meetings will take place. Somebody, however, must eventually take the decision to stump up the money for ever-escalating advances, recording costs, videos, tour support, publicity, promotion, advertising, marketing and generally throwing the resources of a company behind an unknown quantity with the strong statistical evidence that, in the overwhelming majority of cases, it will all be lost. It takes big brass balls because just a few expensive failures will decimate the bottom line, and the first casualty is often the fool who put his or her career on the line. There is, of course, no alternative, because no record company can survive without a constant flow of new and exciting talent.

After a fairly quiet start Roland eventually signed some of the greatest and most bankable acts of all time, including Hendrix, Cream, the Who, the Bee Gees and Esther and Abi Ofarim, an unlikely couple from Israel whose first release 'Cinderella Rockefeller' went straight to the top of the UK charts and sold millions around the world. Unfortunately, the pressures of dealing with artistic high-flyers and the numerous heavy-handed directives emanating from Hamburg took their toll, and Roland became possibly the world's most amiable drunk. He would arrive at the office at a very early hour and by mid-morning, having completed a full day's workload, would begin nipping at the brandy. By lunchtime he was invariably jolly and sociable, but by the middle of the afternoon his secretary would begin calling all the offices with liquor cabinets with the news that RR was on the prowl and the cabinets were to be locked with the keys 'lost'. By late afternoon it was not unusual to see Roland being carried to his car over the shoulder of his driver.

On one wondrous occasion I was enclosed in my office at Polydor with a poet of some repute who was at that time recording an album for Dandelion at nearby CBS studios with a group of like-minded souls. My visitor had slipped out of the studio for a surreal chat but was, sadly, in the first stages of a complete mental breakdown and totally out of touch with anything approaching reality – in truth, not an uncommon situation at the time. When Roland, who was in the final stages of a regular day, entered my office in search of a top-up he found my poetic friend poised at the window eight floors up convinced he could fly back to the studio. Fortunately the window was shut, and upon spying Roland my guest became convinced that he was Errol Flynn; drawing two small cigars from his pocket he challenged Roland to a sword fight. Roland accepted the challenge, and for several minutes my cramped office became a battleground as the two protagonists sprang from chair to settee with ringing cries and great flourishes of bent little cigars. This was only marginally and briefly interrupted by the appearance of the other five poets at the office door. Not in the accepted means of entering a room: they had somehow contrived to arrange themselves outside the door so that only their heads were visible – stacked vertically and all grinning hugely.

Drinking to excess can be amusing, but it played hell with Roland's career. He worked desperately to quit and eventually succeeded with a series of injections from a specialist doctor who would administer the shots in the office. During this later period I was forced to witness the alternative side of the generally amiable breed that is the German executive. Having just completed a business deal with Roland for Polydor to distribute our Dandelion label, Shurley and I were about to take our leave when we were joined by Horst Schmolzi, Polydor's resident German and Roland's boss. Horst was almost a caricature storm-trooper at times and much given to wearing jackboots both literally and figuratively, though he could be charming when he chose. On this occasion he insisted, over our objections, that the deal be celebrated with champagne. Knowing full well of Roland's affliction and his course of treatment, Horst nevertheless further insisted that Roland open the bottle and pour the bloody stuff. Needless to say, we made our excuses and left before further cruelty could be inflicted. Horst once took me on a tour of the Polydor headquarters in Hamburg and proudly pointed out the offices that had been used by the Gestapo during the Nazi era, yet on another occasion he happily agreed to hire my son Brod for the duration of the summer holidays.

I actually got on very well with our German partners, with the possible exception of Siggy Loch who ran the WEA office, also in Hamburg, and was another one fond of wearing jackboots together with a black cloak, with all that conveys. He was a desperately ambitious man who vied with Ian Ralfini, the UK boss, for control of

Europe, and the pair of them spent more on air fares crossing the Atlantic to polish apples with the American top brass than most folk earn in years.

In Spain I spent some time with an altogether different kind of German, a most earnest but somewhat humourless executive named Christian Lhose, who was very keen to persuade me to place the Elektra catalogue with Polydor for the whole of Europe. He was at great pains to point out the efficiency of the organization and assured me that any Polydor office throughout the world found to be performing at less than optimum would be visited by the company 'trouble-shooter', Wolfgang Smit Panthen. I still have nightmares imagining that I am the recipient of a visit from Herr Smit Panthen, though I learned that young Wolfgang was in fact quite a pleasant and understanding young man. Of course. As an example of the somewhat heavy-handed Teutonic brand of humour the top man at Polydor – a legendary workaholic and former U-boat commander named Kurt Kinkele – was fond of telling his American, and mainly Jewish, peers that his first sight of the USA was through the lens of a periscope.

John Fruin was Roland's successor at Polydor. A man of great integrity and boundless energy, he cycled in to the office from Hayes and was always the first to arrive. A health nut, he insisted that all the staff had flu injections as a precaution against the coming winter and decimated the building as almost everybody immediately fell victim to the virus. I was lucky in that I had been out of the country when the needles were out.

Once established at Polydor John Fruin went on to run that company and MGM Records in Hollywood, commuting across the Atlantic twice weekly. This was at a time when both labels were enjoying a string of smash hits on both sides of the pond with acts such as the Bee Gees and the Osmonds. Nobody could sustain that pace for very long, and eventually John was lured away to head up Warners in London where, within a short time, his undoubted ability earned the interest of the *World in Action* team at Granada TV. They were trying yet again to raise the hoary old subject of chart manipulation. On the basis that if you don't talk to the media you are less likely to be misquoted, John refused to meet the television reporters or return any of their calls.

Around this time John was approaching his fiftieth birthday and decided to celebrate it in style by entering the London Marathon. Amazingly, he completed the course and the following day suffered the expected after-effects of exhaustion, stiffness and dehydration but nevertheless made it into work. Approaching the office looking sallow from the lack of liquids and walking like Frankenstein's monster, in heavy shades, he was accosted by the *World in Action* crew who had been lurking outside the building to demand answers and comments. He, of course, refused, and the programme was eventually transmitted with several shots of Mr Fruin looking like a Mafia don from Central Casting. John swore vengeance but left Warners shortly after.

Somebody who permanently looks like a Mafia don is Freddie Bienstock, possibly the most influential independent music publisher in the world. Of Swiss descent and fluent in several languages, Freddie has beautifully sculpted prematurely white hair, a year-round tan, is superbly tailored and has enough charm to negotiate the skin off a rattlesnake. He could play a cultured gangster without missing a beat but is highly intelligent with all the skill and entrepreneurial spirit constantly to confuse and amaze his competitors. Among the many legends surrounding him is that, at the height of Elvis Presley's popularity, all songs for consideration by the superstar were first 'screened' by Mr Bienstock. If that wasn't a licence to print money it'll do until something better comes along.

Our paths first crossed when I started Biscuit Music, the publishing company set up to protect and exploit the work of writers recording for Dandelion Records. Initially one of his staff offered to take care of the tedious business of legally registering and forming the company as a 'favour', which was most welcome at a very busy time. Imagine my surprise when I scrutinized the final draft paperwork to discover that this fine fellow had written himself in as a director and was not at all fazed by my discovery. Fortunately there was time to rewrite the agreements with just Peel, Shurley and myself in charge. Nevertheless we were in need of the financial backing and administrative capability of a major publisher, and a meeting was arranged with Freddie at his swish Savile Row offices just down the road from the Beatles' Apple headquarters. The initial meeting was promising

enough for me to accept Freddie's invitation for Shurley and me to join him for dinner at the Mirabelle, which was at the time London's most expensive and fashionable restaurant.

Over dinner Freddie was at his smiling and gracious best and after the meal suggested we go on to a club to indulge in a little gambling. As politely as possible we declined his kind offer, pointing out that the music business itself was enough of a gamble for us, whereupon Freddie withdrew a huge roll of banknotes and tried to place it in my pocket with the assurance that the gambling was to be entirely at his expense. With some difficulty we extricated ourselves from the situation, without actually stating that we preferred not to be beholden to him in advance of any contractual discussions, and made our way back to the sticks.

The following day we met over lunch to conclude the discussions, at which point I was amused to be offered probably the toughest and most one-sided contract it was possible to construct. A quick perusal between courses indicated that my signature would entitle our potential partners to considerably more than we were prepared to give up. It was just too complicated and weighted against my company to even begin to negotiate, but extreme pressure was put on me to sign there and then. I, of course, refused and watched my smiling host's mask slip away to reveal an altogether different character. Not for the first or by any means the last time I was relieved to have looked a gift horse in the mouth and narrowly avoided a nasty bite.

15. LIFE AFTER DANDELION

CLIFFORD T. WARD FACES THE FUTURE

LIFE AFTER DANDELION

With the demise of Dandelion my first priority was to try to place those artists who had stayed with us with sympathetic record labels – which gave me an interesting insight into other organizations. Medicine Head were happy to go along with Polydor's plans and immediately scored with two Top Five singles – which at least confirmed that we had been on the right track. At the height of their popularity Fiddler John called, as ever in the small hours, to tell me that he had yet again decided to change management and mentioned two organizations as likely contenders. Since they had equally bad reputations I suggested that he held off a final decision pending a meeting with John Fruin, the managing director of Polydor, who would be able to offer sound advice, particularly since the group was riding high and in a position to be choosy.

I arranged the meeting, but Fiddler John didn't turn up and later informed me that he had signed an agreement with one of the two parties that he had originally been considering. I was horrified, but it was too late to turn back the clock. Biscuit Music had retained the publishing rights to the band, and it was not long before I began to receive a series of approaches from the new management suggesting that I turn the publishing rights over to them. The approaches were initially pleasant and conciliatory, with offers of money and unlimited entertainment on the company yacht, but became increasingly threatening. For my part, it was not a financial decision. I simply didn't trust the new team and felt that ownership of the publishing rights would be safer in our hands. Often I would receive as many as seven or eight calls a day, but somehow I managed to duck and dive for six months until they lost interest.

It is a sad fact of life in the music business, and probably in other areas of artistic endeavour, that artists all too often fail to recognize that aggressive management attitudes, which can be so successful on their behalf, cannot be turned off and on at will. The hard-nosed bastard dealing with third parties is also the hard-nosed bastard who almost invariably screws the artist. I was filled with trepidation, but a few weeks later I met up with the band at *Top of the Pops* and was delighted to be told that everything was wonderful. Even the group's most outrageous demands were being met with a smile, and I was wrong in every respect. One year later Fiddler John was bankrupt, having lost his house and his family. He now lives in Phoenix, Arizona, and has yet to recover fully.

The only record company to show any interest in Bridget was MCA, which was then headed by Dave Howells, who had first signed the Dandelion label when he was at CBS. Bridget recorded just one single for them but went on to cut an album for her old friends Chris Wright and Terry Ellis at Chrysalis before emigrating to New York, where she now has a successful business career and occasionally records.

Kevin Coyne had by now left Siren to go solo, and the new Virgin label looked to be an ideal home. Richard Branson was just starting out and had already signed Hatfield and the North, which indicated that he was not looking for instant singles success. We agreed terms, and Kevin was dispatched to Branson's Manor Studios in Oxfordshire to begin recording.

Clifford T. Ward had released one album on Dandelion and had started on the second when the label closed down. He was the most obviously commercial on our roster but fairly expensive to record, which made it crucial that I find a new home for him and recover some of our costs. Charisma Records, under the guidance of former Fleet Street journalist Tony Stratton-Smith, was a small but highly selective operation ploughing time, effort and huge amounts of money into the as yet unsuccessful Genesis. Strat enjoyed Cliff's quirky brand of romanticism and immediately believed that 'Gaye', a track from the album *Home Thoughts from Abroad*, which had been recorded at our expense with me in the role of executive producer, was a potential hit. He was right, but it took a lot of effort, time and dedication from Strat and his very professional team to make it happen. 'Gaye' went into the Top Ten, so, within a few months of closing down the operation, there were three former Dandelion acts in the charts.

The album and 'Scullery', another track taken from it as a single, also charted. Cliff became in demand for television and press interviews, which made it necessary for him to quit his job as a schoolteacher. He also chose this time to move house to a beautiful Elizabethan building in Worcestershire, to where, for his second album, Lord Lichfield flew in his private helicopter to take pictures for the sleeve. Pretty dazzling stuff for a young schoolteacher with a very young family. Certainly among the most moving songs and performances I have ever heard was Cliff's 'To Debbie and Her Friends', which was about his beautiful daughter who was paralysed below the waist and who scooted around the polished floors on her bottom while we discussed plans and strategies. Twenty years later it is to the whole family's credit that Debbie has a law degree and is married to a lawyer.

Cliff was never a music-biz casualty in the sense that so many were, but in truth he never capitalized on or fully recovered from that early success. Here was a young working-class lad living in a semi in Bromsgrove catapulted to international fame and welcoming titled photographers to his country home where the swimming-pool was under construction. 'Gaye' was even a smash hit in Brazil – though we never saw a penny of the royalty income.

Among the many strengths of 'Home Thoughts' were the beautiful and sym-pathetic arrangements by a talented musician who had provided arrangements for the Beatles among others. Richard Hewson shared production credits with Cliff for the second album and again delivered extraordinary arrangements, though the producer experience was somewhat fraught. Cliff is – ahem – fairly single-minded in the studio, and Richard has pretty strong opinions, too. I was so impressed with Richard's ability and general demeanour that I offered to try to help him create a recording career of his own. This resulted in an offer from Phonogram complete with the provision of an eight-track record desk delivered to Richard's home, where somehow he managed to accommodate it in a tiny box-room already filled with guitars, keyboards and other recording equipment. Though they enjoyed some success later, the Rah Band never quite made it on Phonogram, despite releasing a couple of 'interesting' singles with me handling the vocals. I wasn't too impressed with the results and now have no copies to laugh at, but my son Chet heard one of them recently played every hour on Radio Luxembourg when he was stranded without petrol one night. He said it cheered him up immensely. Richard did eventually achieve a major international hit, but for legal reasons (see the chapter on lawyers) we don't talk about that.

Cliff completed two further albums for Charisma but refused to perform live, and interest within the record company began to wane. On one occasion we attended a meeting by prior arrangement to discuss future plans with Strat, who spent the entire time on the telephone to his racehorse trainer. In the face of that kind of indifference we left the label and, with some difficulty, struck a deal with Phonogram.

The first Phonogram album was something of a disappointment – to them for its lack of commercial success and to Cliff on account of the truly appalling cover art. I did manage to persuade him to make a live concert appearance supporting Twiggy, who was both beautiful and charming and treated Cliff as if he were the star of the show. Though the concert was well received and reviewed, we could never persuade Cliff to go out on the road, and Phonogram began to be concerned about their invest-ment. They felt that Cliff should cut his hair and record in America to try to develop a more youthful image. Cliff agreed in principle and it was left to me to work out the details.

By this time I was also employed as a director of Pye Records, where I had managed to continue the long streak of hit singles success that had begun at CBS, my next port of call after Warners. I was somewhat surprised and not a little miffed to receive a call from Cliff in the middle of a busy day requesting that I visit him urgently to discuss a confidential matter of great importance. Since he had by now moved to an even grander house about four hours drive away, I was reluctant to agree without further details, but he was adamant and I arranged to visit him with Shurley the following weekend. Arriving both tired and hungry, we dispensed with the usual gossip and asked what was so urgent and confidential. Cliff immediately produced a brochure on a yet grander mansion.

'Lovely,' I said. 'Now what is it we are here to discuss?'

'This,' said Cliff waving the brochure. 'I want you to tell Phonogram that, rather than waste money recording me in America, they should buy me this house and I'll be so happy that I'll write some beautiful new songs.' That is, in truth, the kind of insanity that artists conjure up all the time. I was too angry to speak and went for a walk around the substantial grounds of Cliff's current abode while Shurley quietly pointed out to our boy that Phonogram didn't give a toss whether he was happy or sad. They had made a major financial investment and were prepared to invest more. His part of the deal was to do what he was being very well paid to do. In the event we did eventually go to the USA where we had a relaxing and enjoyable time recording an album at a ranch in New England. Sadly, that, too, was treated with indifference by the public, and our tenure at Phonogram was brought to a close.

Phonogram had appointed a promotion manager to publicize Cliff's work. He was the photographer who had originally discovered Twiggy, and he saw in Cliff an opportunity to score again. Justin de Villeneuve tried at every level to insinuate himself as Cliff's manager, and the time in America was fraught, with Cliff reporting to me every promise and overture that the photographer-cum-promotion man made. Each time I assured the singer that he was free to make any arrangement he chose and that, if he felt that the snapper could do a better job for him, then he should follow his instincts. I have always felt that the relationship between manager and artist should be based on mutual trust and respect. There will always be differences of opinion, but when the basics are questioned it is time to call it a day.

I was wrong, of course, as evidenced by a string of successful managers who have made millions from clinging on to disenchanted artists or selling the contracts to competitors or, if all else failed, suing for lost commissions. But you also need to have a life. In the midst of these discussions, and shortly after our return to England, Justin invited me to lunch at a fashionable restaurant – where else? – to discuss the situation. Between table-hopping and greeting a host of a nearly famous folk, he informed me that he should take over management of Cliff's affairs. It appeared that his associate Ken Russell wanted to use Cliff's music in a new movie. In vain I pointed out that if indeed he could broker that deal he was welcome to a commission on the fees involved but that should not affect any of the other aspects of Cliff's career. Imagine if you had a film-producer pal who wanted to use Michael Jackson's music: would you really expect to take on his whole career?

Cliff did sign that long-term and onerous agreement with Justin, Ken Russell never used any of his music and Cliff's career waned to nothing. I got a number of calls from my former client over the next few years complaining bitterly of being ripped off and exploited in the new set-up. The stories were often horrendous but I cannot vouch for their truth. Sadly, Cliff became seriously disabled with multiple sclerosis and died in 2001. His primary source of income for the last years of his life was from the deals that I was able to put together for him almost thirty years ago.

I was unable to drum up any interest in Tractor, which perhaps was just as well. Years later, when the Dandelion catalogue was reissued on CD with considerable success and quite substantial royalties for the acts, Tractor, under the guidance of their former roadie, became obsessively difficult to the extent that I sold the publishing company just to be rid of them; this despite the fact that in the true spirit of Dandelion we had paid them several thousand pounds more than we were obliged to do.

So, where are the rest of them? Beau rose through the ranks at the Halifax and became a fairly important executive. He lost interest in communism when he visited the Soviet Union and was assaulted by guards for having his hands in his pockets while in a queue to see Lenin's tomb and then discovered that his coach party was being bugged. Jim Milne is a respected headmaster; David Bedford continues to teach music and compose; Lol Coxhill still busks and makes an occasional television appearance; the Black-Waddys – as Peel calls them – are threatening to re-form; Gene Vincent is the subject of retrospectives in major music publications; Rod Stewart is a superstar; Kevin, as we've seen, is a success on the Continent; and I neither know nor care what happened to Principal Edwards Magic Theatre.

As time has gone by Dandelion has accrued a reputation far ahead of any of its achievements – though its artists did eventually produce hit records for other labels. It never made money, but that was never the intention. We were, in fact, naïve to the point of stupidity. John, Shurley and I dedicated huge amounts of effort without any thought of personal gain. Our nights were interrupted unceasingly, our houses were invaded, our psyches were pounded, and, inevitably, the only people who made money were the lawyers and the accountants. Every penny had to be accounted for, and every artist and writer received every penny due. John's career at the BBC was put at risk, and my own attempts to scale the corporate ladder were severely curtailed. Why did we do it? It was the sixties, a time when there was still an element of optimism around and people had yet to be bullied into looking for a commercial result from every activity. I don't believe any of us regretted it, though for years afterwards the tax authorities refused to believe we didn't have a secret source of income.

Would we do it again? Well, John probably would.

16.

CBS

CBS RECORDS

It's now 1972, and I've put Elektra, Dandelion and Warners behind me and am about to move on to the next chapter of my life. Leaving Warners at least provided a salutary lesson on the stock market. As an executive for Elektra I had been granted stock options, which enabled me to purchase a few hundred Warners shares at a preferred price. The severance pay from Warners was just enough to pay for the shares so, on the basis that this was 'found' money, I spent the lot on stock and over the next few weeks watched helplessly as the share prices plummeted to less than half of what I had paid. Heaven knows what affects share prices. Would it help to sign Elvis Presley? I never found out, but the wise counsel of my wife was to put the shares away and forget about them. Accordingly, I turned the shares over to my bank with instructions to sell at any price at the start of the next financial year while I got on with coping with the real world.

In fact the shares had doubled in value by the time of the sale, reaping a fairly handsome and most welcome profit – but you have to have nerves of steel to play that game. They are probably worth twenty times that price right now, but then again perhaps not. I read recently that when David Geffen sold Asylum Records to Warners he was paid in shares valued then at $40 each, which, in no time at all, plummeted to $5. That would make your eyes water.

Though out of steady employment we decided to move house just as the seventies 'gazumping' fashion was at its height. That's a lot of fun. Music people are a mixed bunch with a fair share of rascals, but compared to estate agents . . . We advertised our then home in the London *Evening Standard* and the phone rang incessantly, with cars full of interested purchasers lined up around the block. Eventually the house was sold to a policeman whose wife wept and begged for more time when they ran into trouble raising the finance. Meanwhile the price of the house we wanted was escalating daily. The fellow who sold us that property arranged transport for a number of pop personalities and told us of how he had supplied John Lennon with three tractors to go with his newly purchased farm. Twelve months later the tractors were languishing untouched and still in polythene wrappers. He also mentioned a midnight call he'd recently had from George requesting the immediate supply of a full table-tennis set with which to entertain his friend Eric, who had just arrived. When it was pointed out that after midnight no sports or games shops would be open, the phone was slammed down. Driving out to George's house in some trepidation the following day he was somewhat surprised to discover a table-tennis set, polythene-wrapped, in George's hall. Apparently a director of Harrods had obliged but, by the time it arrived the stars had become bored with the idea. I have no idea whether either of these two tales is true, but the sheer emptiness of the lives portrayed strikes a chord.

Shortly after moving in to the new house I received a call from Dan Loggins, the head of A & R at CBS, suggesting that we meet in the shelter in Soho Square in London. All very clandestine, but I never discovered the reason for the secrecy. Danny suggested that I join CBS as marketing manager and offered to set up a meeting with the directors. Having had a pretty miserable experience with that company before when they distributed Dandelion, I was not keen, but Danny insisted that the new management team was totally different.

Danny is an American as, I discovered, were Dick Asher, the new managing director, and Maurice Oberstein, or 'Obie', his deputy. They were all friendly, enthusiastic and, being Americans, anxious that I should bring a little local expertise to the operation. They were also an odd trio. Danny was the beautifully coiffed and groomed brother of Kenny, who was a great big star back in the States, both as a solo act and with Loggins and Messina, whereas Dick was a tough ex-Marine major with a degree in law. Obie's father had been a prominent record man with whose encouragement Obie had enjoyed considerable success as a music-business entrepreneur, and he was one of the great mavericks of the industry. While at CBS Obie would resolutely do his own thing in the teeth of opposition from the US bosses, who despaired of his eccentricities. When, later, he became chairman of CBS in Britain his office was littered with urine-soaked sheets of newspaper as he housetrained Charlie the dog, who often appeared with him on television. Obie also just happened to be the brightest and most Machiavellian executive in the music industry, so his eccentricities were tolerated through gritted teeth. (It obviously did him no harm since he 'retired' from CBS and was instantly appointed chairman of Polygram and of the British Phonographic Industry.)

Despite my misgivings I agreed to join, and in so doing committed myself to the most horrible period of my business life. This came about for many reasons, one of which was the relationship between Dick and Obie. To say that Dick and Obie did not get on would be an understatement, and this is best exemplified by an occasion when Dick involved me – reluctantly on my part – in a piece of company politics while the three of us were attending the annual CBS jamboree.

In genuine awe of his bosses – unlike Obie – Dick was, nevertheless, ambitious and always expected a call to return to the head office in New York. In preparation he had to appoint a successor-in-waiting to the position of managing director and, on more than one occasion during my time at CBS, sounded me out for the job. Under normal circumstances I might have accepted, but the most obvious choice was Obie, whose well-founded reputation for political chicanery and Machiavellianism was such that to overtake him in the career stakes would incur an enmity leading to a life of looking over one's shoulder – most likely to remove the stiletto. I refused the offers on a number of occasions and was rather proud of my circumspection. On this particular night, however, at dinner in the middle of the entertainment, Dick plonked himself in the vacant chair next to mine and, with all the tact and discretion of Sherman tank, loudly informed me that he was about to be recalled to New York and that I was his choice as successor. I will never know if he saw Obie sat on my other side. On hearing Dick's bellowed proposal he flung back his chair and marched stiffly from the banquet hall. When he hadn't returned several hours later I feared the worst and persuaded some of the staff to search the waterfront where he was eventually found in a seedy bar somewhat the worse for drink.

Anyway, from day one the pace at CBS was such that, after just two weeks, I called in sick with stomach pains. After a couple of days in bed I called Dick Asher to say that I was recovering and could probably make it into the office before the end of the week. Dick was all solicitude and instructed me to stay home the entire week. He did suggest that I might wish to peruse the paperwork that had accumulated in my absence and offered to send it along. What arrived by taxi just an hour or so later was two giant tea chests full of paperwork. And I had only been there two weeks!

The paperwork was mainly sales and promotion reports, computer print-outs and a series of internal memos in revolting brown envelopes from my new staff, each one polishing apples and telling me how clever they were. These latter were dealt with by returning them to the senders without comment but with a graded system of coloured stars attached, just like we had at school: gold for excellent, silver for good, etc. That swiftly put a stop to the self-seeking memo pushers, but, with an open-door policy, I was never able to stem the ceaseless stream of staff seeking advancement, raises or just encouragement.

Dick Asher was a true workaholic. Apart from being managing director of CBS UK he played an executive role in Columbia Records International (CRI). Arriving at the office at around 7.30 a.m. and working at breakneck pace, by the close of the normal business day he would be joined by a second secretary while he dealt with international affairs. It was quite usual to pass the office at midnight and see him still at his desk. On one occasion Obic called me up to help him measure a telex that Dick had dictated. It was full of legal and technical detail and was eighty feet long.

While undertaking this stupendous workload Dick insisted that he be copied in on every letter or memo, either internal or external. On his copy he would scribble a comment or question that would be returned to the sender in one of those bloody buff envelopes. These comments often demanded a reply, which I would scribble beneath the scribble. All too often my response would draw a further response to which I was expected to respond. A classic exchange entailed twenty journeys between our two offices to the point that the purpose of the original note was entirely forgotten. I was just one of a staff of close to a hundred – all copying Dick and responding to his comments. It certainly kept him in touch with events, but at what price to him and to his staff?

CBS was coasting on album success when I joined. They had had a recent hit with Mott the Hoople's 'All the Young Dudes' and a low chart place for some dreadful British pop group whose name I have completely forgotten, but very little other singles action. Simon and Garfunkel or Dylan were in the charts but by that stage in their careers they could have charted albums in brown paper bags. A challenge was due.

The very first priority, however, was to get some action on an album by Abi Ofarim who, after Esther and Abi, was now solo and a personal signing by Dick. I went into the studio with Abi and remixed a potential single, which at least got some attention for the album, but it was not enough, and the artist returned to Switzerland, where he is now no doubt enjoying the fruits of his 1968 worldwide smash hit 'Cinderella Rockefeller'.

The days at CBS were taken up with endless meetings: staff meetings, advertising agency meetings, marketing meetings, A & R meetings, artist and manager meetings, and all the time the telephone rang and the paper piled up. Anybody not connected with the record business will probably be astonished to learn that actually listening to records was very low on the priority list and generally undertaken at home in the evenings and at weekends when one's time should have been spent with the family. Those occasional evenings, that is, that were not taken up with attending gigs or receptions. That may sound like heaven, but, believe me, one evening spent holding a glass and nibbling on rubbish while scanning the faces for media people and wearing a bright, interested smile becomes very much like another.

The CBS team was highly talented but working as individuals on individual projects rather than as a team, and my first task was to weld these creative mavericks into a cohesive unit. It was never going to be easy, but, with careful manipulation of the various well-developed egos, we slowly began to recognize our various strengths. The two main labels were CBS and Epic, each with a product manager, a press officer, two promotion men and, of course, secretaries. We also handled a number of acts and labels that fell outside of the two main labels and these, too, had a full complement of staff. Sleeve design and specific artwork were handled in-house, and another important department within my area was Artist Relations, which arranged meeting, greeting, accommodating and generally taking care of the many visiting and local acts. Artist Relations, under the capable leadership of Derek Witt, also arranged most of the venues and catering for the various parties and receptions. Try accommodating some of the great superstars for any length of time and you wonder how Derek hung on for so long before the inevitable nervous breakdown.

The most senior plugger was Paddy Fleming. Years earlier he had been my boss at Philips, but he accepted the change of rules with good grace and was highly regarded by everyone in radio and television. If we really desperately needed a television appearance for an act of almost any calibre or reputation Paddy could always arrange it. He is the only promotion person I had ever known who had television producers lining up to buy him a drink. The reverse is almost always the case, and both Television Centre and Broadcasting House are always thronging with promotion people desperate to buy a drink for anybody in order to justify their expenses. Paddy has now retired, but his son Nick carries on the tradition. Having been head of the department at Philips, Paddy found it difficult to share responsibility at CBS with his equally senior colleagues, and a great deal of my time was spent soothing ruffled feathers.

Record plugging is a desperately difficult job. Despite the proliferation of radio stations, very few are prepared to play anything but established hits and, with over a hundred singles and almost as many albums released every week, the competition for airplay is ferocious. Every major label releases at least five records a week, and the poor promotion person must try to introduce each one to a bored producer while trying to maintain interest in records that might be up to three months old. All this with the artist, manager, agent and someone like me constantly bitching about the lack of exposure. With television the opportunities are even fewer, and a dedicated plugger is prepared to sell his or her soul or anything else for a spot on *Top of the Pops*.

Pluggers will dress up and take part in almost any stunt to attract producers' attention to a particular record, but one of the great promotion coups was achieved in much simpler fashion by Dave Most. Faced with the problem of plugging 'Tiptoe

Through the Tulips' by Tiny Tim, he realized that simply playing the record stone cold to any individual producer could be disastrous. In those days Radio 1 producers were hidden in tiny little offices with barely enough room for a desk, record player and a filing cabinet. The plugger, having managed to bypass the jobsworth at the entrance, would walk along the long corridor knocking on cubicle doors and hoping to find a producer not on the telephone, in conversation with another plugger or listening to a competitor's product.

As a result of his engaging personality – and possibly using the influence of the string of hits produced by his famous brother, Mickey – Dave managed to persuade several producers out of their cubicles and into the main office where he put Tiny Tim on the turntable. After a few bars somebody giggled, somebody laughed and in no time everybody was falling about over the sheer eccentricity and effrontery of the record. They all loved it, and it became a huge hit, owing in no small part to the magic of a dedicated plugger.

The product or label manager's job was to schedule the new releases in conjunction with the A & R department, get details of the artists in order to have a press release and biography written, devise, cost and submit a marketing campaign for each record to me and liaise with the management with regard to tour support and appearances; in general, to take care of business for each single and album released on the label. The then CBS label manager, Tony Woolcott, is now a very important honcho at CRI. The third label manager, Andrew Pryor, is now managing director of one of the EMI companies, and the very level-headed and cool label manager at Epic, James Fisher, suffered a nervous breakdown and was hospitalized for some time. It is a high-pressure business, and James, I fear, was not the only casualty. Perhaps I pushed too hard, but I, too, was being pushed.

Former music journalist Lon Goddard handled the press department. He did an excellent job but was never able to satisfy Dick Asher, who appeared to labour under the impression that he could dictate copy and reviews to the music and national press. Even a front-page headline story with pictures failed to satisfy him, and he would complain constantly about the tenor of the piece or the size of the photograph. Lon was distraught and seeking alternative employment until I suggested that Dick's problem was likely to be his low profile in the business. Other chief executives were the subjects of in-depth interviews in the trade press, so perhaps a few articles about Dick might ease the pressure. Thereafter Lon took care to plant quotes, arrange the odd interview with photo and ensure that at every reception Dick was introduced to every media person present. It couldn't have worked better. Our press officer became a hero, and Dick sang his praises so often to colleagues that Lon was offered a job with a rival company on highly advantageous terms. As I have mentioned elsewhere, the average record company executive is at least as ambitious for personal glory as the most successful artist.

I have a theory that in any new company it takes about three months to learn what the job is about and another three months to start producing results. And so it was at CBS. After six months in the job I decided that it was time to concentrate on more singles success and made an appropriate announcement at the annual sales conference to an enthusiastic reception. The machine was well oiled. We had a great supply of product and the weekly marketing meeting I hosted was becoming a very productive forum. The first move, which encountered great opposition, was to stop sending free copies of every single released to chart shops. This was a practice that had grown out of the necessity to be able to assure complaining artists and managers that their records were indeed available in shops, I believed it to be self-defeating, on account of a chart shop being thus able to supply even a modest demand without any real effort, interest or outlay.

I determined that free copies of singles would only be supplied at an early stage in the life of a record, for which some demand had been created by airplay. Most retailers are fairly lazy and do not respond to enquiries about new releases. If, however, I reasoned, they had been asked a few times for a record and then received half-a-dozen copies gratis they were more liable to take notice and fill the resultant sales on their chart returns. This meant, of course, that we had to be quite ruthless with new releases and, apart from truly exceptional circumstances, if a new release received no airplay or television exposure it was dropped from the priority list.

The priorities were determined at the Friday marketing meetings, which everyone in my department attended with details of airplay, television appearances, sales, tours or any other cogent bits of information. We gave every release full attention and every chance, but the losers were dropped, the possibles encouraged and the winners maximized with full, major-league back-up. It worked in spades, and CBS became the top singles company in the country for the first time ever.

One hit followed another. The Three Degrees, after an initial failure, became huge, Mott had a smash hit with 'All the Way from Memphis', and, by wearing a cowboy hat and boots, I was able to focus the team on country music and grab a couple of massive hits for the great Charlie Rich. Charlie agreed to visit and sang to an invited audience. He was most gracious but no stranger to the bottle and looked as though his face could shatter into a thousand pieces. Few British record-company people recognize the importance of country music but, with some encouragement, we were able to bring home another number one, this time for Tammy Wynette. The great country stars are very aware of their fans, and Tammy on tour would often greet hers with sincere and well-informed enquiries about members of their families. Even the old hands such as Andy Williams benefited from this new-found energy and once again enjoyed the top slot with 'Solitaire', as did Art Garfunkel and many other artists.

Billy Paul and Harold Melvin spearheaded the massive popularity of the productions of Messrs Gamble and Huff and, at the suggestion of one of the promotion team, we created a separate division and a new label identity for the Sound of Philadelphia with Greg Edwards in charge of promotion. That, too, was extraordinarily successful, and we fêted the two producers with an exclusive lunch attended by all the top BBC producers. Gamble and Huff were intelligent, knowledgeable, very creative and made great friends with everybody. The label flourished, but the talented duo got into severe financial difficulties back in the USA a few years later.

Greg Edwards was very handsome, a brilliant promotion man and an excellent disc jockey; so good in fact that I was able to help him get a job at Capital Radio in London, where he brought great style to the presentation of black music. He was also somewhat unpredictable, had a complicated love life and carried his colour like a huge burden –

which may explain his subsequent somewhat erratic career path. He could have been a giant.

With all the singles chart success the album sales boomed, and CBS must have been one of the most profitable companies in Britain if not the world. With much fanfare I was offered a directorship, which was pleasing – but I should have demanded more money. All of that success with no increase in expenditure was literally earning millions for CBS, and if I have one piece of advice to aspiring executives it is to get it while the getting's good. It is rarely offered, and a company on a roll becomes awash with dosh, so why not get some of it? It was not until I started Strange Fruit Records and was responsible for manufacturing along with everything else that I realized just how profitable a record company could be. And CBS owned the factory and the distribution.

They had a varied roster of artists on the label. For instance, in contrast to, say, Leonard Cohen there was David Essex. I never met anybody with more instant and natural sex appeal. His rather fussy and besotted manager Derek Bowman brought him into CBS and, as they toured the building with David in his hugely unfashionable drainpipes and brothel creepers, the jaws of just about every female literally dropped.

At the time, David was appearing in a hit musical in London's West End and had just completed filming *That'll Be the Day* with Adam Faith and Ringo. When we met he had already been signed to CBS along with his producer Jeff Wayne, and a decision was needed about the first single release. David and Jeff wanted to release 'Rock On', but the execs at CBS were reluctant, since this track was already on a compilation film soundtrack album that was currently being advertised on television with sales already in excess of a quarter of a million. In advance of a final meeting with the artist and producer Dick Asher asked me to support him and the rest of the team in selecting an alternative as the first release. It all made sense until I heard an acetate of 'Rock On', which sounded to me like a smash hit under any circumstances, and I pretty much staked my job on it. With many misgivings from the experts we went with 'Rock On'.

David was obviously such a potential superstar that I took the unprecedented step of appointing our top plugger Steve Colyer to work exclusively with him. Steve did a fine job, but, in the process, curiously became something of a clone of David to the point of aping his accent, his haircut, his clothes and even his earring. Steve seemed completely unaware of this bizarre turn of events and even approached me with a request that he be allowed to trade in his company car for a beaten-up old Mercedes like the one driven by his hero.

Selling David to the public was relatively easy but entailed a lot of dedicated effort and expense. First, we needed great publicity shots, and David Bailey was hired to shoot the singer in a specially created white suit. The photos were sensational and provided the basis for the whole campaign. Derek Bowman had a background in press relations and handled most of this area. Steve arranged a few important appearances at prestigious chart shops such as Chappell of Bond Street, where he broadsided his car across one of London's busiest roads to cause a massive traffic jam that was reported as fan fever.

With this much action in the press the radio stations started to play the record, and it began a swift climb of the charts, eventually peaking at number two. The Americans were unimpressed and refused to release the record, but I was able to corner the

Columbia boss, Walter Yetnikof, at a bar mitzvah for Dick Asher's son and persuade him to arrange an American release, where, on the back of a promotional tour, it sold a million.

At the height of all this activity I was interviewed by the *Daily Mail* and asked to give some background to what was now 'the David Essex phenomenon'. Believing that it could be helpful to David, I supplied some details of the campaign, being most careful to point out that we considered our job simply to bring David's talent and obvious charm to the attention of the public. In a full-page article the reporter suggested that we had in fact manufactured and sold a product, much as one might a brand of toothpaste. David and Derek were very hurt, and I was subjected to a severe bollocking from Dick Asher. It's really no wonder that the top acts employ press agents to protect them from the 'scorps'.

With a smash-hit record and a starring role in a terrific movie, David gave up his stage role and began to tour. He remained charming and affable, and my two young daughters still recall their visits backstage where David showed them courtesy and kindness, welcomed them, chatted with them and finally ushered them back to their seats without them ever feeling dismissed. That's quite a trick when you are about to give a performance in front of thousands.

On one occasion Obie, who was a fan of Queen's Park Rangers and a friend of their captain Gerry Francis, invited Gerry up to one of David's gigs at Leicester's De Montfort Hall. Gerry was also captain of the England football team at the time, and it seemed like a good photo opportunity to have them pictured together as examples of youthful success. It was, but it also put the pop business in some kind of perspective when David walked out to an ovation from a few thousand fans, with Gerry in the wings used to performing in front of close to a hundred thousand critics at a time in his England shirt.

David continued to enjoy great success and to take with him on tour the Real Thing, a band I was later able to help to achieve the top slot when I moved to Pye Records. I wish that David had continued along the raunchy path of 'Rock On', but later releases became much softer and more obviously commercial; a short-term ploy in my opinion – but what do I know? Having twice put my job on the line to further David's career, and dedicated the efforts of my entire staff to that cause, David and his manager were so impressed with my work that at Christmas they presented me with . . . a jar of cheese.

Andy Williams is the mellowest of men. Always polite and quietly spoken, he seemed to float just an inch or so above the ground – which is a beatific state if it can be held. When we met he had been one of the biggest stars in the world through his television series and a string of hit records. Though the hits had dried up, he was still a massive draw, filling concert halls around the world and in great demand as a guest on television shows. None of that, however, sold records in any worthwhile quantities, and that was the game we were in.

When I took home the most recent Andy Williams album to give it a listen, which was not considered a priority item, I was struck by the track 'Solitaire' and became convinced that it could be a major hit if Andy were available to promote it. So on Andy's next UK visit I apprised him of my thoughts and virtually promised him a chart-topper if he would cooperate. Together we consulted his diary, which was itself a revelation. Over the following few months he had set aside time for several golf tournaments including his own Andy Williams Classic. Each tournament required his presence for a minimum of four days plus travel times. There were a great number of concert dates around the world, two weeks for a skiing holiday in Switzerland and just a few days left in which to film a seven-week run of the *Andy Williams Show* for US network television. Thinking this must be a mistake, I queried the dates with Andy who assured me that with careful planning the series could be shot in just a few days. Those of you who remember the show will recall that it always featured a top star in a guest appearance slot usually performing a new release, a few moments of badinage, a number of songs from Andy, a duet with the guest and a closing song from the host; all done in a relaxed but highly entertaining style. It seemed impossible that seven shows could be recorded and edited in just a few days, but Andy explained that all seven opening songs would be recorded in one day, with another two days to film all of the guest spots, chats and duets, and another couple of days to film the closing sequences and any retakes. Now that is a true professional. How he remains so relaxed is a mystery. Perhaps those herbal cigarettes help.

He did return to do the Michael Parkinson show and was superb. The record, as predicted, went to number one, which was just as well since Dick Asher had expressly forbidden me ever to promise an artist the top position. The album sold in truckloads and gave Andy's career a valuable new impetus. I've since learned that he subsequently scored a $3 million advance from Columbia when his contract ran out, which probably enabled him to enlarge his valuable collection of contemporary art. He was thrilled and presented me with a beautiful crystal decanter suitably inscribed.

Hoping to give Clifford T. Ward's publishing income a boost, I asked Shurley to drop off a copy of Cliff's latest album to Andy in his suite at the Savoy on the off-chance that he might find a song to record. Andy assumed that his visitor was a 'gift' from the record company, which could have proved highly embarrassing, but he quickly and graciously recognized his mistake. Well, that's what she told me.

I would have liked to believe that we had struck up a long-term friendship, but a couple of years later I went to see Andy performing at the Grosvenor Hotel. With some difficulty I arranged for a backstage visit with a couple of new colleagues, but upon being presented to Andy it was apparent that he didn't know me from a hole in the wall. Ah well . . . Those herbal fags again?

Another potentially embarrassing occasion arose when Leonard Cohen called to say that he was planning to release a batch of his romantic poems on disc and would like to discuss the project. I was not a great fan of Cohen and, though he wrote some superb songs, I generally preferred other people's versions and in particular those recorded by Judy Collins. Her version of 'Dress Rehearsal Rag' remains one of the most chilling performances ever. Still, you don't refuse an offer of that kind, and I ended up alone in a room with Lenny reading aloud some of his most romantic work. He has a magnificent speaking voice and read with great warmth and sincerity. Far from being embarrassed, I was both moved and touched, becoming an instant fan. On the evidence of that meeting I completely understand the fascination he has for women the world over.

One of his best friends at that time was fellow Canadian Joni Mitchell, who then had an image of being all sweetness and light; rather less so now. I have a theory brought about from long experience that those acts with the softest image are all too often very difficult and, conversely, the hard-edged ones are often the easiest to work with. I cannot recall any exceptions to this rule and one day tried it out on Mo Ostin, the chairman of WEA, by enquiring how he found working with Joni. Mo was adamant that Joni was a pleasure and a joy to work with.

'What, all the time?'

'Never a problem,' said Mo.

'Never?' I pushed and recounted a particular instance of another artist with an unblemished image.

'Well, there was this one time,' said Mo. 'I was asleep at home when the phone rang at about 3 a.m., and it was Joni. There she was holidaying on a Greek island where she could find just about every one of Lenny Cohen's albums in the shops but none of hers – and what the hell was I going to do about that at three o'clock in the goddamned morning? And another time she . . .'

Simon and Garfunkel are probably the most successful recording duo of all time, and, since they split up, Paul has gone on to even greater success as a solo artist – though in the early days of the separation Art matched him hit for hit while enjoying a new career in the movies.

It was not always so, however. As so often happens, the original success came about almost by accident. Wally Whyton was with Paul in a pub in England when Paul drew out a crumpled cable from the USA requesting his immediate return to promote 'The Sound of Silence'. It had been recorded with Garfunkel as an album track and, owing to substantial airplay, needed to be remixed and released as a single. Paul was at that time resident in Britain and reluctant to give up what was turning out to be a moderately encouraging career as a troubadour. Apparently Wally, Donovan, Cat Stevens and a few other chums convinced him that it was worth giving the partnership another try.

They were an unlikely couple, and it was only surprising that the partnership lasted as long as it did – particularly since Paul wrote all the songs. When the final break came, Paul returned to London with a view to relaunching his solo career on his old stamping ground. A date was booked at the Royal Albert Hall, which immediately sold out with fans and critics eager to be in at an important new stage in the career of one of the truly great writers and recording artists.

However, Paul's triumphant return to London almost fell at an early fence. He is very diminutive in stature and, as is often the case with short people, rather sensitive on that score. For the big occasion he brought with him a hand-made white suit, which he possibly felt would show up well on the vast Albert Hall platform. On the night, Shurley and I took our seats in an auditorium literally buzzing with excited anticipation. Show time came and went with no sign of the star and, as the minutes ticked by, anticipation turned to restlessness in the absence of any apologies or explanations. The festive crowd started to become surly, with an outbreak of slow handclapping. Fearing a disaster, I slipped backstage and discovered a scene that almost beggars description. Staying at a top London hotel, Paul had left his beautiful suit with the valet to be sponged and pressed for the big occasion. Unbelievably the suit had in fact been washed and had shrunk to fit a small child. Paul was simply refusing to appear. He didn't need the money and he certainly didn't need the humiliation. He is, after all, a sensitive and creative man, albeit with a hang-up about his height.

Seeing no contribution I could make I returned to my seat, and good sense obviously prevailed as we were rewarded with a stunning concert by an artist dressed in a T-shirt and jeans. It was a brilliant performance, and straight after the show Paul hosted a backstage party for friends and press at which the first question from the assembled reporters was 'Do you have trouble getting served in pubs because you are so short?' It was also the last question, as Mr Simon stormed out. His solo career flourished, and I next saw him at a CBS sales conference in Toronto where he gave a fairly muted show beset by technical problems in front of several hundred record people from all over the world. He later appeared at the London Palladium where the same show was transformed into a thing of great beauty, building slowly with the addition of further musicians for each song into a moving climax. I congratulated him at the after-show party in a nearby restaurant, where he murmured his thanks in that usual distracted professional manner, but when he knew that I had also seen the Toronto show he was full of questions.

The only sour note of the visit was when his lawyer visited the CBS offices and Dick Asher, who was terrified of artists or their earthly representatives, paraded all of the directors as if we were to be presented to royalty. And that was just for the lawyer.

Art Garfunkel's other job is as a professor of mathematics at Harvard – and doesn't he look the part? At the start of his solo adventures I ran into him at Black Rock, CBS's headquarters in New York, where he quizzed me about the lack of chart action on his first solo single. I pointed out that the record was being played daily on national radio and had been well reviewed but that sales were slow. This rather eccentric academic expressed considerable surprise, since he felt that, as the song in question was a ballad and the current top-selling record in Britain was also a ballad, his offering should be a comparable hit. The fact that the other ballad was sung by Donny Osmond was not considered relevant. I was spared the embarrassment of further discussion by the appearance of a young woman holding a glossy photograph of Artie that she asked him to autograph for her. He scrutinized the photo, stamped his foot and demanded to know where it had come from. The somewhat flustered secretary indicated a filing cabinet, which Artie immediately emptied with shrill cries of horror. As we left he was systematically tearing all of the offending pictures into four and dumping them into a flaming wastepaper basket. He does, nevertheless, have a superb voice and eventually hit the top spot with 'Bright Eyes', written by Mike Batt.

Mike Batt was a spirited young hustler making a pretty good living from having written the theme song and the incidental music for a successful afternoon children's show on BBC television called *The Wombles*. The Wombles were a collection of furry animals living on Wimbledon Common. He compiled an album of music from the series and sold it to Jack Florey, the sales director at CBS, for release as a budget-priced record for children. Though ultimately selling in millions, the music is of no great significance, but the effort and circumstances surrounding its transition to multi-million status may be of interest.

'The Wombling Song' was played over the opening and closing credits of the show, and Mike persuaded the A & R people at CBS to release it as a single in the hope that a few radio plays and the odd review might gain some promotion for the album. The A & R people hated it.

As marketing director of CBS it was part of my function to evaluate the various planned new releases and decide on the amount of promotion expenditure and marketing effort each release would receive – subject, of course, to re-evaluation as the early reactions from radio, press and sales became available. Every record company will tell you that they alone have a true commitment to every single release, but the truth is that very early in their careers most records are allowed to die without a fight. Staff and marketing budgets are finite, and every company will put the most effort behind releases by established hit-makers and just hope to get lucky with some of the rest. All too often, new acts and management think it is enough to get that initial contract and release, when in fact that is just the start of the project and, unless they have a champion at court prepared to fight their corner, they have to rely on luck. One of the most difficult jobs of any record executive is at the start of each week when the weight of the new release schedule demands that a high percentage of current releases be consigned to the bin.

When I took the white-label of 'The Wombling Song' home to have a listen it just happened that my four children, aged between four and sixteen, were all in the house together. They were all familiar with the song through television and spontaneously began to sing along. In my book any record that can cross that age range is a sure-fire winner, and I determined that the Wombles become a top priority.

At CBS the rest of the staff, including the other directors, thought I had lost it but indulged me, and initial results confirmed their suspicions. No reviews, no airplay and no sales. We tried to persuade BBC television to announce the availability of the single following each programme, but the Corporation would have none of it, so the pluggers and their families would phone the Beeb after every show pretending to be punters wanting to know if a record was available. Eventually we got the station announcements but still no sales.

September became October, and it was getting late to establish the record in time for the all-important Christmas sales period, but without airplay that was looking impossible. In a series of almost daily meetings Mike, to his credit, made himself available for just about any daft promotional activity, including being dropped by helicopter and appearing at record stores in a very hot, furry Womble suit made for him by his mum. We even bought quantities of tickets to the pantomime at the Wimbledon Theatre and invited the children of various radio and television producers to be our guests. The coach was waylaid crossing Wimbledon Common by Mike dressed in his Womble suit, thumbing a lift and distributing records and stickers to the bemused kids. Nothing.

In desperation, having given away hundreds of records and Womble dolls, I turned to ace PR guru Peter Thompson, whose clients included the Oliviers, Queen and Genesis. Peter stated quite categorically that it would be impossible to obtain any press coverage in the run-up to Christmas; he would, however, be happy to take on the account in January. Exactly what we did not want to hear, but you have to trust the professionals. We floundered about over Christmas – there were, of course, plenty of other hits to work on. Though the budget album was still selling in reasonable quantities, there was no interest in the single.

Immediately after Christmas I engaged Peter Thompson to handle the press, and within a few days he obtained a double-page spread in one of the national tabloids and on the same day a full-page-with-pictures in the London *Evening Standard*. A truly astonishing result from a remarkable man. Somehow that triggered a radio reaction, and we began to pick up the odd radio play, initially as a joke. Tony Blackburn and Dave Lee Travis began coming up with Womble jokes on Radio 1, and eventually one of them appeared in a Womble suit on *Top of the Pops*. At that point the floodgates opened and the record shot to the top of the charts some four months after release, beginning a couple of years of Womble madness. The budget album was swiftly withdrawn and re-released at full price, whereupon it, too, went gold. Mike went back into the studio to record a follow-up single, 'Remember You're a Womble', with my four kids helping out on the backing vocals. That, too, was a smash hit then and again recently. Mike went on to write and produce many more hits for himself and others. When 'Remember You're a Womble' was re-released in 2000 and again made the charts, my daughter Bee had a hard time convincing her son, who wanted to buy a copy, that she and her brothers and sister had sung on it. What goes around . . . ?

Shortly after I left CBS – for the first time – I read an interview with Mr Batt in which he stated that the success of the Wombles was due in large part to the unflagging efforts of the A & R director Danny Loggins who 'had played the record to his four kids and was so impressed by their reaction'. Danny at that time was not married and had no kids but was still in a position to be of use to Mike's career. I, and by extension my kids, were not.

Mentioning Danny reminds me that I was always envious of his svelte hair and superbly styled beard. Being something of a scruff, I was intrigued as to how he always managed to be so well turned out. The mystery was solved when Peter Thompson told me that, on offering his – very fashionable and expensive – hairdresser a few promotional copies of our latest releases, he was told that the establishment got all the records they needed from Danny Loggins. It seemed that Dan had three appointments every week! So next time you are told that your A & R man is 'in a meeting' try looking for him in the most expensive barbers.

Liza Minnelli is, without doubt, one of the showbiz greats and has, at last, stepped out from under the shadow of her immortal mum – though her recent appearances suggest that she may have encountered some of the same problems.

When she came to London to promote the *Liza with a Z* album everybody at CBS was under strict instructions not to approach her under any circumstances. This was something of a company rule with the superstars of the label and was possibly initiated following problems with Ms Streisand, who was considered sacrosanct, as were Bob Dylan, Johnny Cash, Leonard Bernstein and a few others. Perhaps the US office considered us Brits too uncouth.

Liza was booked into the London Palladium for a season of solo shows following her international success in the movie *Cabaret*. Rather than rely on the CBS staff hacks, she had employed an outside agency to take care of the press, which is not unusual for stars of her stature. The company – Rogers, Cowan and Brenner – had an unusual approach to public relations: it seemed to revolve around them inviting all of their other clients to a lavish party at CBS's expense, in the hope that the press would attend in the expectation that they would get interviews and pictures of various stars and, in the process, mention Liza. Nice work if you can get it – and it seems to work.

In advance of Liza's visit we did an enormous amount of promotion, including arranging the party as well as dealing with the invitations to that and the Palladium shows, plus a unique display of huge posters around the main commuter railway stations. With a lot of hard-won radio exposure and some judiciously placed advertising, the album was high in the charts by the time the star arrived and took up residence at the Savoy. There was indeed a great deal of excitement, at least among the showbiz and gay fraternities, and the Palladium was sold out for the entire run.

Feeling pretty pleased with the results of all the effort – and contrary to the explicit instructions of Dick Asher – I called in at the Savoy to say hello to Liza and enquire whether she had any views on how the campaign was being conducted or any special requests. On being shown up to her suite, I found her with Peter Sellers who was, and remains, one of my heroes. They were both having a ball and pleased that somebody had bothered to come and see them. Liza had no problems with the campaign and was happy to let me get on with it.

The party – in fact a champagne breakfast – was arranged for the early hours of the morning following the opening night, which was a black-tie event and sold out, with tickets changing hands at ridiculous prices. The show itself was a revelation. Liza dominated the stage with a truly breathtaking *tour de force* of singing, dancing and sheer charisma. Shurley, who was brought up in the business, was starry-eyed and speechless with admiration. The audience was in raptures and calling for encore after encore, which went on way past midnight. Eventually even Liza had to quit and, as the final curtain fell, we sped across Regent Street to the exclusive restaurant where breakfasts, suppers and champagne cocktails awaited a couple of hundred fortunate guests.

As befits a great star, Liza kept the celebrity assemblage waiting for a couple of hours while she unwound, dressed and made up. Together with movie stars such as Sellers and Michael Caine, there were a number of important agents and managers at the party. They can be very productive to a record company, and Dick Asher, who was paying for the spread, knew he should seize the opportunity to introduce himself to the glitterati. However, he was by nature a rather shy and clumsy man, and his natural diffidence held him back. Not so his American wife, who had no such qualms. As each famous face entered the room she goaded poor Dick forward as if with a cattle prod while hissing instructions before turning on the gracious hostess act. Fellow directors, employees or anyone without influence were studiously ignored.

Came the moment of Liza's triumphant entrance and Dick was at last on home ground as he busily tried to marshal his troops into proper presentation order. Liza, meanwhile, circled the room meeting and greeting with shouts of joy old friends whom, it would appear, she had not seen for years. She is an extravagantly extrovert person both on and off stage, and the room rang with her bellows of laughter and squeals of delight, while Dick and his wife became ever more agitated. Occasionally she would sneak a glance in our direction, but it was obvious that she did not relish the formality of the line-up of record-company people. Eventually deciding that it could no longer be avoided, she turned towards the predatory pair, who advanced with outstretched hands, brushed past them and threw her arms around my neck. 'Clive, you old mother-fucker,' she boomed. 'How was the show?'

Sheila Asher never voluntarily spoke to me again – and that's another reason to adore the lovely Liza with a Z, of course.

Mott the Hoople had a massive hit with 'All the Young Dudes', which was written and produced by David Bowie, and had a good follow-up with 'All the Way From Memphis'. They would occasionally come into the CBS offices to discuss promotion and sleeve art, with singer Ian Hunter sitting stony-faced behind his ever-present shades. I was never sure whether he was aloof or just dumb. Possibly the latter, because just as 'Memphis' was climbing the charts and the band was offered a spot on *Top of the Pops* they, at the last minute, refused to appear unless they could turn up at the television studio in a brace of white Rolls-Royces – the transportation to be arranged and paid for by the record company, of course. Probably, as my colleague Tony Woolcott pointed out, they only wanted the Rollers to take their old ladies shopping, as there was never anyone around the studios to impress. Still, the cars were provided, the band went on, the record was a hit and no doubt the band had the bill deducted from their royalties.

After they disbanded, the drummer, Dale Griffin, became a producer for Radio 1 and, until recently, produced many of the sessions recorded for the Peel shows. Dale doesn't talk much about his time with Mott, but he did tell me that when signed to Island Records, prior to moving to CBS, he asked Chris Blackwell, the owner, for a new set of drumsticks following a particularly successful concert and was refused. Events like that go some way to explaining why artists take every opportunity to turn the screws on the back of success.

For reasons best known to himself in his role as radio producer Dale always wore a very straight three-piece business suit that tended to confuse the various punk and thrash musicians, who assumed they were dealing with an Establishment figure with no knowledge of the creative process. He also adopted a most authoritarian manner in the studio and took some delight in leaving the mikes open and listening to the mutterings of the young hopefuls who had no idea that he had been there and done that.

The sleeve art for Mott's first CBS album was created by Roslav Szabo, a talented and temperamental Pole who wore a black cloak and cut a romantic figure with his Eastern European accent and manners. The sleeve was a work of art featuring a stunning head design that won awards in Britain but which was not used in the USA where they wanted the usual photo of the group up front.

On one occasion Szabo set up a meeting with the members of the Clash to discuss their album art. In true street-cred fashion, the band turned up late and pointed out that they did not subscribe to the bourgeois concept of punctuality. They had in fact been busy protesting against the system by snapping off car aerials and otherwise demonstrating their anti-Establishment credentials. Roslav agreed that such gestures were important. He, too, had engaged in similar pursuits as a youth, but in his case it had been pretty much confined to throwing Molotov cocktails at Nazi tanks as they patrolled the streets of his beloved Warsaw.

Even with all the unprecedented success we were having, Dick Asher never let up for a moment. Every Tuesday morning the directors met to discuss new signings and general business. This also happened to be the time that we received news of the charts and we would try to delay that information in order to get some business concluded before Asher began bitching and moaning about the chart positions. With as much as 40 per cent of the Top Fifty being CBS acts his response would be 'Aw, shit! Where's the Three Degrees? Fuck it. Why can't we get our shit together and bring home a few hits?' Grown men were close to tears, and sweaty armpits were the norm. I once asked Dick why he pushed so hard and he responded that, unlikely though it may indeed be, he was unable to rest until 'CBS has the entire Top Hundred singles and albums!'

Another appealing little trick of Asher's was to invite me into meetings with artists and managers to discuss marketing plans. Regardless of the calibre of the act under discussion, he would promise '100 per cent total commitment', with billboards, press advertisements and possibly even a television campaign. 'Just go upstairs and discuss the details with Clive,' he would say as he ushered them to the door. As they left full of eager anticipation he would often call me back and whisper, 'Don't spend a dime,' before firmly closing the door. I quickly learned to tap-dance verbally.

Though a brilliant businessman, a workaholic and a slave-driver, Dick had no social graces and was remarkably clumsy. Just before I joined the company he arranged a staff meeting to introduce his latest signing, Donovan. Don dressed for the occasion in a beautiful white suit and somehow managed to keep his cool when Dick accidentally knocked a glass of red wine all over him.

I had my own problems with Donovan, however. On one occasion Dick asked me to accompany him to a meeting with the artist and his agent Vic Lewis. (The occasion was, by the way, also a lesson on how never to try to best a tough Jewish agent.) As we arrived Donovan was about to leave and, after a brief discussion on the progress of the album, he reluctantly agreed to allow me to visit the sessions and report progress. Just what I needed at the end of a long day! There followed another discussion about the artist's forthcoming trip to South Africa, which was, at that time, a country blackballed by the Musicians' Union on account of the apartheid system. Donovan wanted to announce the tour to the British press, but when he was told that this would result in a ban by the union he simply refused to go to South Africa and said that he would cancel the tour.

Vic Lewis was aghast. He explained that the promoter of the South African tour was waiting in the next room to meet Donovan and that the contracts had already been signed. 'You've signed them, not me!' was the artist's response as he swept out. Vic excused himself and walked downstairs with the artist to a waiting car. Upon returning, he excused himself again and called in the hapless promoter, while Dick and I exchanged anxious looks. Vic exuded bonhomie, apologized that the artist had to leave early and assured the promoter that everything was in order with the artist looking forward to a successful tour. 'Everything' apparently included large fees for Donovan and first-class liner tickets for Mr and Mrs Lewis plus tickets for an important cricket match. The promoter was delighted and stood up to shake hands as, baffled, Asher and I looked at each other in amazement. 'There's just one thing,' concluded Vic. 'You will, of course, be arranging a press conference on Don's arrival?'

'Of course,' was the reply. 'It will be an important media event.'

'Good,' said Vic with a smile. 'And you know that Donovan, being who he is, will attack your government and its appalling apartheid policies?' The promoter went white and protested that he would lose his licence and possibly go to jail. Vic was sympathetic but pointed out that, as an established folk artist, Donovan was not about to pass up such a golden opportunity to attack an oppressive regime. Under the circumstances Vic might be prepared to cancel the concerts and tear up the contracts, but there was the consideration of his substantial agency commission plus, of course, the first-class passages and tickets for the cricket match. The poor promoter jumped at the opening and guaranteed Mr Lewis all of the lost commission and perks if he could be let out of the contract.

'All right,' said Vic with the air of a magnanimous gentleman. 'But just remember that you owe me, and if I want you to book some of my lesser acts then I will expect you to come through.' The totally outmanoeuvred promoter agreed instantly, thanked Vic for his cooperation and fled. The only time that Vic had in which to concoct the whole thing was on the short walk down to the car and back. He probably never gave the incident another thought, but Dick and I were almost legless with admiration approaching awe.

After the meeting, I set off for my visit to the studio where Donovan was recording. My brief was to be the company spy, and both the artist and his producer were only too aware of it. At Morgan Studios I was kept waiting for over an hour while the red recording light stayed on, despite the occupants being made aware of my arrival with a telephone call from the receptionist. This was obviously nonsense and a deliberate putdown. Even a symphony orchestra takes a break within an hour, and cooling my heels in a dingy part of north London when tired and hungry is not my idea of a good time.

Eventually I was admitted and immediately subjected to a typical hippie-smartarse-superior bout of condescension. 'Now this is a studio,' said Mr Wonderful, 'and this is a microphone and that is a recording desk.' I had by that stage in my career produced a couple of hit singles and a number of albums and really didn't need this patronizing shit.

'And this is the sound of me leaving,' I replied and went home angry and humiliated. I mentioned the incident to Obie, who observed that, as marketing director in charge of promotion, advertising, press exposure, matching review copies with release dates and the like, I was in a position to exact my revenge when the album was finally completed. I simply don't recall how the album fared, but artists who deliberately antagonize their record company executives are taking unnecessary chances.

One of the benefits of being a multinational corporation such as CBS is the access it can provide to local talent from around the world. This can also become a pain in the neck, since the relevant British or American A & R person has to deal with dozens of recordings that, though successful in their local markets, are highly unsuited to a broader audience. A considerable degree of diplomacy is required in order to keep the foreign affiliate at bay and on good terms.

Such was the case with Swedish band Abba, who were highly thought of in their native Sweden but whose first British release 'Ring Ring' failed to get any support from within the British company or from any of the media. All that changed, however, when they won the 1974 Song For Europe with 'Waterloo'.

Having three of the finalists in Brighton that year, I was obliged to watch the show and was galvanized into action when Abba won. For the next few days virtually all other activity within the company stopped while the sophisticated CBS team sprang into action. Not every Eurovision winner becomes a smash hit, and the days following the competition are crucial. Thousands more of the record must be pressed and distributed overnight; a champagne breakfast press reception and separate interviews must be arranged; additional promotion copies are delivered and sent out along with updated press releases, photos and biographies; every dealer is telephoned to advise and solicit orders; posters are designed, printed and distributed; and all of this against a background of hysterical calls from every major newspaper, radio and television station across Europe. How the artists cope is very often a guide to their likely longevity.

Amidst this madness Bruce Lundvall, the head of American A & R, who was visiting at the time, arrived and watched with amusement. Stig Anderson, Abba's manager, offered the record to Bruce for a nominal royalty and no advance in order to obtain an early US release – and Bruce turned him down! I was astonished and pointed out that the record would sell several million copies in Europe alone and the group would, in all probability, score as big in America as the New Seekers had with 'I'd Like to Teach the World to Sing' a few years earlier. Bruce was adamant that this was not 'an American record', and I concluded that he was just another arrogant American A & R man. In fact he was right. It took Abba several years and some costly tours to capture that market.

Abba, as we know, went on to score a string of hits with massive international success, and even now the show featuring their music is breaking box-office records around the world. They would be guaranteed millions for just one more record or tour, but it doesn't seem likely.

A rare and somewhat heart-warming event occurred some years into their success at the time when their publishing deal ran out. In the early days, when Stig was struggling, his publishing interests in Britain were handled by an elderly but honest publisher who also handled Jonathan King's publishing. Carole Broughton, a capable and talented person, who also acted as Jonathan's secretary, administered the catalogue. Choosing honesty and dedication over what must have been millions in offers of advance money, Stig renewed his deal with his old partner. By coincidence Carole also handled the publishing interests of the Zombies, one of whom introduced Abba to Britain in his new role as CBS A & R man. Another case of what goes around comes around?

I was involved on CBS's behalf in the Crystal Palace Festival in 1974 in some way, but all I can recall of the event was a few twerps trying to swim the lake and Unity McLean, who worked for me in Artist Relations, knocking on Jeff Beck's trailer door and, on introducing herself and asking if there was anything the band needed, being told, 'Well, *you* can fuck off for a start.' Nice. I was also involved in an open-air concert featuring Sly and the Family Stone, the Kinks and either Edgar or Johnny Winter – I can't remember which – at the White City Stadium in west London, which is now the site of the BBC's headquarters. Not many people showed up, possibly on account of Sly's reputation as a no-show, and the day was perhaps most notable for being, I believe, the first time that Ray Davies announced his retirement. I do, however, have some great eight-millimetre footage of my four kids looning about in cloaks and bell-bottoms which now embarrasses them enormously.

Despite all the success, parties, receptions, travel and hanging out with CBS's world-class artists, life with that company was joyless. The pressures were enormous and unrelenting. Asher asked me to become his deputy, and I responded, with one of those rare memorable epigrams, that I had heard of power without responsibility but what he was offering was tantamount to responsibility without power. I had great respect for the entire CBS team. My own staff was exceptional, my colleagues were generally dedicated and professional and my bosses, from Walter Yetnikof down, were ruthlessly competent. However, the music was generally bland with none of the danger of the Doors, the excitement of Love or the naked emotion of Judy Collins. The job was done. From being an important also-ran CBS had become market leader in both albums and singles. What was left? A tortuous climb up the greasy executive pole for more money, responsibility and aggravation? It was time to move on. Australia beckoned, and I needed a rest.

I made my decision known to Dick Asher, who accepted it with good grace and asked for suggestions for my successor. The obvious choice was my senior label manager Tony Woolcott but, despite my recommendation and his obvious qualities, he was rejected. The reason offered was 'Have you seen the way he dresses?' As the scruffiest person in the entire organization I failed to see the significance of Tony's apparel. Another person was appointed, and Tony left in a huff to take up a senior position with Chrysalis Records. As I had predicted, my replacements were unable to sustain the momentum, and I watched with interest as CBS began to lose out on market share and, more importantly, failed to bring home a number of potential hits. Someone else, a very pleasant man, replaced my replacement, but he, too, was unable to stop the decline in sales, so they begged me to come back – and I went back. But more about that later.

MARKETING

It has become fashionable to sneer at marketing and, when one sees the multi-million-pound campaigns of the car industry with barely a mention of the capabilities of the vehicle, one can sympathize.

Car marketing has become all about lifestyles and aspirations rather than performance or price. Movies are not far behind, and the latest celluloid attempt to emulate the excitement some find in computer games is promoted with millions of dollars of smash-bang-wallop trails. It is no longer unusual for a film company to spend 40 per cent of the overall budget on marketing alone – sometimes something in the region of $40 million. Great news for the advertising industry, but that kind of spend all too often means that the product itself has to be aimed at the lowest common denominator.

A friend who ran a reasonably successful advertising agency once confided that his father had advised him not to enter the advertising field since it was chock-full of bright young men and women. He suggested a career in sanitary plumbing or something similar where there was less competition. That was before the advent of the current proliferation of television channels stuffed with commercials made, it would seem, by morons for morons.

The music industry has followed the movie business in most respects but, fortunately, not yet in terms of marketing expenditure. The 'Now That's What I Call Music' series of compilation albums started down that road but appears to have curtailed expenditure of late as it has passed the fifty mark. I was involved with the groundbreaking Tellydisc series of two-minute commercials for albums back in the eighties. This was an early attempt by the television companies to break into the direct response market and, though successful in shifting albums, it never became a commercial reality. The idea was for the television company to supply airtime in return for a piece of the action rather than the normal exorbitant fees. We had a lot of fun before they woke up, and perhaps it led to the current and growing proliferation of channels devoted to shopping.

Marketing is divided into what are known as above-the-line and below-the-line expenditure. Above-the-line relates mostly to those visible posters, press advertisements and radio or television commercials. Most artists and managers only see or care about above-the-line campaigns and will fight the record company for more with little or no regard for the crucial below-the-line activity.

Below-the-line covers creating a biography, writing and distributing press releases, receptions, photography and reproduction, mailing out hundreds or – in the case of dance records – thousands of records to clubs, press, radio and television stations and the very expensive services of promotion people, or 'pluggers' as they are known. For a new or unknown act add in the cost of new clothes, hairstyling and makeup plus tour support.

There is little doubt that the best route to success comes through building a following and a reputation with live performances. Classic examples of this are Eric Clapton, who was deemed a god before he ever recorded a note, and the Beatles, who were rejected by record companies despite creating hysteria among audiences when on stage. The problem for new artists today is that most venues of any worth are only too aware of their own importance and expect to pay nothing to an unknown; some even levy a charge for an appearance. The same applies to the big touring acts who demand payment from the support act. The larger record companies recognize the need to be seen and heard and will often pay for the exposure – as an advance, of course.

Daunting though this may be, it should not deter the ambitious artist or entrepreneur on a limited budget. Rehearsals can be done in the garage or local scout hut and, with a degree of competence, it should be possible to find a pub or club in the area willing to take a chance on you. When the artist or group feels ready to record there are plenty of competent and cheap studios all over the country able to offer reasonably professional services to a budget. It is absolutely essential that the act is well rehearsed, as the studio clock never stops ticking and a budget can be blown just getting an acceptable drum sound. (The Way We Live recorded a magnificent album for Dandelion in a friend's loft.)

There are a number of magazines that list studios, but I would recommend the *Music Week Yearbook* as a starting place. Once having successfully recorded, the same publication is also an excellent source of information on getting records pressed. Initially a new act will need to press around five hundred copies of a single that, with cover art and the cost of mastering and art repro, will come in at around £500.

The first fifty or so copies of the CD will inevitably go to the artists and their friends and family. Some will go to likely venues for future dates, and the balance will be used for marketing. Send, or preferably take, a copy of the record, together with a photograph and a biography stressing the local nature of the act, to the local newspaper, whose editor will be keen to write a story and a review. Try to come up with an interesting tale for the readers, and you have started a marketing campaign.

Assuming that the review is favourable, take a box of the record to each of the record stores in your area and, if finances permit, make up a small poster for display. Any exposure is a complete waste of time if the public is not able to find the record easily and quickly. You will almost certainly have to leave the records on a 'sale or return' basis, which means that you will be paid only for records sold and will be expected to collect those left over.

The next step is to send or take copies of the record to the nearest local BBC or commercial radio station. Try again to come up with an interesting localized story and make the artists available for an interview. Be civil but persistent. All radio stations are under constant pressure from major record labels and professional promotion people to get exposure for the acts, and airtime is precious. It is, however, one of life's greatest thrills to hear your record played for the first time on radio and well worth the effort and likely initial rebuttal. If you now have a decent press review and a confirmed broadcast go back to the shops and give them the details.

With any degree of success on local radio or press, spread your activities to the next town and do the same things with stores. If the record 'has legs' you may see a small surge in sales and know that you are on to something. Do not be discouraged if the results are slow. You are up against very wealthy and sophisticated record companies with deep pockets and highly paid professionals. Who ever said it had to be easy? Some of my own marketing successes came from carefully monitoring local radio plays and store activity. I always used the analogy of fishing (though I've never actually fished): you cast a baited hook, and when something bites you reel it in very carefully. It is a matter of persistence and

gathering up the isolated interest to make up a movement.

If the record is original and arresting, try for a session on one of the Radio 1 programmes. The pay is reasonable and the audiences can be huge. A session on John Peel's programme has been the launch pad for hundreds of successful acts, but John is very choosy and listens to so much that he is mostly attracted to the unique or at least unconventional. There are other session shows that may be more suitable. Try them all. The act will need to be ready and rehearsed to record at least four songs.

With good press reviews, some local radio and possibly a session recorded it will be time to try for the big time. This can take the form of seeking a contract with an established major label, where you will be expected to sell your soul for a pot of gold, or a smaller label with intact principles and ability but little money. Alternatively, a distribution agreement with a national distributor will allow you to remain in control of, and pick up the costs of, all further expenditure. These are major decisions that need to be thoroughly thought through.

If the record is now getting national airplay you will urgently need to have a video available for television. This is a big-time expenditure. A major company will pick up the cost as an advance, and one of the smaller semi-independents will almost certainly stump up – but it has to be done urgently before any interest in the record simply fades away through lack of exposure. There are still a few television slots available, the most effective being *Top of the Pops*, but these are almost exclusively confined to current chart acts or artists with established reputations.

Whichever route you choose, every record dealer and major multiple across the country will have to be contacted and made aware of the potential hit and from where it can be ordered. The established companies will have telephone sales people to undertake this task and, here again, they will have lists of shops connected to the charts, to which they will often send free copies to sustain any initial demand. Going through an indie distributor will entail close monitoring of daily sales, together with the cost and responsibility of ordering and maintaining sufficient stock. This is crucial, since few things kill a record quicker than it being unavailable for even a couple of days. The public is a fickle creature, and there are always hundreds of other records clamouring for attention. An indie distributor will help with this task, but beware of over-enthusiastic ordering. You will have to pick up the manufacturing bills, and a stack of unsold records will eat into any profits when the dust has settled.

Once a record has charted the heat is really on, and the artist must maximize any success through press interviews and photographs, which, in an ideal world, will be handled by a professional press officer or PR person. The established labels have this kind of expertise available as part of the service along with sales, promotion and dozens of other necessary areas of creativity. The job of the manager at this stage is to filter out many of the demands on the act to enable the artist to decide on, rehearse and record that crucial follow-up single or even, if the hit is big enough, embark upon an album. All the while the clock is ticking and the bills are mounting, even if only as advances.

And that's just the bare bones of marketing in Britain. Overseas markets are no less important, but a good licensee in each territory will almost invariably handle these details. Here again the established companies will have arrangements in place, though the smart artist or manager will have held back from the contract the more lucrative territories such as North America and Japan. With a chart record there will be no shortage of offers from these territories, but each one will need to be examined and negotiated.

With a smash hit the availability of a video becomes even more crucial. There simply aren't enough hours in a day to satisfy the international demands for television exposure, and a video will at least keep the ball bouncing for a few weeks. It is occasionally, but only rarely, possible to achieve hit sales outside the home territory without cracking the home market. The expression 'big in Japan' is not just a joke or the name of one of Liverpool's finest forgotten bands. It can happen, and only a fool would ignore the possibilities. There is no formula. British bands – Bush, for example – can be multi-million sellers in America without ever being accepted in Britain while fabulously successful acts like Slade and T. Rex spent months touring the States without any real success. Even the Beatles' first few British hits were rejected by American Capitol, which is why they appeared there initially on a couple of small labels. Somebody obviously had faith and was eventually rewarded. The Beatles' first French concert at the Olympia in Paris was generally written off as a disaster, while Elton John sprang to world fame as a result of his appearances at the Troubadour in Los Angeles, where the media adored him.

Sadly, the days of a smash hit occurring from the odd radio play are virtually gone. Occasional airings on radio can generate initial interest, but to achieve full potential requires a deal of marketing skills and deep pockets. It can still be done, and every week a new star is born, as evidenced by the ever-changing charts. The trick is to maximize the initial success through professional help, which is available but which, like everything else, has a price.

Illegal fly-posting was for a time effective but has now become more difficult since the authorities can pursue the company employing the fly-poster. Nevertheless it is still popular and is probably still the domain of a shadowy figure known only as Vincent or more likely his assistant Terry the Pill. Together they had the London operation sewn up during the early seventies and, for a fee, would undertake to fly-post the entire London area. In reality this usually meant a fair number of posters appearing in the West End and the area around your offices. Any entrepreneur going into competition with Vincent and Terry was likely to find their posters torn down overnight and, while engaged in their necessarily nocturnal activities, would, more often than not, feel a tap on the shoulder followed by the gentle enquiry 'D'you like 'ospital food then?'

Marketing can be as modest as a card in a newsagent's window or as grand as a full-blown radio, television, press and poster campaign. The best answer to those who doubt its efficacy is to ask them which brand of cat or dog food they buy for their pet and why they chose it. It's for sure they didn't taste it first.

On a visit to Austin, Texas, recently, a terrific singer, backed by a wonderful band, transfixed me. The bass player's eyes constantly surveyed the room, apparently seeking out anybody not obviously enjoying the performance. You had the impression that, should you not be seen to be having a ball, he would very likely come over and give you a smack in the mouth. That's how live rock and roll should be, but, as Peel is fond of saying, with the music business now so commercially organized you are more likely to receive a highly publicized and marketed smack in the mouth.

BRIBERY, CORRUPTION AND SEX

A recent rumour circulating around this subject is that of a major record company supposedly sending a daily supply of cocaine by motor cycle messenger to one of the top disc jockeys at Radio 1. It may, of course, be true, but I have been hearing variations of this story for more years than I care to remember without ever seeing anything to substantiate it?

As a director of major and highly successful record companies and owner of a couple of smaller labels, I can honestly state for the record that I have never witnessed nor been party to any form of direct bribery. Had it happened, I would have been responsible for signing the expenses, paying the account or finding the cash, and it simply never took place. The stakes are just too high. Any disc jockey or producer at a major national radio station is very well paid and is unlikely to jeopardize his or her position for less than many thousands of pounds. One or two radio plays on one radio show is extremely unlikely to create a hit, so it would be necessary to find several corrupt broadcasters and a small fortune to have any effect. That kind of money could be better invested in an artist's career in other ways.

The situation is different in the USA where the thousands of radio stations employing thousands of presenters, many of whom are required to sell advertising space to supplement their income, can generate a regional break-out that

can be broadened out, state by state, into a national hit. In his superb book *Hit Men* Fredric Dannen provided chapter and verse of how organized crime influenced the record industry there by supplying money and drugs to broadcasters through a network of so-called independent promotion outfits. That book sent shock waves throughout the American record industry, which took immediate steps to clean up its act, though the word is that the bad guys are creeping back into the business.

Corruption in the British industry, if that is what it is, exists in a more subtle form. Obtaining radio or television exposure is in the hands of experienced pluggers. It is their job to at least try to ensure that the broadcasters hear the record or records that they are promoting. Not an easy task, given the number of new discs, each one desperate for attention, released every week of the year. Having been, at various times, possibly the least successful plugger in the business I know just how difficult this can be – and just how rude and downright offensive the recipients of this attention so often are.

To facilitate a reasonable relationship with the broadcasters, record companies arrange parties, theatre tickets, exclusive previews of new releases by hit acts, tour jackets, sweatshirts, days out at special events and, in the distant past, visits to a 'house of pleasure', along with the expected Christmas gifts, which usually consist of liquid refreshment. Almost anything in fact that does not take the form of drugs or cash.

It used to be that the promotion people would wander the corridors of Radio 1 trying to find a producer or disc jockey with a free moment to listen to the current project. This was ended when it was discovered that promotion people often outnumbered legitimate staff in the building and work was being disrupted. It then became necessary to make a formal appointment to see a producer before the jobsworth on the door would allow entry. At around this time Radio 1 instituted a playlist of records due to be featured that week, which was posted on the notice board in the reception area. This quickly became known as the 'Wailing Wall', as disappointed pluggers scanned the lists for a sight of their current projects.

I keep referring to Radio 1 in this context, since it is virtually alone among radio stations in influence. Television is another matter altogether. It has always been close to impossible to gain entry to a television station without an appointment, and the attitudes of the security staff at BBC Television Centre is legendary, with even established stars being brusquely refused admittance. Accompanying artists to an appearance on *Top of the Pops* was always a struggle. Despite the influence of MTV, that particular programme remains the pinnacle of a plugger's aspirations, and for years it was under the control of a man with a particular sexual

preference. Smart record companies would ensure that he was targeted by their best-looking young men, and a record by a pretty boy was always in with a shot, though I was never aware of anything illegal taking place. Here again the stakes are far too high. Any respectable record company even reasonably suspected of illegal activities would have to answer to shareholders if not the authorities.

Expense accounts for pluggers can be enormous but are always documented by receipts. They probably spend more on expensive lunches in a month than most folk earn in a year. And those are the most successful. By treating a producer or disc jockey to an expensive lunch at a fashionable restaurant they can at least ensure the recipient's undivided attention and hopefully establish a relationship that will stand them in good stead. Over lunch gossip will be exchanged, reputations will be demolished and the name of the current project will be mentioned almost in passing. Each party knows exactly the purpose of the lunch but it is rarely referred to.

I once saw legendary plugger Johnny Wise actually pin Tony Blackburn to a wall with his arm across Tony's throat and an unctuous smile on his face while he extolled the virtues of a particular record. When the hapless DJ eventually escaped the smile dropped from Johnny's face like a raindrop from a windowpane. It was an unpleasant experience to watch, but one could not fail to be impressed by the man's dedication. How much more successful might Tim Buckley have been with the benefit of someone like Mr Wise on his case? Little did I know that I would one day become his boss at Pye.

The late and sadly lamented Teddy Warwick, who was a senior producer at Radio 1, was fond of telling one of the great bribery stories. Out of the blue, one Monday morning he received a huge tin of whitewash followed almost immediately by a telephone call from Mr Wise enquiring whether it had arrived. Teddy confirmed the arrival of the tin and expressed some surprise and bewilderment regarding its purpose. With heavy irony Johnny pointed out that no Pye records had been played on the station that weekend, which, in his opinion, constituted a whitewash. Teddy chortled and informed his caller that, as he was in the process of whitewashing the outside of his entire house, he would be happy to arrange further non-appearances for Pye records in return for further supplies. Was that bribery or corruption?

Of course it may be that, even after a lifetime in this adult and cynical industry, I was still blue-eyed and innocent with bribery and corruption rife around me – but I cannot see how. Rather like sex, I was unaware of any particular excesses.

To paraphrase the great Sid Perelman badly, I am certain that the average employee in the music industry is at least as interested in sex as his or her counterpart in less glamorous businesses. There are groupies, to be sure, but most of those I encountered were pretty desperate creatures eager for attention from any quarter and certainly not the stuff of erotic fantasy. Here again I may just have been unaware of the action taking place around me. My assistant at CBS would always point out any lady in the building walking badly and aver that this was due to cutting her feet on a broken vial of amyl nitrate close to her bed following a night of drug-aided sexual frenzy. A bit of a stretch, I thought, when she might just have been suffering with bunions.

Sex does play a vital role in music, and many of today's male stars owe something to tight trousers and an enhanced crotch, but that is just one side of the coin. Jonathan King always referred to the then current boy band as 'Dickless Wonders' in the belief that they appealed primarily to very young girls who had no notion of or preferred not to think about male equipment. At least as many bands have directed their acts at the gay or bisexual community and artists such as kd lang and Courtney Love are evidence that it is possible for the girls to enjoy success through talent alone.

As a producer, manager and company director I was approached by any number of female artists, including one very famous model. I even managed the careers of a couple of women, but I was never aware of any sexual advances or offers. It was a somewhat different story in the realm of record promotion, where the female practitioners seemed to feel that flirting was an integral part of the game. One of these girls, who had a very famous and wealthy father, would flirt outrageously with everyone and I wondered if she enjoyed it or just found it paid off. Why she bothered I'll never know. Given a rich daddy I would have been out of there in a flash. Well, that's what I would like to believe.

Another female promoter was extremely attractive, sexy and flirtatious. She worked in the Polydor building with me and was the object of much erotic fantasy among the male staff. One day she came on major league to my deputy and invited him back to her place for an after-hours drink. In a state of some excitement the pair drove out to Muswell Hill and entered her apartment, which, it being winter, was in darkness. Switching on a low light our gal suggested that her guest relax with a drink while she went off to – you've guessed it – slip into something more comfortable. My chum barely had time to sit down before the heavy curtains were swept aside and out sprang four young men armed to the teeth with acoustic guitars who began to play at him. It was, of course, a set-up, and the group had hired her to arrange an audition in the hope of getting a contract. Embarrassed and confused, my assistant sat through a couple of dreary songs before making his excuses. There are better ways to get attention.

I seem to recall that John Peel was at that famous photographic session for the sleeve of *Electric Ladyland* by Jimi Hendrix, which featured a whole collection of naked ladies. On another occasion Peel spent an uncomfortable couple of hours sat at the opposite end of a bath to a naked woman for a sleeve picture. John kept busy replenishing the soapsuds, but his companion displayed no such modesty. The album, a compilation of tracks by various artists from our Dandelion label, was called 'There Is Some Fun Going Forward', and it is only as I write this that I understand the concept of picture and title. As a pretty famous person John was the object of a considerable degree of female attention – but then I have read that Henry Kissinger had legions of female admirers, so it is more likely to do with power and celebrity than it is to do with music. I mean – Henry Kissinger?

To close this chapter on a less than serious note and perhaps to indicate that little has changed over the years, I have to relate the story told to me many years ago by a woman of my acquaintance. She had been having a fling with one of the members of the Deep River Boys, who were one of the very first successful black groups back in the mists of time. The relationship came to an abrupt end when, sharing a room on tour with her favourite band member, he confided that the pinnacle of his sexual ambition would be to take her fully clothed from behind while she leaned out of the hotel window. Ever eager to oblige she submitted to this rather bizarre request but was mortified when, some way into the act, she saw her lover waving to her from the ground floor outside the hotel. And they said that romance was dead.

17. AUSTRALIA

AUSTRALIA

In early 1974, following my successful – but near terminally exhausting – period at CBS, and in the face of a draconian tax bill, we decided to have a look at Australia with a view to possible emigration. We had heard great tales of people in our business enjoying a new, healthy and less stressful life there and decided to check it out.

The flight to Australia takes close to twenty-four hours, but on the way out we broke the journey with a few days in Singapore and Bangkok. Singapore was very clean and unbelievably hot, but Bangkok was pure delight. The people are both beautiful and charming. The day we arrived was their New Year's Day, and everywhere we went we were daubed with a mixture of flour and water by crowds of laughing, happy souls. Our young daughter Sam literally stopped traffic as the locals poured out of shops and offices to wonder at her. And this from possibly the most beautiful people in the world. It was a truly magical few days full of laughter and beauty surrounded by more gold in the temples and in the stores than it is possible to imagine. On the day we left, very early in the morning, our waitress dropped a pile of crockery, and the entire restaurant staff, including the manager, fell about laughing. Just like in a Little Chef.

Australia was something else. We arrived in the early hours at the best hotel in Sydney, tired, hungry and somewhat apprehensive, having been told that a couple of species of local spiders were fatally poisonous with no known antidote. Upon entering the room Shurley noticed a creature halfway up the wall and enquired of the bell-boy what it might be. 'Aw, fuck me,' he shouted, springing across the room and flattening the beast with one blow. 'This room was supposed to have been fumigated!' We were then told that there was no restaurant or room service available before breakfast, which was not for several hours. Not even a cup of coffee. Welcome.

The following day we began to explore the city, which was very pretty but rather like London in the fifties with lots of Greek restaurants and espresso-coffee bars. The nation was in the grip of an election campaign, with politicians making speeches on television promising that if they were elected they would curtail the influx and influence of 'whinging Poms'. Welcome indeed.

Following some fraught negotiations with Avis, we rented a car with a severely buckled front wheel that we were assured was drivable and anyway the only one available and wobbled off to Manley Beach, which appeared to be populated by people who had lost an arm or a leg to the marauding sharks. The motel was almost empty, but when we requested a replacement for the non-functioning television in the room the manager muttered 'bloody Poms' and reluctantly wheeled in a replacement.

Having previously written to business acquaintances advising them of our visit and requesting a meeting, I began telephoning to make appointments. The first call was to the managing director of WEA in Australia, with whom I thought I had a good relationship, and we agreed to meet later that week. I then called on the CBS and Polydor offices where we had licensed Python Lee Jackson and Medicine Head, both of whom had charted in Australia. At one of these meetings, towards the end of the day, I was ushered out fairly smartly and informed that the office was closing early since the following day was a national holiday. Before I left I enquired if the company had managed to get either of our current hits on to a K-Tel compilation album and was told that this had not been possible, which was disappointing. On returning to the motel that evening one of the first television commercials I saw was for a K-Tel album featuring our two hit tracks. With a meeting planned for the following day out at WEA I assumed, since I had heard nothing from my friend, that it was going ahead despite it being a public holiday. I duly trekked out to Warners to keep the appointment and found the place locked and barred. The next day I phoned my friend who said, 'Yeah! Fancy me forgetting it was Anzac Day. Well, I'm a bit tied up for the next couple of weeks but . . .' I quietly replaced the receiver and called the airport. We left after just five days with no regrets. When you are so obviously unwelcome why hang around? I don't blame the Aussies. In fact I'm not too wild about your average Pom myself and have to admire the directness of the Australians we met. I only wish we Brits were allowed to be as honest.

18. EVERONE'S GONE TO THE MOON

LEFT TO RIGHT: JONATHAN KING'S SECRETARY, CAROL, SHURLEY AND JK, VENICE

EVERYONE'S GONE TO THE MOON

The real Jonathan King is very different from the public image he projects. He is charming, witty, great fun to be around and one of the most honourable men you could ever hope to meet. So don't believe everything you read.

After we returned from Australia I took a call from JK suggesting that we meet for lunch to discuss my taking on the job of managing director of his UK Records label. My only knowledge of him at that time was of a sneering, opinionated record producer and disc jockey who had parlayed a hit, 'Everyone's Gone To the Moon', into a career. Before accepting the invitation I called John Peel for advice. 'You'll like him,' he said, and that was good enough for me.

Over an expensive lunch JK offered me complete freedom to run the company as I saw fit, with the proviso that he had sole responsibility for A & R. How could I lose? Lunch drifted into dinner and, after agreeing generous terms, JK suggested that the next day I should go into the office and introduce myself to the staff, as he was leaving immediately for New York where he had another office.

The next day I duly turned up at a scruffy little office near Tottenham Court Road and introduced myself to the staff of three as their new boss. They did not seem particularly surprised – but then one of them was JK's brother Andy, who was no doubt used to some odd behaviour. Andy was in charge of radio promotion and, though very able, he was considerably in the shadow of his famous brother. The office boy, Jeff, who also had a famous brother, Keith Chegwin, spent most of his day holed up in a cupboard with dirty magazines. Jeff eventually became a successful record producer and publisher, while his brother drifted off into a period of drink and obscurity but is now, happily, back on our screens.

I heard nothing more from Jonathan for about a month, by which time we had a chart entry with 'I'd Love You To Want Me' by Lobo, which, despite having been a hit in the USA, had originally been released in Britain without success by Philips through Phonogram. Somehow JK had persuaded them to let him have the rights to the record on the basis that he could make it into a hit and thus allow Philips and Phonogram to get the benefit of increased album sales. Try doing that now!

JK called again from Peru or somewhere and, on learning that we had a chart record, suggested that we were coping admirably and that his presence was not needed. A couple of weeks later he called again from some other exotic place and, on being told that we now had two records in the charts, he once more decreed that we appeared not to need him around. The second hit was by First Class, which was a made-up band of session men. By the time JK called again we had three records in the Top Twenty, which is pretty good for an organization consisting of four dedicated souls and an absentee owner. Still Jonathan felt his attendance to be superfluous and continued on his travels.

As part of learning about my job I needed to view the contracts and, while perusing the distribution agreement with Decca, noticed that they had omitted to take up their options for the current year. This meant that to all intents and purposes we were out of contract and open to offers. With three records in the charts, UK was the hottest current label and likely offers could be measured in millions. When next JK called I apprised him of the situation in some excitement. His response was that if I was unhappy with the efforts of Decca I should approach them and try to rectify the situation rather than just penalize them because some poor clerk had forgotten to send an option letter. He was quite aware of the millions he was passing up but was prepared to act honourably and respect an agreement signed in good faith. I truly cannot conceive of another executive in our business taking the same approach and only hoped that I, too, could learn from JK's decency. (He will probably hate that bit of information being made public as he has always worked at and cherished his reputation as the Antichrist.)

The next time I heard from the boss we had four records in the Top Twelve and had no further new releases lined up. It was now a full three months since our initial, and so far only, meeting, and JK felt it was time to get together. Not in the office, however. He suggested we meet in Venice and that I should bring Shurley at his expense. Venice was wonderful, and JK was in magnificent form. He has an ability to touch complete strangers and charm them. Everywhere we went he carried a small pile of books that waiters in cafés and restaurants would carefully take from him and place on adjacent chairs before attending to his every wish. Not because he was famous – I doubt that anybody in Venice knew who he was. Yet he would stop at outdoor tables and ask diners if he might sample whatever they were eating; nobody was ever offended by or refused him.

To celebrate our last night in that most beautiful city, where no motor cars are allowed and conversations are can take place at normal volume, JK arranged dinner at one of the best restaurants. He arrived in a stunning white suit that he referred to as his 'Death in Venice' outfit.

Back in London JK drove everywhere in his white Rolls and never to my knowledge used a parking meter. He would always park up on the pavement, and I never saw him get a ticket. Perhaps it's like that for all Rolls drivers, but I doubt it. About once a month he would hold audition sessions at another office where hopefuls would turn up with cassettes of their efforts. They were usually greeted with 'Hello. Who are you and who do you hope to be?' – a somewhat daunting but friendly greeting. Often there would be a line stretching out of the door and down a couple of flights of stairs, but each cassette was listened to for about twenty seconds before being rejected. Jonathan believed that he could tell a hit inside ten seconds and allowed a further ten seconds for grace before ushering them out of the door. He further believed that by taking instant decisions he was saving a lot of time and had at least a 50 per cent chance of being right. Would that more 'Um and Ah' people would be so decisive.

One of the strangest meetings I have ever attended occurred following the next big hit from 10CC, 'Wall Street Shuffle'. Decca – which distributed UK and were responsible for all marketing costs – was owned by Sir Edward Lewis, a gentleman from the old school who was very fond of JK. Sir Edward also owned Decca Radar together with a huge empire of radio and television manufacturing and heaven knows what else. Having had a run of hits, 10CC and their manager Harvey Lisberg – whom JK always referred to as 'Harvey Calling' since that was how he always announced himself on the telephone – decided to play a concert to promote the release of the new album. Not surprisingly, they asked us to supply a few thousand handbills to publicize the album; an unusually modest request by today's standards and one I passed on to the Decca marketing department for action. Hearing nothing and with the concert dates approaching I once more called Decca, believing that perhaps my request had been mislaid. Not so. They were awaiting approval for the expenditure from Sir Edward. I found this hard to believe and impossible to accept, since the total bill was unlikely to exceed £40. 'Just tell me yes or no, and if necessary I will pay for the things out of petty cash,' I demanded to no avail. They were unable to take such an important decision without Sir Edward's approval – and this was the company that had the Rolling Stones, the Moody Blues and God knew how many other international smash-hit acts on the roster. Unable to believe the information, I sought a meeting with Sir Edward and hustled over the river to the magnificent building he owned on the Albert Embankment.

A uniformed commissionaire met me at the door and ushered me into one of a pair of lifts, the other one of which was clearly marked 'For the use of the chairman'. The commissionaire confirmed that indeed the only time that particular lift was allowed to be used by anybody but the chairman was during a Test Match at Lord's when the chairman, naturally, would be otherwise engaged.

Sir Edward occupied a huge office overlooking the Thames, and he sat behind an impressive desk surrounded by framed photographs of himself with various members of the Royal Family. He was most gracious and polite with that top-drawer manner that effortlessly made me feel like a small spiv. He was, nevertheless, some way into his dotage and launched into long-drawn-out tales of his past successes when he was forced to fly tons of Vera Lynn records into Britain from the USA to meet the wartime demand and was granted special dispensation from the government to so do in order to keep up morale. He followed this with tales of the massive orders for Al Martino treated in the same way owing to a post-war shellac shortage, as my eyes glazed over and a leap into the river below started to appeal. When at last I was able to introduce the subject of £40 worth of hand bills and the ability of his marketing staff to take such minor decisions, he reminded me that he was in fact the chairman of the company and quite able to take command of such matters. A wonderful example of British management in full flow. Not many years later the empire disintegrated and Decca Records, which for years had been one of only two companies controlling the British record industry, was bought by Polygram. Very sad. I think I eventually bought the handbills for 10CC out of petty cash.

Having been in charge of marketing at CBS, where Dick Asher demanded huge advance orders for relatively minor albums and made life miserable if they were not achieved, I was pleased at last to have an album of 10CC's greatest hits to market and an opportunity to elevate UK Records into an album label. I reckoned without Decca which, despite my screams and pleas, seemed content with an initial sale of about five thousand albums. They believed that demand would grow over the weeks and months. At CBS we would have targeted an initial sale of a hundred thousand and expected to double that within a month of release. Decca wouldn't even print more than five thousand sleeves in anticipation of demand. Hardly surprising that 10CC was wooed away by another label.

With the hits still flowing in Britain, JK asked me to look at the US operation, where Decca's subsidiary, London Records, were our licensees. That was even more of an uphill struggle and, compared to contemporary outfits such as Atlantic or CBS, it was close to impossible to see how they could survive. They were living off the Moody Blues and Al Green without giving anything back. Still, we had a great time in New York where we went to plush eateries such as the Four Seasons with JK wearing a tuxedo and tennis shoes long before that became fashionable. We also went to a show starring my old friend Harry Chapin, who introduced us to his dad who was playing in the pit orchestra. In JK's absence I stayed in his West 57th Street apartment, which had numerous security locks and a cable television with a hundred channels. They were almost all crap and not anything to look forward to.

One of my first tasks was to meet up with the company lawyer Paul Marshal, who Jonathan warned me was very expensive and charged by the hour. It was, nevertheless, important that we meet and that I be briefed on the American situation. Time was indeed money, so I set my stopwatch as the meeting commenced and stopped it whenever we were interrupted, which was just about every minute. Paul took call after call from some of the biggest names in music and films, advising, commiserating and counselling. At the conclusion of our two-hour meeting my stopwatch informed me that we had spent a total of twenty minutes on UK Records business, and I mentioned to Paul that we would expect to be charged just for this time. We got along fine after that, and it amused the hell out of Jonathan.

As we progressed back in Britain Jonathan was a fund of innovative ideas – most of which were unworkable, but his enthusiasm was infectious. He still made forays into the studio and emerged with recordings by bizarrely named invented groups such as 100 Tons and a Feather. As JK once famously said on his television show, 'Nobody ever got rich by overestimating the intelligence of the British public.' He was subsequently inundated with sacks of mail all agreeing that 'they' were stupid. At the first sniff of a hit everybody – well, the three of us – would be encouraged to 'hit the phones' and call every radio producer, disc jockey, record dealer and columnist to try to bring it home. There were, naturally, a number of failures but enough hits to ensure that both Jonathan and myself were in some demand.

While at CBS I had been asked by a very senior colleague, whose wife had made an unexpected office appearance, to go to a nearby hotel and present his apologies to a certain lady who would be waiting for him in the bar. This I did with some reluctance and forgot about it. While I was working for Jonathan I received at home by registered mail an anonymous letter full of foul language and accusing me of having an affair with the wife of a well-known music publisher. The letter further pointed out that the publisher in question had friends from his early days in Chicago who would be only too happy to arrange my sudden death. I figured it to be from some crank, showed the letter to my wife and threw it away, somewhat surprised that it should have been sent by registered mail. The next morning a similar letter arrived addressed to Shurley, and this I took to the police. Threatening me is one thing but never include my wife. It is extraordinary just how upsetting a poison pen letter can be – and these were truly venomous.

Later that morning I took a call from my former CBS colleague asking if I had received a letter from the publisher named. It transpired that the publisher, who was quite elderly, had in fact written the letters after having his wife followed and it being reported that I was the object of her liaisons. I only met the lady for about thirty seconds, which may go to prove something, though I'm not sure what, other than never to get involved in other people's lives. The ex-colleague suggested a meeting with his attorneys, but I wanted no further exposure to his complicated personal life – mind you, having met his wife on several occasions I could well understand the reasons for his dalliance. She was the worst kind of executive wife, one who went out of her way to humiliate those lower down the pecking order. In a rare moment of candour she once confided to me that she kept her hair in perfect order by tightly wrapping her head in Scotch tape every night upon retiring. It must have been like sleeping with human flypaper.

At UK I began to get phone calls from Larry Uttal, who had had phenomenal success with Bell Records before selling the company and was about to set up his new label, Private Stock. He called regularly with increased offers of salary and perks that eventually included substantial stock options. All this on the strength of my reputation as a fixer of hits, as we had never actually met. When we did eventually meet it was some months later at MIDEM, the music-biz trade fair in Cannes, where JK introduced us and Larry gave no hint of recognition until I reminded him that he had offered me stock in his company. There truly is nothing like a few hits to give you a reputation either as an artist, a producer, a writer or as an executive.

In Cannes Shurl and I stayed at a fairly modest hotel overlooking the beach front, while JK stayed, as ever, at the hugely expensive Negresco in Nice, driving along the coast to Cannes in the white Roller every day. He always travelled in style, and his secretary Carol always booked him into the Negresco even when he was broke. She was amused and a touch concerned one year to take a call from JK in Nice asking her to phone the manager of the hotel to ask him to rearrange the room since it was not up to the usual standard. At the time JK was severely overdrawn with little prospect of change. For some enchanted people life is simply too short to travel anything but first class.

As we were due to leave Cannes JK arranged to collect us and drive to Nice airport. Shurley is always late, so Jonathan parked the Rolls squarely in the middle of the single-lane road in front of the hotel and watched with considerable amusement as the local drivers, being quite unable to pass, screamed and hooted while traffic backed up for at least a mile. When Shurley finally emerged JK simply smiled and waved at the enraged motorists as we progressed to the cause of their rage. Grandly we drove off, with Shurl and me cowering in the back and JK exchanging pleasantries. At the Negresco we encountered a sad sight as JK mounted the pavement to park between the hotel and the rows of cars lining the road. It was Richard Burton dressed in a camp little fur coat and leading two fussy little dogs. He was very drunk and had great difficulty negotiating the glass doors to the hotel. When he finally worked out how to gain entrance he handed the dog leads to a porter, snarled abuse at him and lurched off. Tragic really and, as JK commented, a demonstration of the acid of fame dripping on to a soul.

A period of high farce was when Phonogram tried to lure away 10CC and Jonathan took to staking out their offices late into the night to see who was visiting whom. On a couple of occasions I was asked to join him on his lonely and secretive vigil. He was not too difficult to find since the stakeouts were conducted from the comfort of the Rolls – registration number JK100 – parked as ever up on the pavement while JK watched television in the back seat. Somehow it would not surprise me to learn that our security services operate in a similarly discreet fashion.

Phonogram did, of course, win the battle for 10CC but were forced to pay our man an override royalty on the massively successful singles and albums that were to follow. At this time our deal with Decca was close to ending, and we were in need of a new licensee, but without our only established album act UK Records was again reliant exclusively on the energy and ability of the chairman. We finalized a deal with Polydor Records but I believe that both JK and I had started to lose a bit of enthusiasm for manufactured product.

With the situation worsening at CBS, Dick Asher took to calling me every couple of weeks to ask me to return on pretty much any terms I cared to name. Quite often JK would pick up the phone and say, 'Hello, Dick. Are you still trying to get Clive back?' It was impossible to embarrass Dick, however, who was, to say the least, single-minded. Eventually I began to think that Jonathan might be losing interest in UK Records, so, since the company would be nothing without him, I began to consider Dick's proposals. When he told me that he was returning to America and leaving Obie in charge of the British operation I agreed to return.

It was with some sadness I left UK Records. They never achieved any great success in the years that followed, but I put that down to a diminution of Jonathan's enthusiasm rather than any lack of marketing flair. I probably had more sheer fun working for JK than at any other time in my business life. He is a genuine one of a kind and thoroughly deserving of all his success. We have run into each other from time to time and he is still as engaging as ever. He spent some time as a consultant to Walter Yetnikof in America, which must have been, to say the least, testing, and he had his BBC television programmes and a column in the *Sun* to keep him busy. The last time I heard him working he was hosting a show on Talk Radio and being very nice to callers. I do hope that was just a passing mood, as JK's rudeness and acerbic wit remain a national treasure.

Since I originally wrote this chapter JK has been accused and convicted of crimes that allegedly occurred over a quarter of a century ago – in fact during the time we worked together – and he is currently residing at Her Majesty's pleasure for the next seven years. I am happy to state for the record that at no time at all during the close relationship that was then in place between Jonathan and my family were I or Shurley ever aware of any inappropriate behaviour. He remains a gentleman and, in a recent correspondence, has assured me that, despite the horrendous injustice, he is determined to come out of the experience a better person and that the next half-century will be 'even better than the first'. I believe him absolutely.

Anyway, as they say, you can never go back. But go back to CBS I did, and after a few months the company was back on track as market leader.

During this time I was handed the task of launching Bruce Springsteen upon a largely unsuspecting British public in what became known as the hype of the decade. Actually it wasn't that much of a hype. A few fairly dramatic posters around London, a strictly limited supply of cheap tour jackets, a couple of adverts in the music press, a couple of concerts at London's Hammersmith Odeon and the media hyped him themselves. If only it was always that easy.

Twenty years on, 'the Boss' goes from strength to strength, but back then he had released a couple of commercial duds and *Born to Run* was his last best shot – with a little help from a quote by Jon Landau, then a writer for *Rolling Stone*, along the lines of 'I have seen the future of rock and roll'. Jon later became Bruce's manager.

Those who had seen Springsteen performing live in the USA had been truly impressed, and among them was Mike Appleton, the producer of the *Old Grey Whistle Test* – the most influential 'serious' rock programme on British television at the time – who offered to film one of the Odeon concerts for later transmission on the BBC. This was a bit of a breakthrough. Appleton did point out that Bruce's act was very low-lit and would require the provision of especially sensitive cameras to capture the full magic. When the great man finally arrived I was introduced to his manager, Mike Appel, who turned out to be the most unpleasant person I have ever encountered – before or since – and that's some achievement in an industry swarming with creeps and ego-driven crazies. I relayed to him the television producer's requests for super-sensitive cameras, with, of course, the assurance that the rental charges would be paid by the company. This produced the foulest, most disgusting stream of personal abuse I have ever heard in a lifetime of living with masters of the art – let alone had directed at me.

It seemed that Mr Appel believed that he and he alone knew absolutely everything about everything and all others – and this writer in particular – knew nothing about anything, though he said, or rather screamed, it in much more colourful language. Rather than come to blows, I immediately left the meeting and telephoned the head of CBS in New York with a request that I be taken off the case, since we were obviously incompatible and I feared that blood might flow. The incredible response was – and if you heard this in a movie you would not believe your ears – 'If that man demands that you take one million dollars, tear them up and throw them out of your window you have my full authority to do it.' I later discovered that Bruce was halfway into recording *Born to Run* when somebody at CBS, thinking of the earlier unsuccessful albums, got cold feet and pulled the plug on further recordings. His manager had financed the completion of the album by selling all his personal possessions and even his apartment. The album was reluctantly released in America and quickly set the charts alight, leaving the CBS execs with egg on their faces and Mr Appel's grip firmly on their balls.

Swallowing a certain amount of pride, but taking care not to have anything further to do with the monster manager from hell, I returned to the fray, and eventually the sellout concerts were filmed. It was a very hectic and taxing time, as Springsteen was only one of a number of important current projects, so that by the time we took our seats at the Odeon I was exhausted. So tired in fact that halfway through the performance Shurley nudged me with the information that I had been fast asleep and snoring, as had our two companions, Obie and Andy Williams, who at least could offer the excuse of jet-lag.

It was, in truth, a lousy performance and one that Bruce hated. He ceremoniously burned the film footage immediately after the show. Too dark I believe. At the backstage party I was asked for the only time in my career to provide a girl for an artist. It seemed that one of the band was in some need. Since pimping was never my speciality I was unable to help. It all ended happily, however. Both the single and the album charted here, Bruce sacked his manager and went on to become one of the world's most respected performers.

I thought I had a good relationship with Obie and wished him a happy Christmas as he went off on one of his exotic holidays while calling in at the New York head office, Black Rock, on the way. The next day, just a couple of days before Christmas, he suddenly returned, came straight to my office and said, 'The people at Black Rock said that one of us has to go and, me being a good Jew, it's you that's walking, not me.'

In shock I asked him what was the reason, and all he would say was, 'Ask Dick. He came back on the same flight and will be here shortly.'

When Dick eventually arrived he had no explanation beyond saying that some day I would laugh about it. I pointed out that, with no reasonable explanation offered, I would sue. CBS agreed and even suggested a figure. Dick then went further, offering me the choice of CBS jobs in three other countries and, as head of Columbia Records International, he offered me managing directorships in Canada or Australia. When I refused he offered to set up and finance my own operation in Los Angeles. Baffled, I pointed out that he was firing me and at the same time offering more senior positions. He agreed that it was an odd situation and suggested that I discuss the matter with the chairman Walter Yetnikof, who was due in the following day.

Meanwhile I cleared my desk and telephoned Shurley, asking her to come and collect me. Great stuff just days before Christmas. Walter did call and professed himself as baffled as me. He did offer to call his chums at other companies in the USA and, sure enough, a few came through with job offers, though none was suitable. I got enough money in settlement to pay off my entire mortgage and soon found new employment, but to this day have never received an explanation. Some idiot even suggested that I had been 'caught with my hand in the till', but a stiff note from my solicitor elicited a fulsome apology. My hunch is that Obie, who was the most devious person I have ever known, feared or resented my presence and got rid of me. I've seen him do the same thing to a number of managing directors at CBS and again later when he became chairman of Polygram. Oddly enough, we remained friends, but sometimes it doesn't pay to be seen to be too good at your job when you work for nervous Americans – or Brits for that matter.

CBS Records subsequently became a subsidiary of Sony and is currently one of the very few profitable record companies in the world. With that fantastic back catalogue and the advent of CDs it should be difficult not to remain successful, but all too many other great companies have achieved that dubious distinction. I value the time I spent there, despite the traumas, but discovered that I still had much to learn.

SALES CONFERENCES AND MIDEM

Record companies' annual sales conferences usually take place in late August or early September and, for various reasons, are the high point of the year. They are the opportunity to present to the sales personnel and the attendant trade media the important new releases that will hopefully be available over the following three months leading up to the Christmas bonanza period.

The large corporations will invite employees from all around the world, arrange accommodation in first-class hotels and spend huge amounts of time and money to ensure that everybody feels part of a team, working together for the greater good.

Every conference is preceded by months of frenetic activity by middle management, label managers and A & R personnel trying to schedule important new recordings for pre-view, together with artwork and accompanying notes to ensure that the sales team are well equipped to spread the word. Wherever possible, artists are invited along to meet and dazzle the assembled company, in the expectation that the personal touch will generate extra effort and commitment. Those artists with new product to release and the – increasingly rare – ability to perform live are invited to perform a short set to the largely uncritical audience, which, of course, involves the provision of sound equipment, lighting and proper staging. With the

current emphasis on video it is also crucial to all releases that the accompanying videos are ready, which entails discussions and negotiations with directors, producers and studios.

Enormous pressure is exerted upon artists to finish recording on time, on sleeve designers, on the video producers, on managers to finalize promotion activity and, of course, on the company label managers to coordinate and present the packages. A major company will have upwards of a hundred releases to preview over the few days of the conference, and the weeks leading up to it are a tightrope of tension, excitement, hard work and long hours, frustration, sleepless nights and the occasional nervous breakdown. The sales people, for whom all this activity is generated, are generally unaware of these efforts and tend to treat the gatherings as opportunities to get drunk, laid and ask awkward questions.

Conferences in North America are even more sophisticated affairs and reach a level of indoctrination quite outside the experience of the average Brit. Great artists appear, there is much political manoeuvring among the executives and the sales people are encouraged into a frenzy of company worship. I recall a salesman tottering with the aid of crutches on to the stage at a theatre in San Francisco to receive the 'Salesman of the Year' award. In a voice throbbing with emotion, he accepted the award and hobbled off the stage to ecstatic applause. He returned moments later to grab the microphones and say to the assembled disciples, 'If there is any one of you out there who does not, every morning of his life, look in the mirror and thank God for working for Columbia Records, then I tell that person to leave this theatre now, take a taxi to the middle of the Golden Gate Bridge, stop the taxi and throw your fucking self off.' The few Brits in the audience shifted uncomfortably and looked at each other in horror as the theatre erupted with seemingly genuine glee.

On another occasion the Columbia corporate machine was in full flow with a triple-screen presentation of the various aspects of Columbia corporate activity, including, of course, television, radio, music, musical instruments, toys and other merchandise. As the cameras panned in to show the massive output of Columbia Books, the publishing wing, two black promotion men seated in front of us, resplendent in Afros and gold chains, could contain themselves no longer. Leaping out of their seats and giving each other high fives they hollered in unison, 'Let's read.'

The entertainment on these occasions is often magnificent. In Toronto in 1975 we had full sets from stars of the calibre of – an admittedly somewhat muted – Paul Simon with full orchestra, along with Harold Melvin and the Blue Notes. The leading country stars perform in a separate place and are accompanied by an immaculate group of the top session men. The Columbia machine really can deliver.

Despite the availability and superb professionalism of the artists on show, the real entertainment for many of the executives is the sight of so many of their colleagues deeply involved in the double-dealing, back-slapping and political chicanery that is apparently essential to keep a career on track in the USA. At one point I was summoned to meet one of the great and good only to be stood in a line of directors who all but curtsied when introduced to the great man. Following this, I was soundly admonished by my chairman for having the effrontery actually to engage the godhead in a short conversation. I forget who the man in question was, but he was certainly important enough to strike everybody dumb as he progressed as if on wheels along the line of sycophants.

The sales conference I enjoyed most was one at Stratford-upon-Avon, which I attended while at CBS. There I had the great pleasure and privilege of meeting one of the very few true giants of the music industry, Goddard Lieberson. Much has been written of Goddard – or 'God' for short – and how he financed and recorded great musicals like *My Fair Lady*, his nurturing of major classical talent like Leonard Bernstein, his knowledge of and fondness for jazz and his all-round charm, wit and sophistication. Dave Brubeck told me how, as a struggling jazz musician, he had been courted by Columbia Records and arrived to discuss a contract only to be confronted by a team of lawyers, accountants and A & R men. Goddard headed the group and, on learning that Dave had no legal representation, offered to switch sides and act on Dave's behalf in the negotiations. How could the jazz man refuse? Goddard physically moved to the other side of the conference table and negotiated what was then the most lucrative agreement ever offered to a jazz musician.

At the time of the Stratford conference, which was my first for the company, Clive Davis had just been very publicly fired and Goddard had been dragged out of retirement to hold the fort until a replacement could be found. There was great anticipation surrounding his visit, and he managed to exceed even his majestic reputation. Tall, slender, white-haired and dressed to kill, he bounded out of the limo smiling, shaking hands and exuding that special kind of charismatic magic usually associated with the most successful movie stars or politicians. Speaking entirely without notes and addressing several hundred total strangers, he managed to be the wittiest, most forceful speaker I have ever seen or heard. It was with considerable trepidation that I followed him on to the stage to give the keynote speech and, with one eye on the great man, outlined my strategy for securing Columbia's place as a leader in the race for singles success. With a vast catalogue of well-established American artists to draw upon, CBS UK's album success was virtually guaranteed, but the British company was in danger of becoming complacent and needed, I felt, the danger and excitement of a full-blooded attack upon the singles market. I was delighted that Mr Lieberson was the first to shake my hand and warmly congratulate me on the speech. My admiration for him was to be confirmed when I found out that Shurley, who had driven me to the conference and had been introduced to Goddard briefly in the elevator before driving on to Yorkshire, encountered him a little while later at a zebra crossing in town. There he addressed her by name and wished her a good journey. That is style.

By contrast, a few days after this, Goddard, Dick Asher, Obie and I were driven to lunch in Soho by Dick's driver in the company Rolls. The driver was instructed to return at 2.30 to take us back to the office for further meetings before Goddard flew back to the States later that afternoon. At half past two there was no car or driver and, after an anxious period of hopping from foot to foot and peering around corners, we eventually returned to the office by taxi, late and with schedules in disarray. Eventually the driver walked past Dick's open office door and, on being asked with some severity just where the hell he had been, responded that Mrs Asher had needed the car for a bit of shopping. Dick was always, in his own words, 'a nervous Jew' and at that moment probably saw his professional future disintegrate.

Even with the best of intentions and careful planning, not every sales conference works out, as I discovered when I was at Pye.

Following a run of hits from Barry White, Gladys Knight, the Real Thing, Melba Moore, Sheer Elegance and others, it appeared that the main thrust of our hit acts happened to be black and this, we figured, would be an appropriate theme for the annual sales conference. It seemed a good idea at the time to link it all together under the title of 'Black Umbrella' with appropriate brollies, folders and sales paraphernalia for the salesmen.

The presentation was well received and introduced by Jim Davidson, who was just starting out and happy to appear before Louis Benjamin, who was also boss of the London Palladium. The other smart idea was to arrange a reception at Shepperton Studios and invite all of the club disc jockeys that had been so pivotal to our success. Big mistake.

The regional promotion people invited local club jocks to the party and laid on coach transportation. The problems arose when the first couple of coaches arrived and disgorged a few dozen young men who gave every appearance of never having seen food or alcoholic beverages in their miserable young lives. Within minutes they decimated the place, ate all the beautifully prepared food and became legless. In next to no time we ran out of food, drink and promotion packs, which were ground into the floor as further coaches full of hungry, thirsty and enraged DJs arrived looking for freebies and a good time.

In desperation I sent out to the local off-licence for further supplies, while the other directors (who had carefully organized private stashes) looked on and enjoyed my obvious distress. The Real Thing and Greg Edwards were there, and it is to their everlasting credit that they managed to retain their good humour amid the mayhem.

The last straw was when a Mancunian disc jockey stood in front of me, his face obscured by cream – save for the two green candles emerging from his nose – swaying perilously and threatening never to play another Pye record in his life. 'Is that a promise?' I snapped and swept out leaving others to deal with the mess. Not my finest hour.

As mentioned earlier, when it comes to the press it is not possible to overestimate the amount of liquor required if the media are to remain friendly. Just like starting a new business venture, triple your budget and never expect civilized behaviour.

Perhaps the best ever sales conference story occurred in Hawaii when Michael Jackson's *Thriller* was in full flow and selling millions of copies. The top executives from around the world met for a week and agreed that the smartest thing they could do would be to stay there and do nothing in case, by returning, they might inhibit the apparently unstoppable sales of the album. That's a true story and says a lot about sales conferences, executives and the power of a smash hit.

MIDEM (or Marché International de l'Edition Musicale), the world's biggest music-industry fair, takes place every January in Cannes – it is also one of the best ligs in the biz. On my way home one year I was about to board a plane at Nice airport when my arm was grabbed by a fairly prominent young music publisher. 'Sandie Shaw is on your flight,' he said in a state of some agitation. 'Can you please tell her that she is going off with my tickets and credit cards and I have no money to pay for the car, the hotel or the flight home?'

I found Sandie, in first class, of course, and explained the situation as her erstwhile companion waved frantically from the tarmac. She peered keenly out of the window, contemplated briefly, then, with a barely perceptible shrug, leaned back, closed her eyes and said, 'Fuck him.'

I was reminded of this story recently when I heard the star relating how she had become a Buddhist in a Radio 4 interview and now offers counselling. What you see in the wunnerful world of the music biz is very rarely what you get.

MIDEM attracts thousands of music people to the French Riviera, ostensibly to meet and conduct international business – but mostly to get laid, stoned, drunk and ripped off. The Palais des Festivals – where they also hold the Cannes Film Festivals – becomes a huge bazaar, where all of the people you have been trying to avoid all year eventually track you down and try to pick your pockets. You, in turn, are, of course, trying to find and pick the pockets of all those people who have been avoiding you all year. Does that sound like fun?

The major companies like WEA and Polygram rent expensively decorated and furnished stands in order to meet up and negotiate with clients old and new the deals that can have a dramatic effect upon artists' careers. The smaller companies also rent booths and pretend that the world is beating a path to their door. Nobody is fooled, but the organizers and the hotels and the hookers make mountains of money, and the participants can claim vast sums in expenses for pretending to be working.

Of course there is some work done by thrusting independents such as Beechwood, Pinnacle and Windsong, who take export orders for records that are only available in Britain. One year I was fortunate to be in the company of one of the truly great men of the industry, Nesuhi Ertegun, on the Warner/Atlantic/Elektra stand. Sons of the Turkish ambassador to America, Nesuhi and his brother Ahmet built Atlantic Records into one of the all-time excellent record labels before selling out to the mighty Warners. In the early seventies Atlantic had much of the cream of the world talent, including Cream, Aretha, Led Zeppelin and Crosby, Stills, Nash and Young, so just about every record company in the world wanted a piece. Nesuhi, who was by then in his sixties, saw everybody and greeted each visitor by their first name with genuine warmth and a friendly hug.

Starting at nine in the morning, with appointments sometimes scheduled for as little as four minutes, he sailed through the day renegotiating detailed and complex contracts without ever referring to notes. Millions of dollars were committed, and in one memorable instance an old sparring partner was squeezed into the schedule for an appointment lasting only one minute, though he was not made aware of the brevity. At the end of a very long and stressful day Nesuhi was as fresh as a daisy and I was shattered. That kind of education is without price.

An amusing event occurred at one point in the day when I repaired to the men's room where I was quietly singing to myself while washing my hands. Nesuhi appeared at my side and asked if I had ever considered singing as a career. This from the man who recorded Ray Charles and Otis. Ten years earlier I would have killed to hear those words, but it never happens when you need it.

Most evenings at MIDEM feature a black-tie concert, where emerging acts perform live to an international audience in the expectation that their careers will expand into other markets. The only one of these very showbiz events I ever attended featured Lesley Gore on the comeback trail after the barren years that followed 'It's My Party'. It doesn't always work.

One year I travelled to Cannes in the company of a very young Elton John and his equally young manager Steve Brown. Elton was a sensation at the airport, in his colourful ensemble and platform boots, and had just broken through in the USA with his first smash hit, but he was still virtually unknown in continental Europe and the rest of the world. The MIDEM concert was to be the platform from which his international

career was to be launched. A couple of nights later I was taking a midnight stroll along the beautiful Cannes seafront and saw Elton clomping along La Croisette in floods of tears. Apparently he had been due to top the bill at that evening's concert but the performer who was playing second top billing had refused to stop playing. After two hours the audience had left and Elton never got to play. He was convinced that his chance of international stardom had gone for ever.

One of the attractions of Cannes in MIDEM week is the horde of good-looking hookers who descend on the town to service the free-spending artists and executives. Many solicit business from the driving seats of open-topped Mercedes, and it's a rare man indeed who is not at least momentarily flattered to be accosted by a beautiful girl in a beautiful car. It is, however, a fairly well-kept secret that many of these beautiful young ladies are in fact beautiful young men. One very famous former lead singer of a hit group, who made a successful move to executive status, learned this the hard way. In a moment of commercial passion, after money had changed hands, he ran his fingers through the young lady's hair only to have it all come off in his hand and be faced with a fairly miffed transvestite. He refuses to divulge what happened next.

Another year this same fellow indulged a fantasy in Cannes by engaging the services of two hookers to share his bed. Rather than fulfilling an erotic dream, he describes how the two ladies chatted to each other throughout the fairly brief engagement. Not understanding French, our chum deduced that they were discussing what they were planning to eat that evening and how it was to be cooked. He was virtually ignored, except for the financial arrangements, and does not recommend the experience.

On another occasion a whole group of Warner executives was invited to dinner at one of Cannes' most exclusive restaurants for a clan get-together. It was a large party that included various company lawyers and directors of the publishing and record divisions. Though informal, it was very much a family affair, and so it was with some surprise that we discovered that one of the group, who is now a very successful artist manager and must only be referred to as X, chose to invite a local lady who could most politely be referred to as a 'party girl'. The young woman spoke little English, and her presence rather upset one of the WEA top brass Phil Rose, who took it upon himself to score a few points off the hapless X.

Over dinner Phil decided to lure the lady away from X with numerous references to the imminent arrival of 'Frank', who would be filming in Cannes and who was looking for a number of local girls for small parts. X never had a chance, as his partner for the evening turned her full attention to the man who just might get her a part in a new Sinatra movie. I imagine it's a line that has been well worked.

On the walk back to the hotel arm in arm with his new partner, Phil confided to X that he suffered from an intermittent sexual problem, inasmuch as the essential bit of physical equipment was moody and occasionally prone to failure. Would he, X, that is, please wait in the hotel lobby while Phil took the young lady up to his room? In the event that, having made a start, he was unable to complete the engagement he would call down to seek assistance. Incredibly our man accepted – the climb up the corporate ladder is not without sacrifice – and hung around the lobby while the rest of us pretended to bid each other goodnight. In fact we all trooped up to Phil Rose's suite, where we sat in darkness in the room adjoining the bedroom trying to stifle giggles.

The bedroom contained two single beds. Tony Roberts, who ran the WEA publishing operation in London, slid under the covers of the bed furthest from the door while Phil's new partner – and now co-conspirator – allowed herself to be partially disrobed in the half-light. After a decent interval Phil called X on the house phone and told him that, as he had feared, he had been unable to satisfy the young lady, who was now seriously aroused and in need of satisfaction. Would our man hurry upstairs and oblige?

He would, of course, and was met at the door by the partially dressed beauty who immediately began to undress him while murmuring presumably naughty French words of encouragement. In no time at all our boy, naked except for his little black socks, flung himself on to the unoccupied bed ready to sacrifice his honour for the company good. At that point Tony sprang out of the other bed and switched on the lights as about a dozen of us piled into the room whooping 'Surprise' and smacking the company stand-in on his hairy naked arse.

In fact X took it all in good spirit and later claimed that he had eventually bedded the lady. When questioned whether he had in fact spotted Tony in the adjoining bed, he replied that he had been aware of a third party but had assumed that it had been his boss, who perhaps got off on that kind of thing. A real team player, X, and his career goes from strength to strength.

Every year people return from MIDEM with similar tales of drunken madness, but it remains a good place to sell your wares, establish contacts and generally fly the flag. The bar at the Martinez has certainly been the scene of countless deals with millions of dollars, pounds, francs, marks and yen negotiated to the sound of popping champagne corks. Why the people involved choose to conduct so much business there rather than in the comparative sanity and sanctity of an office is beyond me. But then I'm a bit of a miserable old sod who has managed to keep some of the money I made, rather than throw it all away trying to impress my peers. Different strokes . . . ?

A few of the truly high-flyers hire yachts for the duration of the festival, but as a general rule they are to be avoided. There is no easy escape from a yacht, and all too often those who put on the biggest front are the ones who have the most to hide. When one of our most successful Dandelion acts took on new management I was invited on to the company yacht in Cannes to discuss a new publishing agreement. I refused the offer, and over the following weeks was subjected to a series of increasingly threatening offers and propositions, which ceased only when one of the directors ended up in clink for using a gun to terrorize his staff.

Crucial advice to anybody planning a visit to the MIDEM festival: take bundles of cash. The locals hike the prices of everything, and a beer and sandwich will set you back a fortune. I shudder to think what they charge when the film festival crowd checks in.

19. GOODDAY PRODUCTIONS

MICK ROBERTSON
The first single The Tango's Over

CBS 2615

MICK
ROBERTSON

CBS

the music people

GOODDAY PRODUCTIONS

Goodday Productions was a little side project that I worked on in 1974 while still at UK. Peter Thompson, who was and may still be the finest PR expert in Britain, and I had worked together successfully on the Wombles. Among Peter's clients at the time was a very handsome young man, Mick Robertson, who was then presenting the children's television programme *Magpie*. With his spectacular good looks, tall slim build and relaxed presentation, Mick was building a substantial and dedicated following. This being a good era for pretty young men, Peter suggested that we turn him into a pop star. There was a lot of that about at that time.

In truth the project was little more than a scam, but with Mick's established popularity, Peter's expertise with the press and whatever I was able to bring to the table we figured we just might be able to sell the package. First, we needed to find out whether Mick was game and could actually sing. He was and he could. After a bit of time in the studio we felt that, though he could never truly claim to be a singer, he had a light but pleasant enough voice and could, at least, carry a tune.

Jonathan was supportive and happy to allow me to pursue the project in my spare time, though, since we were looking for serious money, chose not to be involved himself. I touted the concept around the usual companies and eventually accepted a substantial deal from Dick Asher.

With a three-album deal and money in the bank we looked for a producer who could bring out the best of Mick's admittedly limited vocal abilities and cover any deficiencies with lush orchestral arrangements. We chose Richard Hewson, with whom I had worked on Clifford T.'s albums and who had contributed string arrangements to some of the best of the Beatles' recordings. The next task was to find original songs, and these were provided by Richard writing the music and Shurley, with occasional assistance from me, supplying the words. I believe the term is 'in house'.

We very nearly made it. The first single, 'The Tango's Over', with a lot of press, some radio play and a couple of television showings of the video that CBS paid for, reached fifty-something in the charts and it looked as if we were on our way. Looking back through the file, it is difficult not to be impressed by the effort that went into the marketing and promotion, under the direction of CBS's Arthur Sheriff.

Richard and Mick wrote the second single, 'Then I Changed Hands'. It, too, started out well, with an appearance on *Top of the Pops*, but at this time Shurley and I were travelling extensively and Dick Asher was about to return to the USA, leaving the company in the hands of Obie. The record died through lack of availability and, not being in the country, I was unable to prevent what looked very much like sabotage. Obie would do things like that.

With Dick, who had made the original deal, back in America, the album came out to good reviews and press coverage but little support within CBS. The corporate writing was on the wall for all to see. All managing directors of major record labels desperately need to make a name for themselves by signing successful acts, and their successors almost always concentrate all of their own efforts on finding and signing their own stars. Any act that has yet to make it at the time of a record company management change had best look elsewhere for support and encouragement. It happened to me a couple of years later at Polydor with Band of Joy, as we'll see, and is no doubt happening to other ambitious acts right now.

Obie, in his Machiavellian way, refused to honour the three-album deal and pointed out that if we chose to sue CBS had a fleet of lawyers on the payroll who would keep us dancing until long after our money and patience ran out. He was probably right, and life was too short to put it to the test.

In an interesting coda to all this, as is often the case we did not use all of the recordings for immediate release and were amazed later to hear one of our 'out-take' tracks released as an instrumental single – under another name, of course. I went back to the studio and, sure enough, there was our original sixteen-track master tape with the track in question carefully removed. The studio advised me that the producer, who was, of course, a familiar figure and whose visits were not questioned, had in fact removed the track in a nocturnal visit.

The record went swiftly to number one in several countries, and we decided to sue since we had paid a considerable amount of money for the recording, which made this a clear case of theft. Had the producer simply asked our permission we would have gladly given consent to its release on the basis of a small share in the profits. But he didn't, and we were pretty angry. Our lawyers were confident that we had an unassailable case but soon discovered that the producer had leased our recording to a production company that had, in turn, leased it to another company, which had arranged for it to be distributed by a major company. We now had four adversaries all of whom denied any responsibility – and that was just in Britain.

Confident that justice would prevail, we pressed on, but having incurred several thousand pounds' worth of initial legal costs we were then informed by our lawyers that this was a David-and-Goliath situation in which all the parties were prepared to fight and the costs were liable to be astronomical. Apparently in such a situation, and supposedly to avoid frivolous actions, the complaining party is required to pay into court a sum sufficient to cover the likely costs of the case should they lose. Failure to do this meant that the case could not proceed. To raise that kind of money would have bankrupted both Peter and me, so we were reluctantly forced to withdraw. Our lawyers, of course, were keen to proceed in the belief that it was a case we could not lose, but we've all heard that one before. A cautionary tale perhaps but just another first-hand example of how the law protects the rich and powerful.

Anyway, Mick carried on with his television career, Peter continued to be the best at what he does and, just for fun, I organized a deal with Phonogram for Richard as an orchestral act and even contributed a couple of vocal tracks. Shurley gave up a promising career as a lyricist and over the following years would smile when a few pounds in royalties arrived in the mail.

If there is anything to be learned from this it is the usual 'get the money up front'. Only lawyers profit from litigation. To achieve any kind of record success every act needs a champion within the company. And the higher up the better. Had we, any of us, though of it as having any great artistic merit we would have been devastated. But it wasn't even rock and roll.

CHARTS

A great deal has been said and written about chart hyping. Most of it is uninformed and sensationalist, but that has not prevented a number of careers from being ruined on the strength of accusations. As somebody who may not have invented chart hyping – but certainly helped to develop it into a sophisticated marketing tool – I've never quite understood what all the fuss was about.

It is perfectly possible substantially and legally to influence the makeup of the music charts, and anyone in a position of responsibility in a record company would not be doing their job if they did not make every legal effort to so do. Of the tens of thousands of records released every year the great majority disappear without trace, and the overwhelming mass of even regular record buyers are aware only of those that appear in the charts or which are advertised on television. Since television advertising is so expensive, it is generally limited to the promotion of sure-fire winners by established acts or to compilations of past hits. This makes it even more crucial to have chart recognition, as an appearance on a successful television-advertised compilation album can be very lucrative.

A national body, drawing on sales information supplied by selected retailers across the country, compiles the official chart. That was not always the case. The first-ever UK record Top Ten was published in the *New Musical Express* and was pretty much what that paper chose it to be – with, no doubt, some consideration given to what was being advertised that week. There were, however, only about half-a-dozen record companies operating at that time, so the choice was somewhat limited. Those record companies were astonished to discover that an appearance on that chart added tens of thousands of sales, and they determined to create an 'official' chart that they could control.

The British Market Research Bureau was appointed to select and draw sales information from a base of record dealers and collate the information on a weekly basis. Key dealers were asked to provide the information at the close of business every Saturday. They would – for no reward whatsoever – count up every record sold that week, enter the details on a form provided and scurry round to the local post office to ensure that the information was received in London by the following Monday. With the help of (probably) an abacus the figures were totalled up and the resultant chart was published in the then only trade magazine, *Record Retailer*. Accurate or not, the chart had an immediate impact with huge additional sales coming in from the major record chains, and television shows such as *Top of the Pops* refusing to book new artists until their record had 'charted'. The game was afoot!

Let me now state categorically that, to the best of my knowledge, it has never been possible to manipulate or 'fix' a record into a high chart place, say twenty or above, but at the lower end . . . The 350 or so dealers who supplied the sales information were usually independent, ranged from very professional specialist record stores, such as Reed's of Peckham, to the 'mom and pop' stores that just sold a few records on the side. The list of participating stores was supposedly highly confidential and changed regularly as stores dropped out and were replaced, but any marketing person worth his pay knew exactly which shops contributed and which person in each shop was responsible for supplying the details. For those without this inside information the going price for a list of the 'chart shops' was a few hundred pounds. I understand that there was a ready market for these details among artist managers and agents anxious to do right by their clients, but a lot of people paid out a lot of money for completely fictitious lists.

In those early halcyon days there were about five thousand independent record stores across Britain; there are less than a thousand today. With national sales limited to, at best, a few hundred copies of any new release in the first couple of weeks, it was obvious that any reported sales through the relatively few chart shops would make an impression.

It is generally believed that all chart records sell in tens of thousands, but that is only true of genuine Top Ten hits. Weekly sales of records, in the charts but outside the Top Twenty, are measured in hundreds, and any record showing comparable sales through the chart shops is pretty much guaranteed a chart place. The first trick is to get the disc into the influential shops. This is never easy, since each retailer is faced with an alarming choice of new releases every week and knows only too well that most of them will never succeed and that any over-ordered stock will simply gather expensive dust on the shelf. In the absence of a big name, extensive airplay or specifically local interest, most shops will not order a new record until it is asked for by a customer, since they will be required to pay for it even if it never sells a copy. Just a few wrong decisions in a year can put even the best of shops out of business.

The simple answer is to supply new releases on a 'sale-or-return' basis, but this can be self-defeating if every company is doing it and the records stay on the shelves taking up space that should accommodate hits. There is little point in supplying several thousand copies of a record that just lies there, and no amount of clever advertising will shift a record by a new artist without airplay or a following – unless, of course, it already happens to be in the charts.

To create sales for or at least awareness of new artists, I hit upon the idea of a series of short in-store public appearances by them. Up to twenty personal appearances in a day can be undertaken with judicious planning and a good driver. Each appearance would be advertised and promoted in the shops with an inexpensive poster, there would be signed photographs to give away and, of course, a supply of the new waxing for those who wished to buy. The public were generally curious enough to attend, the record was played continuously in store and any ensuing sales were recorded and sent on to the chart compilers, since, naturally, these events took place only in chart shops. In almost every instance a modest chart appearance ensued, which led to radio plays and orders from other shops that had to have stocks of any new chart entry. We were somewhat limited to how many shops could be covered in a few days, and by the availability of the artists, but in this way we achieved early and lasting success for artists as diverse as Marty Wilde, the Springfields, Frankie Vaughan and Jimmy Dean.

If artists were unavailable for a shop tour it was sometimes possible to drum up interest in a new record by visiting the stores with just a poster and a sales pitch – but the record had to be good. While working as an independent hustler I was hired by Robert Stigwood to promote 'Wrapping Paper', the first recording by Cream. This was right at the start of psychedelia, and nothing had prepared me for my first meeting with the band, who were hanging around Polydor Records' reception area, bearded, pony-tailed and bedecked in Carnaby Street militaria. They were reasonably civil but somewhat nervous, giving no hint of the world superstars they were soon to become and seemingly not terribly interested in the fate of their first recording.

Without the availability of the group, who were tied up in the studio, and armed only with a few cheap posters and a test pressing of the record, I set out on a tour of London's chart shops where I played the disc and, where possible, displayed a poster. The promotion was successful, and the record entered the charts in the mid-forties. Robert Stigwood was delighted but pointed out that, owing to a factory problem, no copies of 'Wrapping Paper' had yet been delivered to the shops despite its appearance on the charts. I then switched my attention to the Midlands-area chart shops and at the end of another week was pleased to learn that the record had moved a couple of places up the chart. Unfortunately the pressing problems continued and still no records were available to purchase, so I moved the operation up into the north of England, where my visits were greeted with some scorn, since I was now promoting a record that was enjoying chart success without a single copy having been sold. Another week of hustling around the chart shops of Yorkshire and Lancashire produced another upward chart move, and at this point the record was finally released, only to drop out of the chart within a couple of weeks. Three weeks of chart activity without a single copy having been sold convinced me that, far from being an accurate reflection of sales, the charts really indicated the tastes and preferences of the relevant retailers – many of whom were young girls easily impressed by a visit from someone with even a tenuous connection to the artists.

Over the following years I was able to use this information to good effect with a series of perfectly legal marketing strategies that enabled me to move CBS Records from virtually nowhere to a dominant position in the singles charts with nearly half the Top Fifty. At Pye Records I was asked by the chairman, quite seriously, to slow down the succession of hit singles, for fear that the momentum could not be maintained. He was right: I left and the hits dried up.

There are, and always will be, unscrupulous or desperate people who will try to get records into the charts by the simple expedient of going out and buying hundreds of copies in what they hope are the right shops. This is transparent, expensive and illegal – though I've never understood just why. Following all the chart success, and on the heels of yet another investigation into chart hyping, I was invited on to a television programme to discuss the problem, in the course of which I stated that I believed the 'buying in' of records in order to obtain a chart position was no worse than the Bank of England buying up the pound when it is under pressure. The programme was watched by the heads of all the major record companies, who subsequently dissociated themselves from my remarks – at least publicly. Incidentally, Frank Bough, who interviewed Dave Cash and me for the programme, was all chatty and matey before the start but switched to shouting and hectoring immediately the red light came on. An interesting technique.

Over the ensuing years the methods were refined and became more sophisticated, but the basic premise for chart success remains. The records – or books or whatever – have to be available in the stores and a demand must be created. Nowadays it is not unusual for the dedicated entrepreneur to create a dance record at home with a synthesizer, press a few hundred copies and supply the right specialist shops with copies on a sale-or-return basis from the boot of a car. With exclusive access to the records the enthusiastic specialist shops will often promote them to interested customers and report the sales to the chart compiling company. Very often this can result in an appearance in the specialist chart or even at the lower end of the regular charts, at which point the major companies will swoop in with offers of mountains of cash.

Music is now so fragmented that low chart places often indicate a strong but limited specialist interest that does not translate into a crossover hit – and a lot of major company fingers have been expensively burned picking up the rights to a dance hit of strictly limited appeal. In recent years the collection of sales information from a much wider sample of shops is undertaken electronically by the use of barcodes. It should be foolproof, but I guarantee that a number of individuals have, or claim to have, found a new way to massage the results. I hope so. With a million pounds or more still possible from a number one record the rewards are too tempting.

A recent 'investigation' into chart fixing by the *Roger Cook Programme* that covered two weeks of primetime television in 2000 proved that nothing had changed over the past quarter-century. Despite the expenditure of tens of thousands of pounds on recording, filming, marketing and hyping what was in fact not a bad little record, our undercover hero was able only to force the record into the low eighties in the charts. They should have given me the money. With that kind of dosh I could have guaranteed at the very least a Top Forty place – and in the seventies both *World in Action* and the *News of the World* tried to prove it.

The Cook programme was full of shadowy figures claiming to be able to influence the chart and making veiled references to the possibility of buying support from disc jockeys. In fact the promotion team behind the record appeared to have done a splendid job with considerable press, radio and television coverage. I am surprised that the record didn't do better and would ask serious questions of the distributor.

It all seemed a curious waste of time for what was supposedly a serious investigative television programme. All the money and effort simply demonstrated that, just as in any business, there are fringe people ready to make unsubstantiated claims and take money from gullible suckers. And even if it had all worked, so what? Who would have been hurt? Surely not the idiots who buy records just because they are in the charts. They must surely be happy with anything. Possibly the radio and television people who compile their programmes based on what is apparently popular, rather than exercising any form of taste or judgement, might feel a little put out, but I guarantee they won't change. The only genuine losers in the whole chart hyping scam are the other artists, producers and record labels who are kept out of the charts by the phoney few. But who ever said it had to be easy?

20. PYE

PYE RECORDS

Somewhat shell-shocked from my abrupt and unexplained CBS termination I was relieved to receive a call from Louis Benjamin, chairman of Pye Records, offering me the position of marketing director. The job carried a decent salary and a Jaguar with free petrol and parking, which made the decision a little easier.

Pye Records, by the time I joined in early 1976, was struggling. It had been a highly successful company with a long list of hits by Sandie Shaw, the Kinks, the Searchers, Status Quo, Acker Bilk, Lonnie Donegan, Petula Clark and many more. Pet alone had provided the company with over thirty hit singles, starting way back in 1954. Years before that, when we were both around ten years old, I had shared a stage with this precocious young lady as we entertained limbless ex-soldiers in a charity concert. With her anxious father watching from the wings Pet sang and did excellent impressions. I sang 'The Minstrel Boy to the War Has Gone' which, in retrospect, was perhaps not an ideal choice. Years later, when Shurley and I were stranded in Paris without a room, the president of Pet's record company loaned us the singer's apartment for a few days. It was very grand, as befits a great star who, even now, is selling out theatres around the world.

Pye had been the first company successfully to challenge the dominance of Decca and EMI before launching the first of the 'budget' labels with the Golden Guinea series that had rocked the industry in the late 1950s. By this time a part of the ATV empire, it was stale and languishing, with very few hits and a poor image. Not the most attractive proposition but certainly a challenge.

On my first day Louis Benjamin played me an acetate of the group Sheer Elegance, who were managed by the adopted son of Lord Grade – the chairman of ATV – and were thus being given rather special treatment despite their obvious shortcomings in terms of appearance and presentation. I somewhat hesitantly suggested that the record might well be a hit and was immediately ushered through a small door leading to the ATV part of the building and on into the office of the great man. Wading through several inches of carpet I was introduced to His Lordship, who sat behind a vast desk almost hidden by a cloud of cigar smoke.

Benjy introduced me and said, 'Go on then. Tell him.' Lord Grade was at the time by far the most powerful and respected man in the British entertainment industry, with control not only of ATV and Pye Records but Moss Empire Theatres, several film companies, ATV Music – which owned the publishing rights to Lennon and McCartney's songs – and was behind the most popular show on British television throughout the the late fifties and most of the sixties, *Sunday Night at the Palladium*. Not a man to upset. I confirmed what I had said to Benjy about the hit potential of the Sheer Elegance record whereupon Benjy said, 'That means we do not need to spend any money on it.' Adopting my best marketing bluff I disagreed and pointed out that, having had one minor hit, this record could consolidate the group's following and, with a reasonable campaign, it might be possible to move them into the more lucrative album market. Rising from his desk, preceded by the largest cigar I have ever seen, Lew Grade put his arm around me and said, 'The boy is right. Spend a little money now, and in no time we've got another Queen.' Since Queen were then considered to be one of the most musical and sophisticated acts around, and Sheer Elegance most certainly were not, I wondered, not for the first time and certainly not the last, what kind of Alice-in-Wonderland world I had entered. Fortunately the record, 'Life Is Too Short Girl', was a sizeable hit.

Later that day, while in discussion with my new staff in my new office, I heard a small cry followed by a loud bump from the corridor. Leaping out of my chair to discover the source, I was assured that it was just one of the other directors, who always got drunk and fell over at that time of day. The executive in question was very able and important but was also prone to soiling the office furniture as a result of over-indulgence. I further discovered that, if my weekly marketing meeting went beyond noon, the staff became restless and invented excuses as to why they had to leave. It seems that by noon, because the pubs were open, the meeting was eating into serious drinking time.

The managing director of Pye was an abstemious and serious individual whom I had known several years earlier when I had been a salesman on the road and he had been the head buyer for a large record chain. Walter Woyda had been a difficult man then and the years had not mellowed him. He loathed me for my lack of subservience and tried ceaselessly to have me removed, despite the unprecedented success that the company began to enjoy.

The hits that had marked my tenure at CBS quickly began to flow at Pye, and the rare weeks that did not show a new chart entry were followed by a week in which we had two or more new entries. At one point Benjy invited Peter Prince, the A & R director, and me to lunch to ask us to slow down the rate of hits for fear that we may not be able to sustain it the following year. We were staggered and pointed out that this was what we did and the only way we knew how to slow down would be to send us on extended leave. 'You're a pair of difficult buggers' was Benjy's response. 'You don't have to deal with the board.'

Benjy always lunched at the Cumberland Hotel opposite the ATV offices and used the ATV entrance to the building while we returned via the Pye entrance and lift. Upon arriving on our floor, we discovered Walter, who was excruciatingly insecure, pacing up and down awaiting our return from lunch with the chairman. 'Well?' he demanded. 'Do I still have a job?'

To his credit Peter paused briefly, appeared to consider and said, 'We'll let you know.' Peter Prince was one of the best A & R men with great ears for singles. I mentioned this in a trade paper interview once and Peter asked me if I had meant 'like Mickey Mouse?' He went on to become managing director of Tamla Motown in Britain, but the last I heard was out of a job and struggling. I hope he's fixed up now.

The Brotherhood of Man were a decent little club act who got lucky with a Eurovision winner and a funny dance that translated into a smash hit around Europe. I initiated exactly the same process as I had with Abba with similar results and the record – 'Save All Your Kisses For Me' – went on to become the top-selling record of 1976. Over the next twelve months they managed two further number ones but somehow lacked the appeal of what were obviously their role models. They were managed by an ex-boxer who had an odd habit of ending telephone conversations by saying, 'Kiss, kiss'. Very disconcerting since his earlier career had left its mark and he was built to last. He was an industrious man who kept the group busy performing and earning throughout their hit period, which, by not giving them enough time to write and record, may have accounted for their inability to consolidate into an album act.

Stevie Wonder was blessed with a smash-hit album at this time with one stand-out track that was getting all the airplay. He apparently refused to allow Tamla to release it as a single, and Peter Prince had the bright idea of getting Tony Hatch to cover the song with an unknown singer and a similar arrangement. This resulted in another number one, which is an example of an A & R man doing his job.

Barry White visited the UK to play a few concerts with his Love Unlimited Orchestra. He is a huge man – there's a photograph in which he manages to make me look petite – with a huge female following, and every seat was sold out within hours (and many of them were left somewhat damp after the concerts). He is a true professional and a very amiable man.

With extraordinary singles successes including three number one hits from the Brotherhood of Man and more from the Real Thing, Barry White and Carl Douglas, plus smash hits from Gladys Knight, Simon May, Tony Hatch, Andrea True Connection, the lovely Melba Moore and others, Pye replaced CBS as the top singles company, which gave me a certain satisfaction. It also elicited a creepy telegram from Danny Loggins at CBS, congratulating me on bringing 'the Selwood magic to Pye'. (This from a man whom I once overheard saying about himself, 'This is one Jew who ain't marching to the gas chamber,' in reference to discussing future plans with me – which I thought, to say the least, a tad disrespectful to the victims of the Holocaust.)

While working at bringing home the hits, I wrote a rough draft of a proposed script for a television soap opera based on the music trade. I submitted it to Benjy with a request that he pass it up the line to one of his colleagues at ATV if he thought it had merit. He copied me in on the note that he sent with the script to one of the ATV senior producers. It was most complimentary about my prowess and experience but attached to it was a note addressed to me and assuring me that, in his opinion, the current run of hits was due to the earlier efforts of a departed promotion man, Johnny Wise, and was his legacy. Since it had been several years since Mr Wise had left the company I put it down to a mischievous sense of humour. The script was not accepted.

Liquor played a big part at Pye but never in front of His Lordship, who would stride about the company, cigar in front. It often appeared that the cigar would come around corners before the man. At the end of the day it was not unusual for Benjy to invite his fellow directors into his office for a drink before leaving. I only rarely attended these meetings, as I am not much of a drinker and was not crazy about the company, but a colleague, who joined the company as sales director, was less fortunate. He was invited into the inner sanctum on his first day and was enjoying his drink when the door burst open and Lew Grade walked in. With practised ease and astonishing alacrity the assemblage slipped their drinks into desk drawers and hidey-holes. All except my chum who rose to be introduced to the chairman with drink in hand. The following day he was informed that 'the Chairman' was concerned by his apparent drink problem.

Another game played at Pye was known as 'Beat the Clock'. This came about because Lord Lew was an early riser and always first to the office where, it was said, he would open the mail to see what was going on. Benjy was also an early riser and would often meet with His Lordship for an important discussion while most folk were still asleep. It was impossible to meet Lord Grade without first clearing it with Benjy, who jealously guarded his special relationship. Other directors who wanted a confidential word took to getting into the office at dawn and playing music at high volume in the hope that Grade, being the only other occupant, would come around to investigate! Benjy confided in me that he always knew when this had happened, as he had a habit of touring the offices of his directors in the early hours and sniffing for the aroma of the trademark cigar. And these were highly paid, extremely influential men.

The following story illustrates the kind of madness that can arise in the higher echelons of the world of entertainment. It was told to me by Les Cocks, who had been a senior executive at Pye before becoming the producer of such top-rated television shows as *The Golden Shot*. In a meeting attended by Lord Grade, Benjy and the head of the publishing group, word came through that the girlfriend of Richard Harris, who was starring in a Grade film currently in production, had written a song to be performed in the movie. All discussions were stopped as the three titans went into a huddle to decide on recording, publishing, royalties, advances and release dates and so on. After an hour or so of occasionally heated exchanges, Les gently enquired whether anybody had yet heard the promised opus. His question was ignored while a deal acceptable to all parties was thrashed out. In the event the song and the lady made a brief appearance in the finished film, rather reminiscent of the old Cliff Richard movies where the train conductor opens the carriage door to discover the source of the noise and ends up tapping his toe.

One of the demerits of the job at Pye was the requirement to attend the private viewings of His Lordship's films. It probably sounds quite glamorous to be expected to sit, in considerable comfort, in the private viewing theatre watching movies, but the reality was that they were generally awful and I had too much else to do. Lord Grade was terrific at raising finance and obtaining worldwide distribution, but this often showed in that the actors spoke many of their important lines with their backs to the camera to allow for foreign-language dubbing. I did usually manage to stay awake, unlike the time I attended a private showing of a Christopher Lee film that was so awful I fell asleep while sitting next to the actor. He is a very big man and was kind enough not to comment, but the lunch that followed was somewhat frosty.

Despite, or perhaps because of, my best efforts, Pye seemed unable to crack the album market. I believed this to be on account of the company being unwilling to invest the kind of funding required – though we did have a top-selling album with the Muppets. I had initially turned it down when it was offered to me by an ex-colleague from the old Century 21 days. I just couldn't see it, but when it arrived I gave it our best shot and it hit the top spot along with the single from Kermit. The Wombles and Kermit, eh?

With little sign that Pye were prepared to expand into the album act area, I began to get antsy again and consider new challenges. Having achieved all I was ever likely to at Pye, I was presented with a demo tape from some friends of Clifford T. Ward. The group, though poorly recorded, had great potential, and I tried to persuade Pye to sign them, which would enable me to bring all my experience to bear in creating a hit album act. In order to help them get a deal with Pye I even paid for the group to go back into the studio for further recording out of my own pocket. It was not to be and, after just fifteen months, in which time we had over fifty chart entries, I decided it was time to leave and try to get my own thing back on the rails.

Benjy was kindness itself and gave me my company Jaguar as a token of his appreciation. A few years later the company went out of business, the factory was sold and that terrific catalogue was put up for auction. It has since changed hands at least twice. Perhaps it was the booze.

HAVE EARS, WILL TRAVEL

In the music business opportunities to travel abound. Until the early sixties everything to do with the British music industry happened in London, and anybody wanting to make a career in music headed for the capital. That all changed with the advent of Mersey Mania when the talent-hungry A & R men flooded into Liverpool signing up virtually every act from that city. Very shortly any A & R person could reasonably justify a week or more living high on expenses in Manchester, Birmingham and Glasgow.

Now it is a truly international business, and talent must be hunted down in places as far apart as Africa and Australia. The last time I spoke with Seymour Stein – who discovered Madonna, owned Sire Records and was then heading WEA in Los Angeles – he had just returned from Europe and was about to leave for several weeks in Africa seeking out acts for his new world-music label

In a meeting with Chris Blackwell at Island our conversation was interrupted by a call from a colleague in Trinidad, following which Chris asked his secretary to get him on the next available flight to the island. Without pausing to pack even a toothbrush, he was on the plane within a couple of hours and expecting to sleep on his friend's floor for the next night or two. Of course, owning houses and apartments in London, New York, Los Angeles and Barbados tends to ease the packing problem.

Apart from the numerous industry events, which commence in January with MIDEM and continue throughout the year wherever the weather is likely to be pleasant, many of the larger labels have started to hold their own in-house get-togethers in exotic places such as Mexico City. The sales, marketing and promotions people get to stay in top hotels in glamorous locations in the name of work.

My first business trip to New York was terrifying. On arrival at Kennedy I asked directions from a uniformed lady and was curtly informed that she was 'a customs officer, not a goddamned information bureau'. The fight for a taxi was handled by a huge, black Redcap, who simply threw passengers into the backs of the yellow cabs that arrived with shrieking brakes. The cabs then hurtled off into the night with the drivers separated from the passengers by a shield of bullet-proof glass through which one shouted one's destination. Settling into a hotel just a few blocks from Times Square and too excited to sleep, I decided to check out the area. The walk up Broadway was like a scene from West Side Story, with steam rising from the gratings and cops twirling night sticks on every corner that was not occupied by hookers or what looked like black gang members. The heat and smells were completely alien, and cheap souvenir shops and sleazy porno emporiums surrounded the theatres.

As I approached Times Square I heard gunshots followed by police sirens and fled back to the comparative safety of the hotel, where the radio informed me that a British tourist had just been shot near Times Square.

Another time in the Big Apple Shurley and I became concerned when our cab appeared to take a circuitous route to the hotel at about two in the morning. Our fears increased when we found we were being slowly driven through a deserted dockland and the cab was cruising to a stop. Just at that moment a police car cruised slowly by and its occupants gave us the stare. Our cabby accelerated away and deposited a relieved pair of Brits at the hotel where we were informed that we had probably taken a 'gypsy' cab and narrowly avoided being mugged.

A subsequent business trip to Los Angeles was almost as interesting. Having a free afternoon, I decided to take a walk around Beverly Hills to admire the beautiful scenery and properties. In Griffith Park I paused to chat to a young woman engaged in painting a watercolour. Noticing my accent she asked where I came from and on being told London she breathed, 'Oh, wow! That's in Europe, isn't it?' So much for Swinging London. Continuing my walk, I was called over into a police cruiser and interrogated at some length. It appears that only potential criminals walk in Hollywood. Later that day I walked up Sunset Strip to my hotel and was again called over by a cop who accused me of 'walking against a red light'. He had been parked on his motor cycle on a hilly side street and simply rolled down towards me wearing a gun and heavy shades despite the late hour. When I pointed out that there was in fact no red light in view he politely enquired how I would like to find my teeth down the back of my throat. 'Oh. That red light,' I whimpered as he fined me $10 on the spot. On being required to produce some identification I recovered some of my composure and pointed out that we Brits had not been required to carry identification since Jerry stopped raining bombs down on us. That gave him pause. He adjusted his gun belt, showed even more of his gleaming teeth and offered, as an alternative, to let me pass the night in the pokey.

I understand that Angelinos are proud of their supposedly incorruptible police force, and they may well be right. I never paid the fine as a matter of principle and, every time I return, there is a frisson of fear that somebody may emerge with a warrant.

Some of our most memorable holiday travels came courtesy of my former boss Jac Holzman who, on selling Elektra, moved to Hawaii. Jack invited us to stay on Maui in a rented villa close to the beach. At that time I was still a 'white-knuckle' flyer, and the flight across the islands in a little prop plane in a blinding storm did nothing to reassure me; nor did the several broken aeroplanes littering the sugar-cane plantations surrounding the tiny airport where we arrived or the two shamefaced pilots being brought back to the terminal following a crash.

Maui was splendid. We rented a motor cycle and explored the island, returning each evening to view the fabulous sunsets from a hammock on the beach behind Jac's villa. Jac was training as a pilot and offered to fly us, with his instructor, to a neighbouring island. We set off with Jac at the controls and Harry and Sandy Chapin along for the ride. After circling a defunct volcano we came in to land, at which point Jac stalled the engines about a hundred feet above the ground whereupon we began to drop like the proverbial stone. Harry Chapin, ever cool, crossed himself and murmured 'There goes the ball game' as we braced ourselves for the impact. The next few seconds were a blur, as somehow, just short of impact, the instructor managed to restart the engines, gunned the motor as we hit the ground and immediately took off at top speed. Jac apologized and explained that it was like falling off a horse: you have to get back on; and he, accordingly, was about to try another landing. Jac went on to get his commercial pilot's licence and in fact started a small airline ferrying passengers between the islands, before moving back to LA where he now flies his own plane around the country. Harry and Sandy Chapin credited Shurley's counsel with saving their marriage, which was going through a tough time, but Harry was tragically killed in a road accident just a couple of years later. He was a good man in a crisis and very talented.

Another holiday at Jac's expense was spent cruising French canals in a barge. One of the highlights was an evening spent at a very exclusive restaurant where the food and wine were exquisite. At the end of the meal Jac and Bruce Botnick – who engineered the Doors' albums – persuaded the silver-haired *mâitre d'* to show them the cobweb-encrusted wine cellar and, after considerable haggling, managed to purchase a couple of cases of the elixir. With whoops of joy my companions carried their prize back to the barge, convinced that they had negotiated the deal of the year. It was hard to believe that a sophisticated and highly experienced restaurateur would allow himself to be diddled, so everyone was happy. And that was a highlight! It was in fact a very restful break with bicycles on board for the more energetic passengers.

A holiday on a luxury yacht cruising the Greek islands may well sound like paradise, but you have to choose your companions with care. Our companions on this trip were Jac, his new girlfriend, who lived on Maui, where she grew marijuana, Jac's new young assistant, the Greek captain and crew and a white-haired carpenter called Roger whose wife was highly proficient at macramé. Roger styled himself a non-Euclidean architect and may have had some influence in the design of a fabulous new home Jac was having constructed in South Salem.

It was a strange trip. Jac was suffering with constipation and piles, the conditions of which he steadfastly reported over breakfast each day, his girlfriend spent pretty much the whole time in her cabin, emerging only in the mornings silently to perform oriental exercises on deck, while

Roger's wife finished another acre or two of macramé. At every port Roger would don shorts and running shoes to hare off at great speed up the nearest mountain. Many of our companions appeared to have a shared sweet tooth, since they had an ample supply of sugar cubes, which brought them much pleasure.

We traversed the islands in some style, but, when a storm arose as we were about to leave Rhodes, we discovered that the yacht was manned by fair-weather sailors who refused to leave port, insisting that to do so would result in a watery grave. Jac's will prevailed and over the hysterical entreaties, indeed tears, of the captain we set off into what fast became a gale. We sailed through the night with the crew cowering in their bunks and, at the height of the storm, Roger lashed himself to the mast and played jazz riffs on his saxophone while the wind howled and the giant waves crashed around him. If you saw that in a movie you would assume that the director had gone mad – but it happened.

At some point in this odyssey we picked up Claude Nobs who ran the Montreux Jazz Festival, had a record label and was a big player in Swiss television. Claude is a very pleasant and talented man who had, in fact, accompanied us on the earlier barge trip, where he displayed a keen knowledge of and fascination with wild mushrooms, which he sought out and cooked. Towards the end of the trip, on a shopping spree, Claude asked Shurley to help him select a traditional Greek silk dress and a gold necklace as a gift for his sister. What they chose was rather special and made even more interesting when Claude turned up for dinner that night in a local restaurant wearing both items before speeding off into the night in an open sports car.

Stopping off at one of the deserted islands, the yacht was a beautiful sight out on the clear turquoise sea, and I decided to swim back out to it rather than wait for the dinghy to arrive. It was a lovely warm day and the sea was calm and tranquil, but I found the going very hard. Though not by any measure a good swimmer, I am fairly capable, but my strength was almost vanished by the time I flopped exhaustedly on to the deck. I mentioned this rather odd occurrence to Pete Drummond some time later, who told me that on that stretch of water two members of Pink Floyd's road crew had disappeared, together with their rowing boat, and were never seen again. It seems that there are strong undertows in that particular bay.

When it came time for us to leave the cruise we watched in some trepidation as the commander of the port, looking for all the world like Napoleon Bonaparte in the prow of his boat, sailed out into the storm-tossed night in a successful effort to persuade the captain of the ferry to come into port. With some difficulty and a degree of athleticism, we boarded the ferry and spent the next thirty-six hours on deck with nothing to eat or drink *en route* to Rhodes, as the lavatories and restaurant were closed and awash with vomit. Glamorous or what?

In search of a different holiday we wound up at a dude ranch in Arizona, which turned out to be one of our better moves. For anybody brought up on Western movies it was pure heaven, and even our then truculent youngest daughter wept when we left. There is really nothing to compare with riding a horse through the desert and mountains with the sun on your back, pretending to be Clint Eastwood. My own steely-eyed taciturn self-image was somewhat shattered when my daughter called out from amidst a posse that my face was the same colour as my bright red Western shirt. We nevertheless fell so in love with the place and the people on every visit that we bought a horse property as a second home. Sure, there are tarantulas, rattlesnakes and other forms of dangerous wildlife, but we feel safer there than in jolly old London, and Paul Beatle seems to agree, as he is a neighbour.

TRASH

BAND OF JOY

21. **SARABEE**

SARABEE

Life at Pye had been a breeze, albeit an unsatisfactory breeze because the company was just not interested in spending the time and money required to build album acts. Whatever the volume of hit singles achieved, they were building on quicksand. Without proven album acts every release requires a new start.

In late 1976, towards the end of my stint at Pye, and in view of my reputation as a hit-maker, Marty Machat, who was then among the most feared and despised lawyers operating in the music business, approached me. He represented a number of big international stars, among them Leonard Cohen, and though our past business relationship had been amicable I was nervous. Indeed, Jac Holzman said to me that if he ever missed being at the centre of the music business, he had only to remember Marty to reassure himself that he had made the right choice.

We met at an expensive restaurant, and over lunch Marty offered to manage me at his usual rate of 20 per cent. He had a special relationship with Polydor Records and, on the company's behalf, offered me a choice of taking over as managing director when the current incumbent moved on or, as an alternative, Polydor were prepared to finance my own production company that it would market and distribute. Having by that time suffered far too many years of corporate politics, I opted for the production money and, with Shurley as partner, prepared to launch Sarabee Music.

I found Marty to be mild-mannered, quietly spoken and courteous, the absolute antithesis of his reputation. The first act we signed was the group I had initially funded and offered to Pye. They were called Band of Joy and featured two members of the original Band of Joy, which had included Robert Plant and John Bonham of Led Zeppelin. I thought they were truly sensational, and when Marty heard the demo recordings he agreed. His eyes lit up, and he immediately decided that they had too much potential to be included in the Polydor deal, which was to be essentially a singles-based project. He shopped the tapes around and came up with a very good offer from United Artists. With a light cough he murmured, 'We really hit the bell this time', and showed us the figures. It was enough to record an album and keep the group together on modest wages for a year.

The band was thrilled and anxious to begin recording. The two original Band of Joy members were Kevyn Gammond, an extraordinary guitarist, and Paul Lockey, who also played guitar and handled lead vocals. Johnno Pasternak, the bassist, had toured with Kevyn as part of Bronco, while Michael Chetwood, on keyboards, was fairly new to the profession but highly talented. The drums and percussion were in the charge of Francesco Nizza, a very tall Italian with a wonky eye that made him one of the most formidable figures you could ever wish to avoid. In fact Frankie was a sweetheart and a truly gentle soul, except when he was behind the drums or in a spirited discussion with his girlfriend, Vana, who was Greek, very beautiful and also over six feet tall. Vana was related to one of the Greek shipping magnates and had her own island. She was a star in her native land where she hosted her own television show and had recorded with 'that fat macho pig' Vangelis, as she referred to him.

Frankie and Vana were both multi-lingual and would have many spirited Mediterranean discussions in various languages, literally over our heads. Occasionally they would pause, smile at Shurley or me, explain that they were not really fighting and resume hostilities at top volume complete with arm and hand gestures. It was, on occasion, like being back in the Blitz.

Recording the Band of Joy album began at the Old Smithy in Worcester with excellent initial results. The new songs were dynamic and interesting, though the performances were a little rusty to begin with but improved substantially as the weeks passed. Marty had meanwhile pulled out of the United Artists offer and agreed a new separate deal with Polydor for the group. The managing director of Polydor at that time was an exuberant Dutchman called Freddie Haayen who had produced one of the few Dutch groups with an international following, Golden Earring. He loved the first recordings and pronounced them to be 'fantastic, fantastic'. On leaving his office after one of these very enthusiastic meetings I encountered Mike Hales with whom I had worked when running Elektra within the company. Mike enquired how the meeting had gone and, when informed of the MD's excitement over the recordings, asked if Freddie had actually jumped on to the table when he deemed them to be 'fantastic'. I had to confess that no such activity had occurred, whereupon Mike shrugged and said, 'Well, that means he didn't really like them.'

We found that hard to believe; even more so when Freddie asked if he could remix one of the tracks with a view to releasing it as a single. How could we refuse the man who controlled the company and had a successful track record as a producer?

We booked into a good London studio and arrived with the master tapes, only to discover that Freddie's idea of a remix was to push all of the faders up well pass the pain barrier and sit at the desk waving his arms about and shouting, as far as we could guess, 'fantastic'. Fortunately he had another appointment and left after about an hour, which gave us time to recover and use the remaining very expensive studio time to some purpose. Needless to say, the remix was junked.

While all this was going on I had found a neat little semi-punk band called, in a then fashionable style, Trash. They had approached me at the suggestion of my daughter Bee, who had heard them at a little local gig. Bee also mentioned in passing that she had rejected an approach from Gary Numan as she felt he was using it as an attempt to get into her knickers! I was never a fan of punk, but Trash seemed to fit the bill, and I put them together with Shel Talmy, who had produced the first hits for the Who – it seemed like a good idea to have a 'name' producer for our first release. Though close to blind, Shel did a reasonable job in the studio, and the end result bore fair comparison with anything then in the charts, without quite catching fire.

I managed to secure an audition for Vana for the leading role in the much-heralded musical *Evita*. She was perfect for the part, with her great style, superb voice, attractive accent and thigh-length boots. It was not to be – but she would have been sensational. I have to believe that the show was already cast.

With the Band of Joy album completed and ready for release in an extraordinary sleeve, it was time to outfit the band in suitable stage clothes and arrange rehearsals for the first live appearances, which were as support on the upcoming Manfred Mann national tour. Polydor had agreed to pay the costs of the tour and for a video to promote the first single, but the anticipated change at the top had taken place and the new managing director, Tony Morris, did not appear to share his predecessor's enthusiasm.

It is a fact of life in the music–biz hierarchy that enthusiasm – particularly from the top – is contagious. With Freddie at the helm Polydor were committed to the Band of Joy and prepared to invest in marketing, promotion and energy. The group still had a lot to learn in terms of presentation, but that's true of every new group. The Manfred Mann tour was arduous, covering Glasgow and Aberdeen to Birmingham and Brighton. The weather conditions were very harsh, with many dramas in the snow, but the band were improving with every show and starting to earn genuine encores.

The album was released to favourable reviews, and John Peel even played three or four tracks on his late-night show, but he sounded less than enthusiastic. Despite our long-term relationship I have never asked John to favour any record in which I have an interest. On the last date of the tour the Polydor promotion team watched from the back and, at the height of the punk craze as it was, they were dismayed by Kevyn's twin-necked guitar, which they deemed old-fashioned despite his extraordinary expertise.

I was then called to a meeting with Tony Morris and informed that he had taken a call from Robert Plant, who claimed that he was the founder and owner of the name Band of Joy. Morris informed me that he was not about to upset Robert Plant, who had apparently threatened all kinds of aggravation, and the company was not prepared to support the group without a name change. The lead singer of Led Zeppelin had, it seemed, suggested that he always planned to use the name for his next group, when Led Zeppelin had run its course. Kevyn and Paul were shocked and felt that they, as founder members, had at least an equal right to the name. Paul was convinced that, back in the early days, he had in fact written the opening riff to what became Led Zeppelin's most famous piece. He may have been right – but try to prove it. I was never thrilled with the original name since it sounded to me like a Salvation Army group and, having just purchased a group car with the number plate Joy 24 K, we decided to go with 24 K as a group name.

Polydor then made it clear that after one album and one single they had given up on the group. They had an option on a second album but decided not to exercise it after hearing the new recordings, which were heavily influenced by punk. Meanwhile the band was still on wages and well advanced into recording the new album. The original advance – which had initially seemed so generous but out of which all recording, travelling, equipment and living expenses had been paid – was now looking pretty sparse.

We recorded another single with Trash, which suffered the same fate as the first, and Polydor pulled the plug on Sarabee Music.

Muff Murfin, who owned the Worcester studios and had many contacts in the Midlands area, suggested that we join forces, and that was the genesis of the Bird's Nest label. As a sixteenth-birthday present we recorded my daughter Bee singing a couple of Sandie Shaw numbers. Bee and her brother Chet then went on the road to promote the single with interviews at local radio stations around the country. They were well received and obtained a bunch of local radio plays, but the record didn't take off. The time was not wasted, however, because Bee and Chet now own a hugely successful group of record companies with albums dominating the compilation charts.

In a break from recording the 24K album I took Vana into John Lennon's house and studio at Ascot, where she recorded a couple of the Band of Joy songs but, despite her talent and beauty, I was unable to drum up any interest. The house and gardens were remarkable.

We then discovered a group called the Wailing Cocks fronted by an extraordinary young man named Andde Leek. After recording a complete album, Andde left the group to go solo. Terrific. The replacement singer was also very good, but neither the original group nor Andde, with whom we recorded another album, ever made it despite some marvellous songs, great gigs and a couple of Radio 1 sessions. I always believed Andde to be a potential star and, in the hope that another label might do a better promotional job, leased one of his singles to Beggars Banquet. That, too, failed to ignite, and years later he recorded an album for Warners, which was produced by George Martin, again without success. A true enigma. Andde has all of the talents, cheek, attitude, looks and songs in abundance. Every time I hear a new Michael Jackson recording on the radio I think it is Andde – and he sounded like that long before Michael's breakthrough as a solo act. He did have a modicum of success as a key member of Dexy's Midnight Runners on their first hit record 'Geno'. He was never paid a royalty or session fee and when, at his request, I phoned the Dexy's management, pointing out that Andde and the drummer were exclusively contracted to my company and seeking payment for them, I was told to back off or have my legs broken.

Along with Band of Joy, we had another great group from the Midlands, Little Acre. Their live appearances were truly exceptional, with large crowds demanding encores and having a whale of a time – all with original material. We recorded an album but managed only to release one single, which was well received and gained a fair amount of radio play but again had no real success. The lead singer, Johnny Higgs, was a charismatic individual on stage but when not in front of an audience had one of the worst stammers I have ever encountered. They were an amiable bunch of miscreants travelling around the country, always broke and occasionally in trouble with the law. On one occasion they told me of the time that the ubiquitous Mr Plant popped up again, joining the group in the local café and showing them his enormous royalty cheque before divvying up the bill between them and ensuring that anybody who had toast with the coffee paid extra.

Band of Joy, now 24K, had meanwhile completed a very expensive album with no record deal in sight. I touted the tapes around and got a positive response from Chris Blackwell at Island Records who promised a US release and tour, but the managing director of the British operation simply didn't want to know. I set up an 'audition' date at a London studio at the request of some of the A & R men and was sickened when the only one to turn up was carried dead drunk from the back of his limo and never even sobered up enough to open his eyes. And I had been a director of that company! The view from the other side.

Bird's Nest continued to record and release records that nobody wanted to buy. The Rowdies were followed by a disco instrumental entitled 'The Ultimate Warlord' by the Warlords, which was Muff in disguise. This was followed by 'Buzz Buzz a Diddle It', a fifties-style rock-and-roller sung by Mysterious Melvyn with Robert Plant on backing vocals. It is probably now a highly prized collectors' item, and, no, I don't have a copy. Muff and I, under the name Flash, took joint vocal and writing credits with a send-up of the reggae hit 'Uptown Top Rankin' – well, we thought it was funny. Chris Squelch joined the list of expensive failures and, with completed but unreleased albums from the Wailing Cocks and Little Acre, we had no money left. My former employers Pye Records distributed the label, but they, too, were in trouble and about to go belly up. In today's market we could certainly have scored an advance, but that was then.

If all of this sounds harrowing and frustrating it's because it was. At the same time it was an exhilarating period of discovery and creation. Here was one of the most successful market manipulators in the business quite unable to find and produce his own hits. Probably I was too close to it all. With other people's product I could exercise clinical, even ruthless, judgement, but when it came to my own productions I simply lost faith. With many regrets and much diminished bank balance it was time to quit.

There are too many lessons here. Perhaps – most importantly – it is crucial to try to control your own destiny in terms of promotion and marketing. The money from a major company can be alluring but only if it is supported with enthusiasm and action. Talent is never enough. The ability to shout and scream and make life unbearable for everybody in pursuit of a hit is as important as good luck and timing. On the other hand, there's always the Lottery.

If, like David Geffen, you can sell your original record label to WEA for $7 million, fail as a film executive for that company, retire, then start a second label with $25 million from WEA plus a further $17 million from CBS for the overseas rights, and collar Warners' best-selling act with which to start the label, all of the foregoing is redundant. But how many King Davids can the world accommodate?

Not being David Geffen I was now close to broke and in need of employment. This was the period of the emergence of video rental as home entertainment, and 'clubs' charging fairly hefty membership fees or deposits were springing up on every high street. Some former colleagues were operating a company called Tellydisc, which sold records that were exclusively available by mail order and that were advertised in a series of two-minute commercials on ITV at peak time. I discovered that the commercials, for which the regular cost of airtime would run into hundreds of thousands of pounds, were provided gratis by the television companies for a share of the retail price. This was an early and a rather brave attempt by the television companies to pave the way for interactive home shopping. By filling up unsold airtime with a Tellydisc commercial they were also able to hold up premium rates to their regular customers. The results were sensational, with over a quarter of a million copies of a specially packaged Barry Manilow double album sold in the first promotion. Of passing interest is the fact that, despite the commercials making it clear that the double album was available only by mail order, a huge demand was created in the shops and the record label was forced into reissuing the original deleted Manilow albums. That turned Manilow's UK career around, and he continues to flourish to this day. Anybody interested in the craft of marketing may wish to note that every direct mail offer has a big retail spin-off.

Since I had good contacts in the video industry, which was at the time mainly run by record people, I approached the Tellydisc crowd with a proposal that they rent video films by mail order, using the same kind of television exposure. The scheme was adopted by the lads at Tellydisc and, more importantly, by the executives at Thames. We formed a new company called Televideo with myself as managing director, and I set about acquiring film titles for the catalogue and a campaign.

With video ownership still very much in its infancy, I came to an agreement with Granada rental shops to include a special offer on the hardware. I further secured something of a coup by obtaining rental rights to the Warners film catalogue, which was then only available for sale at about £40 a shot. John Bentley, who was notorious as a successful 'asset stripper' in the sixties, had recently acquired the video rights to the United Artists catalogue, featuring mega hits such as *Rocky* and *Rocky II*. These were included in the catalogue and formed the basis of our first commercial. John Bentley's partner Bev Ripley was brought on to the board of the new company and turned out to be one of the brightest, sharpest and most amusing people I have ever met. It was and is hard to believe his reputation as Bentley's hatchet man. Bev later opened a chain of video stores, which he subsequently sold to Blockbuster, no doubt making him a few more millions in the process.

The lads at Tellydisc were also very smart but appeared to have no long-term plans beyond making as much money as possible while planning the next 'hit' or 'sting'. They were highly skilled at presentation and hospitality but quite unwilling to go the distance. Life for them was a succession of fast cars, well-appointed offices, beautiful women and spending all the profits just before we made them. It was impossible not to be charmed by their enthusiasm but equally impossible to curtail their spending or to persuade them to focus on the mechanics of a project.

The night we launched Televideo with a much-too-expensive commercial we actually blew the fuses on the switchboard that customers were asked to call. The response was sensational, and we gathered together with the executives from Thames to sip champagne and watch the thirty or forty switchboard operators trying to cope with the avalanche of calls. Despite the response, it just didn't work. Granada was not happy with the ratio of conversions to full rental agreements and dropped out. The shops responded by lowering the club membership and deposit fees, and the public gave us a try but balked at the additional but unavoidable mailing costs. Within weeks we went from one of the most successful product launches ever to just a dribble of business, and Thames and the other commercial stations quite properly refused to provide further 'no-cost' air time.

At that point I should have walked away, but somebody came up with the bright idea of turning our customer base into a universal video club operated through regular retail shops. We would take out insurance against the loss of any tapes, and shops joining our scheme could safely rent films to any customer presenting a Televideo card. The customers were only required to pay us a fiver to enable them to rent from any shop featuring the Televideo sign, rather than pay deposit or membership fees to several stores. It was an excellent concept, but by the time we managed to obtain operating capital from a venture-capital bank, secure the insurance, find the premises, hire the staff and install a computer system the market had moved on and free club membership became the norm. Our brand new operation was redundant virtually as soon as it began.

It seems to me that timing is everything. It took too long to finance, record and release Band of Joy, by which time punk was sweeping away the concept of well-played music, and the same was true in a different sense with Televideo. In fashion-conscious industries such as music or movies – and no doubt in other areas – it is not enough to have a great group or business plan without having instant access to the funds with which to make it happen.

With video technology still very new, a mighty battle raged between the three formats of VHS, Beta and Philips for market dominance. Whichever format won would get a royalty on every machine and cassette sold, and I was engaged in a consultant capacity both by Sony and Philips to persuade the film companies to make their catalogues available to them. We achieved a measure of success but too late to stem the dominance of VHS, which is now being replaced by DVD – another way to sell us the same old stuff again.

Working out of Shepperton Studios we struggled on for a year or so trying to raise further finance and keep the project afloat, but eventually we were faced with closure and bankruptcy. I did find a buyer for the bones of the business, but he, too, struggled to find the necessary finance and, despite having previously been massively successful in his native Sweden and in Holland and Germany, he threw in the towel. By this time I was burned out, exhausted and, following several pointless sessions with a psychoanalyst, spent the next twelve months in hospital trying to recover from the butchery of the National Health Service.

Waking up one morning with severe stomach pains, I was rushed to St Peter's Hospital in Chertsey for what was described as a routine operation. The surgeon was on attachment from the Army and may have had other things on his mind, as it all went horribly wrong. This resulted in a series of further operations over the following months that often left me wrapped in tin foil like a Christmas turkey and all too frequently hovering between life and death. Confidence was not restored when the surgeon made ward rounds with a strong scent of liquor on his breath.

The food was inedible and, given my seriously weakened condition, the ward sister suggested that Shurley feed me with home-cooked meals twice each day. In view of my lengthy stay the state benefit was reduced to £19 per week, which did not begin to cover the cost of Shurley's petrol and food deliveries – and this after a lifetime of handing over a sizeable chunk of not inconsiderable earnings to Social Security. Imagine my delight when, after finally being discharged, I wandered into my local post office to mail a job application and stood in line behind a dozen or so men, many of whom could not speak English, being handed piles of nice maroon twenty-pound notes. My spirits were further raised by a visit from two tax collectors demanding £10,000 in tax and National Insurance payments for the time I spent in hospital. They accepted that I had been unable to earn a living while prostrate on my back and close to death but insisted that Shurley or I should have disputed their original claims – like we had nothing else to do. By this time we were just about to get going with Strange Fruit Records and, as they refused to leave the house without a cheque, we gritted our teeth and paid up.

Over the years I have often wondered if I was being paranoid about that hospital, where the poor nursing staff were forced to do everything literally at a run, but feel somewhat vindicated, though still crippled, by the recent announcement that St Peter's was named as Britain's worst hospital. We did consider legal action against the bastards, but, having spent a few thousand on a second opinion that affirmed I had a clear-cut case for a medical negligence suit, I was reliably informed that the insurers would drag out the case for several years and, in the unlikely event that I lost, I could face legal costs of close to a million. We decided to get on with our lives.

LAWYERS

For the artist, agent, manager, promoter, label owner or entrepreneur, dealings with the lawyers acting either for or against you will become an inevitable and unavoidable necessity. They will be expensive, tiresome and only rarely efficient.

When we conceived Strange Fruit records we honestly believed that it would be sufficient to provide a simple two-page document laying out in clear language our obligations to the artists and confirming the limitations of our rights. In layman's terms, it stated the amount of the advance, the royalties due, the suggested price of the records, the dates upon which the royalties would be due and the countries in which we were allowed to sell the records. Since there were no obligations upon the artists to do anything other than to be paid royalties, we somewhat naïvely hoped that would be sufficient. We also believed that a standard royalty for all would be acceptable; one that allowed us to make some profit and was fair to the artists who had, of course, been paid for the original recordings by the BBC and would consider these additional royalties to be 'found' money.

In general it worked out, but the more successful acts consulted their lawyers who inevitably required inserts and additions to our original agreements along with much improved royalty rates. In fact the more successful the act the easier it became to pay higher royalties owing to the economies of scale, which are as important in the field of music as they are in any other business.

We believed that the whole contractual situation had reached its climax when we negotiated the release of the Queen BBC recordings. Queen were managed by Jim Beach, who was an eminent lawyer in his own right, having been a partner in Harbottle and Lewis, the official legal representatives of the British Phonographic Industry. It would be fair to say that what Jim did not know about the legal side of the business was probably not worth knowing. He examined our by now considerably expanded agreement, made substantial alterations and adjustments, to which we consented, and then sent it all on to his lawyers where the process began again. Following much discussion and negotiation, we did arrive at an agreement that we could live with and with which the lawyers were reasonably content.

Since Queen were at that time one of the biggest acts in the world and were represented by a top lawyer, who in turn used the services of one of the top law firms, we truly thought that the resulting agreement would serve as a benchmark and be suitable for all of the important acts. Don't you believe it. In every instance where we sent out identical agreements they came back full of red ink, inserts and crossings out. And the objections were rarely the same. On one silly occasion we sent two copies of an agreement to the two lawyers representing an act and received one copy back fully signed by one partner just a day or so after getting the other copy returned covered in red ink and with complete pages altered.

It is important to remember that these negotiations were to grant us a licence to release, in a limited form and in limited territories, recordings that were owned and paid for by the BBC. Invariably, they were made in the early days of artists' careers when they were anxious for any radio exposure. The artists were not required to do anything other than give their consent.

When it comes to initiating a recording career, things are very different. The company is at risk for the entire menu of advances, recording costs, videos, tour support, marketing and considerable executive time. They are not about to throw all this away on a promise and will go to great lengths to ensure that their considerable investments are secure. Any contract will contain provisions to ensure that the services of the artist is exclusive for at least the next three or five years, with a minimum number of further recordings to be made available every year on request.

We once licensed a collection of tracks to EMI and were horrified by the size and complexity of the agreement – almost the size of a telephone directory. It was possible to track how the various paragraphs had come into practice from the company being burned at different times, but it seemed much too complex for what was a fairly simple deal. I now understand that the standard EMI contract for video alone is fatter than that old agreement, and that makes it impossible to read without professional advice.

One very famous and successful American lawyer suggests that a new act should sign almost any agreement just to get a foot in the door on the basis that, if successful, any contract can be renegotiated and probably will. Typical American lawyer advice and guaranteed to keep the fees rolling in.

An example of this was when I was working with Jonathan King, who had a number of hits with 10CC at UK Records. Being the honourable man that he is, he believes that a deal is sacrosanct. When Phonogram offered the band a million to switch labels, JK dug his heels in and refused to let them go, despite the fact that the deal they had at UK Records was, to say the least, ungenerous. He believed that the band and their management had signed an agreement in good faith and that they should respect it – just as JK would have respected it had his investment not been successful. We decided to fight. The problem was that our lawyer, Paul Marshall, also represented Phonogram. He also represented Decca Records, who also had a substantial interest as they distributed UK Records throughout the world.

'Mighty Marshall', as JK called him, would then visit the office to discuss strategy, and occupy a different corner of the room as he expounded the conflicting arguments. With his UK Records hat on he would suggest the legal moves to combat the Phonogram offer and then move to another corner to theorize on how they might respond, moving to another corner of the room to lay out the Decca position. We were enthralled and a trifle dizzy. The end result was that 10CC got their million and a massively increased royalty, JK got an override royalty on future recordings and I never was told what Decca got out of the deal, but, since the first Phonogram release was 'I'm Not in Love', there were a lot of smiling faces.

This is a rare example of the negotiating skills of a top American lawyer, but I have a hunch that it would not have been considered acceptable legal practice by a British court had it come to trial, since there was some conflict of interest. Incidentally, Lol Creme subsequently told me that 'I'm Not in Love' had been scrapped by the band after a number or aborted sessions. The master tape was resting in the rubbish bin at the studio when it occurred to Lol, as he drove home after midnight, that the addition of the heavenly voices might be the missing element. There then followed a nocturnal race back to the studio to retrieve the tapes before the cleaners arrived, and when the group appeared the next morning he had completed the multi-track overdubs. The record became 10CC's biggest-ever hit, selling millions around the world.

A fairly typical bunch of 'Manchester whingers', 10CC would sit in my office complaining about how badly life was treating them and then drive off in their various Mercedes limousines. I do wish that I had kept some of the little cartoon drawings that Lol used to illustrate to me just how hard up they were.

Marty Machat was another great American lawyer who preferred to resolve conflict by negotiation. He would often settle differences by inviting the parties to a day at the races where, in a convivial atmosphere, the adversaries were usually more accommodating. Perhaps it is because in the American legal system lawyers are paid on results rather than by extortionate fees. The situation is changing in Britain with the introduction of 'contingency' charges, but it is hard to believe that this will have any effect on the adversarial and confrontational stances of our professionals.

We were fortunate in finding Iain Adam, who is one of the good guys and who has represented us well over the years, along with some of the bigger names in music. He is reasonable and does not try to impress or confuse through jargon.

An altogether different situation arose when I tried to help my friend Muff Murfin in his dealings with Phonogram. Muff owns and runs a couple of studios and produces radio jingles along with countless other activities that keep him busy and prosperous. He had a stroke of luck when he was offered the opportunity to write and produce the music for the British version of *Gladiators* on television and was assured that the music would be used in dozens of trails for the show for some weeks before transmission. He decided to record the background music as an album and release the theme music as a single. Muff offered us the rights to the recordings, but I figured that a major company was needed to fully exploit the hit potential and offered to make a deal for him with a major company purely as a favour.

With that volume of promotion promised, I knew it would not be difficult to set up a deal and, accordingly, approached an old chum, Brian Berg, who was in charge of television projects at Phonogram. Brian jumped at the deal, and we agreed terms on the spot without lengthy discussions or haggling. The problems arose when the deal reached the Phonogram legal and business affairs department who took for ever to issue a contract in which the deal was changed beyond recognition. This is pretty unusual. It is acceptable to discuss and negotiate minor points of a contract with company lawyers, but, having agreed the basic terms like advances and royalties, it is unique in my experience to have these arbitrarily changed without notice. I made it clear to the woman in charge of the Phonogram legalese that I would sign the agreement as discussed or go elsewhere. The response was that I was a prima donna and 'difficult'. As the deadline for the start of the television series was fast approaching and we needed to get a single out in time to meet the anticipated demand, there was not in fact time to seek an alternative licensee, but I thought it best at least to talk tough.

With only days to go to the deadline, a new agreement was received that bore at least some similarities to the original concept, so I signed and returned it, swearing never again to deal with Phonogram. A couple of days later I took a call from the lady, in which she stated that the agreement I had signed and returned was, in fact, the wrong one and that we should revert to the earlier agreements

that I had refused. When I pointed out that I had signed an agreement devised and provided by her company, she said that if I insisted on sticking to that agreement she would be forced to fire her secretary and did I want that on my conscience?

This was insanity and, frankly, I exploded, threatening to cancel the deal and make their shenanigans public. No more was heard from the woman, who was, please remember, the head of the legal department at Phonogram, until several months after the release of the album, by which time it had gone gold, earning my chum much dosh. Then she called him asking if he had a copy of the agreement as Phonogram had mislaid their copy. That perfectly illustrated that the fun for her was in the confrontation and that the eventual agreement was almost incidental.

The bad news is that, increasingly, the lawyers are taking over the running of music and movie companies and they in turn hire more lawyers to look after the nuts and bolts, since they then believe they have moved into the creative area. CBS in the USA has always had a lawyer at the helm, but a lot of very knowledgeable people point to the arrival of lawyers as the start of the decline of the music industry as an innovative and creative force.

All this is probably not unique to the music business, but the process is very obstructive in a creative industry. Lawyers know this, and I've heard that one of the favourite jokes in legal circles poses the question, 'What do you call twelve dead lawyers?' Answer: 'A start.'

22. STRANGE FRUIT

CS WITH JOHN PEEL, 1986

Strange Fruit

Strange Fruit Records
By arrangement with BBC Records and Tapes

Side 2

STRANGE FRUIT

On the heels of the failed video business, and following a full year in hospital flirting with the Grim Reaper, I was finally at home facing up to convalescence and unemployment.

This was 1985, and while I was away punk had happened and the music business had transformed into an animal I barely recognized. Sheer ability and talent had given way to image or attitude, and the new hit-makers were the New Romantics and shoe-gazers. Even as a kid I was a reactionary old bastard, and the current crop had me completely foxed. It is almost impossible to dip in and out of the music business. Those who stay the course and have a reasonably open mind can often recognize and appreciate the evolving trends – or at least employ someone who can. Drop out of the business for even a relatively short time and you may never recover lost ground.

After selling Asylum Records and absenting himself for a couple of years, even the infamous David Geffen found himself out of touch when he roared back with Geffen Records and millions of dollars of backing. He eventually had the sense and the money to hire good young people who turned the company around by signing acts such as Guns 'n' Roses and the revived Aerosmith, who were a far and very loud cry from the 'old guard' acts initially signed to the new label.

Now here was I, flat on my back both figuratively and literally. The year in hospital had exhausted us, both physically and financially, while the only business I knew anything about had raced off into unfamiliar and barely fathomable territory. What to do?

Shurley had continued managing John Peel, and listening to his radio shows on a regular basis at least kept her informed of music trends. John continued to discover interesting new acts that were invited to record sessions at the BBC studios. Many of the groups John featured in session were unsigned to any record or publishing company, and it occurred to me, with my music-publisher's hat on, that they might welcome a modest cash advance in return for turning over to my company the publishing rights to the three or four songs featured on the session. Radio 1 is obliged to pay the Performing Rights Society, the agency which collects royalties on behalf of song writers, each time any song is played on air. At the time the fee was around £30. If the music was not lodged with a publisher, or if the writers were not members of the PRS, the money went into a slush fund to await a claim at some time in the future or, in all too many cases, simply to wait for ever.

I was prepared to attend future session recordings and offer the composers £100 in return for a share of the publishing income, which would at least help them defray the cost of van hire and petrol. Though initially out of pocket, I expected to make a profit on any repeat fees and hoped to get lucky with the odd hit. The Frankies wrote 'Relax' and 'Two Tribes' on the train to London to record a Peel session, and publishing either of those two songs would have earned millions.

Shurley agreed that the idea was worth further investigation and suggested that I meet up with Johns Peel and Walters, since it could work only with their approval and cooperation. Neither of them was overly impressed with the plan, but one of them, I don't remember which, cut right to the chase and asked why I hadn't considered releasing the complete sessions on disc. They were proud of their pioneering work, but the BBC had a policy of destroying or simply losing session tapes, and this would at least provide a reason for keeping them available. I would, of course, need to get the approval of BBC Enterprises, the commercial side of the Corporation, and probably the approval of all of the musicians involved, but it looked a safer bet than hoping for the odd hit.

The first call was to Johnny Beerling, then head of Radio 1, who immediately gave us an enthusiastic green light. He could have just as easily killed the project but was most helpful. Thanks, Johnny.

The next priority was to seek the approval of and work out a commercial arrangement with BBC Enterprises. That only took about six months! The guy in charge was simply never there and his assistant appeared to be permanently at lunch. I would call every day – sometimes several times a day, but the boss never returned my calls. I later learned that he was being treated for cancer and the lunches his assistant in the legal department attended were essentially liquid. I assume that the entire department went into limbo in that period because no other person was prepared to discuss the matter.

I did at last get to meet the man, who received the idea with enthusiasm, agreed a reasonable commercial arrangement, and even offered to print and supply notepaper combining our new logo with those of the BBC and Radio 1. To set the record straight, Strange Fruit is indeed a reference to the Billie Holiday recording of the same name. John, a fan of W.C. Fields and football, suggested 'Bank Dick' or 'Back o' the Net Records'. The latter seemed like a bit of a mouthful and the former, when written down, can be mistaken for Black Dick, which I figured might limit its appeal somewhat.

Apart from the commercial BBC considerations, which granted us exclusive access to the sessions in return for guarantees and a royalty on every session released, we had to provide proof of agreement with the Musicians' Union and the written approval of every participant on every session recording released. Dealing with union representatives is rarely easy, and my earlier experiences dealing with the MU over visiting American acts or prerecording backing tracks for television did not fill me with enthusiasm. To monitor our performance in this regard, the Corporation appointed their in-house union representative, who was fortunately not very bright and fairly lazy. After a few more weeks of negotiations we came to an agreement with the MU whereby we would pay each musician, on each session released, a further session fee in addition to any royalty arrangements. Occasionally the 'musician' in question was just a mate of the band, who turned up and banged an ashtray or radiator to pick up a few bob.

We now had a name, agreements with BBC Enterprises and the MU and some notepaper. We very urgently needed finance and John's suggestions as to which groups we should approach for the first releases, since it would be silly to release sessions that he was unlikely to approve.

Getting money from any financial institution requires the preparation of a business plan laying out in some detail how much is needed, how it will be spent and a reasonable estimate of when it will be repaid, plus, of course, an indication of the likely profits involved and any securities available – your house, for instance. We had to decide quickly how many records we expected to release and how many each was likely to sell; then choose the best route in terms of manufacturing and distribution as opposed to licensing; the likely advances, royalties, mastering and sleeve design costs; what percentage to set aside for marketing, legal, accountancy, travel, telephone; and God knew what else.

In simple terms, to license a label to a major company means giving up any control in return for an advance and a royalty. Our previous experience of licensing to majors clearly showed that they were only interested in hits. They also had extensive catalogues of their own to work on and could not be relied on to spend much time on what was likely to be essentially a collectors' label. The majors have their place and can bring home a potential hit quicker and in greater volume than most of the indie distributors, but in this instance we decided to go with the growing indie trade and opted for manufacturing.

I discovered that an old friend, Adrian Owlet – remember the Gene Vincent episode? – had purchased a record-manufacturing plant out at Slough, and we quickly agreed a keen price for pressing there. This was in the days of vinyl and cassettes, and all the intelligence we were able to gather indicated that we should release each four- or five-track session as a twelve-inch EP. Each release would need to be mastered, cut and transferred to a master disc at a specialist studio, and these costs had to be included in the equation. The paper labels had to be designed, typeset and printed by another specialist for each release, which left the twelve-inch sleeves. With fairly modest anticipated sales, we decided it would be too costly to provide anything but a black-and-white 'generic' sleeve, and we figured that the series was likely to become more important than any individual artists. Even so, every sleeve needed to be typeset and printed with details of the song titles, musicians, producers and recording dates. Even the inclusion of a photograph would bump up the costs, and thus the distinctive Strange Fruit sleeve listing hundreds of recorded sessions in random order was born. Shurley toiled well into several nights listing the hundreds of artists culled from the BBC's session sheets and from memory. These, too, needed to be typeset and checked for accuracy.

With rough costings assessed for advances, session fees, tape-copying, cutting, mastering, record labels and sleeves available and a recommended retail price of £1.99 as a target, we were in the business of pennies and fractions of pennies. Out of the retail price came 15 per cent VAT, a further 40 per cent for the dealer, then 25 per cent for the distributor. From what was left we had to try to make a profit after paying all of the costs plus royalties based on the retail price to the BBC, the artists and to the Mechanical Copyright Protection Society, which collected statutory royalties on behalf of the writers, composers and publishers.

Somehow we persuaded the bank that we could make it work. The first one, Lloyds, turned us down flat, but we later learned that the manager was a misogynist and always refused loans to women – despite our having dealt with the bank for years.

Barclays was our saviour. It demanded the security of a charge on the house, but by this time the train was running and we felt confident.

With the manufacturing and pricing in place, together with just enough finance to survive, we now had to arrange sales and distribution without any indication as to what our first releases might be. The first call, again at Peel's suggestion, was Rough Trade, who had become an important player from small beginnings in the back of a shop in Notting Hill. I had previously met the owner, Geoff Travis, when he had declined to distribute a record by Andde Leek that I had produced, and it was with some trepidation that we drove out to their large and extremely busy warehouse in King's Cross.

Again the Peel connection worked its magic, and Geoff was keen to distribute the label before we had firmed up releases. Unfortunately the Rough Trade staff to whom we were introduced appeared to know little or nothing of the business of royalty accounting, and our enquiries about mandatory payments to the MCPS were met with blank looks. Since this is a basic tenet of record manufacture and distribution, we became concerned about the whole accounting process. There is little doubt that Strange Fruit and Rough Trade Records were a natural partnership at that time, but my background with the major labels had made me all too aware that image and performance were very different animals.

The former sales director at Pye Records, Trevor Eyles, had moved to another indie distributor in the role of managing director. The company, Pinnacle Records, was owned by Steve Mason, who was fairly new to the business. He had bought the company, which had a somewhat chequered past, when it had been close to bankruptcy but had now begun to turn it into a considerable force. A call to Trevor resulted in a meeting with him and Steve where a deal was struck within minutes. Steve even offered a modest advance, which we accepted with a degree of relief. Anybody meeting Steve Mason cannot fail to be impressed by his sheer size, enthusiasm and attention to every detail. In business he is an astute poker player, but beneath that flinty exterior beats a heart of granite. We later realized that he needed Strange Fruit as much as we needed him, but, from our viewpoint, Pinnacle was a hungry, aggressive and well-managed operation.

John eventually, and somewhat grumpily, presented me with a huge pile of 'session sheets' as his preferred choices, culled from trawling through the BBC paper archives. Each session sheet is simply a note of the songs recorded, the participating musicians, the producer and the date. There were no details of where any of the musicians could be found and, since we were operating at the fringe of the Corporation, there was very little help available from the BBC Artists Index, where the details of managers, agents and contact numbers were kept.

Some, such as New Order, were easy to find, but others, the Buzzcocks included, were spread around the world. We tracked down one member of a hit group, who had returned to pumping petrol in an obscure northern town. New Order were brilliant. 'Anything for John,' they immediately responded and turned the details over to their lawyer, Iain Adam, who negotiated such a generous but fair agreement on their behalf that we immediately asked him to work for us.

Contracts are an enormously important aspect of the record business, and woe betide anybody who proceeds without a clear understanding on paper signed by all parties. Handshake deals are fine for failures, but at the first whiff of big bucks somebody always gets greedy. If the prize is really big it usually ends up in the hands of lawyers – and they are always the winners, their fees often swallowing up all the profits. Few lawyers and certainly no inexperienced solicitor could fully comprehend the subtle language or twists and turns. Jac Holzman told me that he failed to sign Pink Floyd to Elektra in their early days because he lost patience with their solicitor, who had previously dealt with house conveyancing. No doubt their current legal representatives have more savvy.

Because we were asking for no further commitment from the musicians, other than their permission to release commercially tracks already recorded, we were able to keep our agreements limited to just one page written in clear English. This detailed the songs, the rights granted, the territory, the period and the royalty rate. As I have pointed out elsewhere, such a straightforward approach was rarely enough, and, following negotiations with various lawyers or teams of lawyers representing various artists, even our simple statement of our obligations grew and grew.

Just as we began to make headway with finding and securing the agreements of the musicians, we received a very stern letter from our man at BBC Enterprises forbidding us to make any use of the BBC and Radio 1 logos on our notepaper and demanding that we scrap any such notepaper in our possession. We were further required to provide a written undertaking to make no further use of any such paper on pain of severe penalties. Since the notepaper in question had been designed, printed and supplied by the same fellow this came as something of a surprise – but was just one of many such eccentricities we learned to accept.

From over a hundred letters and agreements sent out, we eventually received the approvals of the members of New Order, Stiff Little Fingers, Sudden Sway, the Damned, the Screaming Blue Messiahs and the Wild Swans. I was also able to find the original tapes in the basement of the BBC's Egton House, which is a true Aladdin's cave of unique session recordings by some of the greatest – and many of the least successful – artists and groups of the past forty years. At that time no one person had responsibility for the tapes, and all too many were lost, destroyed or still locked up in dusty cupboards across London. Mainly as a result of our activities, the BBC subsequently appointed Phil Lawton as the official curator of the archives. He was a superb choice, being knowledgeable, helpful and immensely enthusiastic. But back then there was nobody, and I would borrow the appropriate keys and spend hours crawling around the basement making lists of what was available and what we might release. I am still a fan and could barely contain my excitement at the sight of the riginal and unreleased recordings by the Beatles, Cream, Floyd and the rest.

With the first six releases decided on, we were able to make a presentation to the Pinnacle sales force, with test pressings of the records, sleeves, details of the prices and our ambitions. It is crucial that any sales force is provided with adequate tools, samples and information to enable them to present effectively to the record buyers. It is often helpful to address the sales team in person, answer questions and try to enthuse them.

This I was happy to do despite still being weak from my sojourn in hospital and exhausted by the negotiations and preparations for the project.

The evening before the scheduled sales presentation I received a telephone message from our man at BBC Enterprises instructing me to cancel the presentation and meet him urgently. As the message was not received until after 6 p.m., with the presentation planned for 10 a.m. the following day, we decided to take a chance and go ahead with the presentation, since to miss it would delay the release for a month – and we were running alarmingly low on funds. Under the circumstances sleep was somewhat scarce that night, but the sales team loved the concept and appeared to be most up and enthusiastic – so much so that we were held up and forced to drive at breakneck speed from Kent across London to meet with our man at Enterprises. Arriving shattered from the drive on one of the hottest days of the year, elated by the sales reception and nervously anticipating the reason for the emergency meeting at the BBC, our man greeted us with the comment that the meeting was 'not important' and he had forgotten the reason for demanding it.

As the day of release approached, we mailed out packages of all six records to every national or local radio station, every disc jockey or producer likely to give us a sympathetic listen and, of course, the record reviewers in the music and national press. At the same time we designed and distributed a striking poster for display in the record stores. The response from radio was patchy but worth the effort and expense; the response from the press was almost 100 per cent favourable, with even the *NME* giving us positive thumbs up. The icing on what was becoming a substantial promotional and marketing cake was when Johnny Beerling threw an 'on air' party with celebrities dropping in on Peel's show to enthuse about the label. It was a starry night and just the launch we needed.

The response from the retail trade was considerably better than we had dared hope. Orders were piling up, and on the day of release we actually shipped eight tons of records. The clear front runners were New Order, with the Damned some way behind in second and the remaining four releases barely reaching the minimum anticipated figure of two thousand sales each. The next releases followed a similar pattern, and it quickly became apparent that we had indeed established a collectors' label with modest sales for every release but the big sales confined to the established hit-makers – proving yet again the old marketing maxim that 90 per cent of your profits come from only 10 per cent of your product. Easy to say, but the hit-makers, Siouxsie and the Banshees, for example, and their record companies were only too aware of their importance.

The Banshees owed a huge debt of gratitude to John, since it was primarily as a result of recording Peel Sessions that they were eventually signed to Polydor. Anybody around London in the late seventies will recall the 'Sign the Banshees' graffiti campaign. Siouxsie herself and her manager were very helpful, but the original band that recorded the sessions had broken up in some acrimony and were not even speaking to each other except through lawyers. This was a very common situation requiring a considerable degree of tact and diplomacy in obtaining all of the signatures of the participating musicians. Annoyingly, while we were still having discussions, the Banshees sacked their manager.

At the time of our first releases the record industry was sharply divided between established major labels and the aggressive new indie labels, such as Creation, Rough Trade and Beggars Banquet. The indies even had their own charts appearing in the trade and music press where our first releases quickly established a firm foothold – much to the annoyance of our major-league competitors.

Most days we toiled through until midnight, but each day was full of excitement, with whoops of joy when we received positive responses from the likes of Robert Smith of the Cure or David Gedge of the Wedding Present. The Smiths eventually came on board and were most welcome, but we never quite repeated the sales of our first release by New Order. I am somewhat embarrassed to recall that when I first listened to the test pressing of the New Order session I thought it had been cut at the wrong speed and called in a fan to check it out.

A huge thrill for all of us was obtaining the approval of Herb Cohen to release Tim Buckley's session. Herb is a doughty and occasionally cynical gentleman, but even he looked pretty wistful as he listened to the cassette copy. Tough old campaigner that he is, he simply needed to assess the quality of the recording and gave us the green light with no strings. Not so my former record company Elektra, who threatened to sue us until we agreed to pay them an additional royalty, as did Tim's former wife through her new partner. Sadly, that session barely covered its costs – but it is the essence of the label.

Another early coup was obtaining the approval to release a Jimi Hendrix session. Alan Douglas, who is a jazzer from way back when, appeared to represent the estate and was resplendent in black cloak and shiny black Western boots. Bee and Chet had recently joined us to help develop the 'Indie Top 20' label, and Chet, who had a background as a salesman in the liquor trade, accompanied me to one of the meetings with Alan. It would be fair to say that my son was somewhat gobsmacked by this larger-than-life figure, but now that he and his sister own several record companies with a considerable staff he has become accustomed to the eccentricities and eccentrics of the music biz.

The Indie Top 20 project came about as a direct result of our releases appearing so frequently in the indie charts. At that time Virgin was spending a fortune advertising the 'Now That's What I Call Music' series on television, and it occurred to me that a similar but somewhat downbeat approach might work well for the indie trade. Many of the titles appearing in the indie charts were strictly one-off, with modest sales and a limited shelf life. To be included in a compilation would at least provide some additional income and exposure. The project was generally welcomed by our colleagues on the other labels, and Bee and Chet were given the responsibility of making it work. They were also asked to handle the 'Night Tracks' series, which dealt mainly with sessions recorded for the Janice Long and David 'Kid' Jensen shows on Radio 1. Neither of these projects was very profitable, but they did provide an excellent learning curve for Bee and Chet, who, when they eventually buggered off to – very successfully – do their own thing, paused only to blag some of the office furniture.

Anyway, the Hendrix release was moderately successful and, since we were scrupulously honest and prompt in our accounting, Alan Douglas offered us a complete album of BBC Hendrix sessions. He, too, had spent years trying to obtain the rights from our friends at BBC Enterprises and had only succeeded with a change of personnel in that organization. We were delighted but, without the means to offer an appropriate advance, turned to Steve Mason at Pinnacle for advice and finance. By this time Pinnacle had become enormously successful with PWL Records, and Kylie Minogue in particular. Steve also owned a well-respected and flourishing heavy metal label, which gave him an inside track on what sales could be expected from a Hendrix release. Imagine our surprise when he suggested an advance based on expected sales of just fifteen thousand copies. It was a derisory figure and not one I was prepared to pass on. As a thank-you to Alan I introduced him to Castle Records who snapped up the opportunity and went on to sell over a quarter of a million. We earned nothing from the deal and were pretty unhappy with Steve for not supporting us. I was recently informed that the same album with additional tracks was just reissued and sold half a million in the USA alone.

Later that year Alan Douglas produced a series about Hendrix for American radio, containing speech, demos, interviews and bits of released and unreleased music. I asked him if we could issue it in edited form on disc in return for a royalty. He agreed, and I offered the project to Castle as a limited edition with each disc numbered, in the expectation that this would make it more desirable to Hendrix fans. Released as a joint project with profits equally shared, it was hugely successful in all three formats. We limited the pressings to advance sales only with no opportunity for reorders, but when the final accounting came in I noticed considerable discrepancies between the sales reported and the quantities manufactured. My protests to Castle met with little response, but there wasn't much I could do except demand a full audit, which would be too expensive and time consuming. I managed to keep back several copies of the CD as potential collectors' items but lost these along with my priceless thirty-year record collection when I was burgled. It was nevertheless a satisfying and rewarding project that amply repaid the dozens of hours I spent editing and mastering the original six hours of radio programming. A couple of years later Jac Holzman created a similar radio series on the Doors and gave me permission to repeat the process, but I was unable to get permission from his old company Elektra. I was sorely tempted to make my first venture into bootlegging, but sanity prevailed.

Following the success of the New Order session, the band allowed us to issue the Joy Division tracks and, within a few months, we had releases from both the Fall and the Undertones, which were reasonably well received, not least by JP since they are two of his favourites. (The Undertones re-formed for one night just to play at Peely's fiftieth birthday party but were unable to perform owing to a death in the family of one of the band.) Somewhat surprisingly, on account of his fearsome reputation, we enjoyed a most amicable relationship with Mark E. Smith. When we eventually released full albums of sessions we tried very hard to come up with a full album from the Fall, but Mark wanted John to suggest the best tracks and John would not be content with less than a double – or even triple – album containing all of their sessions.

Releases by bands such as Twa Toots, Xmal Deutschland and Stump did a lot for our credibility but little for the bottom line. Our distributors, not unreasonably, wanted the big names, but we stuck to our guns and continued to come up with what we hoped was a representative mix of acts rather than simply creaming off the big sellers. That, at least, was what kept us in favour with the many artists and record companies that were keeping an eye on us. A particular pleasure was tracking down and obtaining approval to release the truly historic recordings by Pink Floyd founder member Syd Barrett who, we were informed, was alive and well and living happily with his mum in Cambridgeshire. Syd's brother, Dr Barrett, signed on his behalf and, though we were never able to release the Pink Floyd sessions, the group never objected to our EP of Syd's stuff.

Life was almost unbearably hectic but confined pretty much to the mechanics of the business, and I decided it was time to get out and meet some of the new bands who were setting the pace. Making a rare visit to the BBC Maida Vale studios to meet one of the leading thrash bands, Napalm Death, I was astonished and delighted to discover that this young group of shaven-headed and tattooed individuals in ripped denims and T-shirts were in fact a most amiable and polite bunch of vegans. Yet again I was reminded that, as a general rule, those with the most fearsome public image are often the easiest people to get along with. The reverse is also often true. Can that nice Mr Blair really be such a sweetheart *and* the most powerful person in the country?

To celebrate our first year and fiftieth session we needed something special and were delighted to get the nod from the Cure, who were very hot at that time. Robert Smith was most helpful and personally chose the session from many that they had recorded. It was a bit strange to meet him getting out of his Range Rover in the middle of the day in full make-up but, as they say, 'whatever gets you through the night'. The logistics were somewhat difficult, as the band recorded for Fiction Records, which was licensed to Polydor, all of which had to give their consent, but somehow it all worked out and, for the occasion, we changed the record cover to gold with an appropriate huge poster. Over the next couple of years I tried to get approval for a full album release, but the timing was never right. I sent copies of all the sessions recorded by the band and received from Robert his preferred track listings, but it never happened.

Very few of the truly mega acts ever responded to our enquiries, though we did come close with Elton John, but were unable to finalize things. David Bowie demurred and procrastinated, the Stones refused through their titled management, Paul Beatle never replied, and the closest I got to the Zep was to renew a friendship with their great but ailing manager Peter Grant, who kept himself busy looking after his collection of vintage Rollers. The breakthrough came with an enquiry to the Queen office. Jim Beach who, years earlier, had been our lawyer when I started Dandelion managed the group at this time. He gave us approval subject to interminable contractual negotiations (detailed in the section 'Lawyers'). The only caveat was that the album must feature a full-colour-black-and-white photo, which was to be provided by his office. I had never heard of a full-colour-black-and-white photo, which seemed to be a contradiction in terms, but was happy to oblige. Brian May handed me the picture and was unexpectedly quiet and unassuming. We really needed to get into the areas of albums and CDs, but John was never a great fan of Queen and, fearing that he might object, we started a new label called Band of Joy just for the

Queen album. It exceeded all of our expectations and was our first entry in the regular charts. Pinnacle was thrilled and so were our bankers. Some time later Freddie passed away and the album once again hit the national charts, but this time there was little joy in the event.

With the success of the Queen album on a new label I turned to the sessions recorded for the Alan 'Fluff' Freeman and Tommy Vance shows, which Tony Wilson produced, creating for these a new label identity, Raw Fruit. In general, it would be fair to say that the motivation of the heavy metal groups leans more toward the financial than the artistic and, with rare exceptions, we were never able to obtain cooperation from any of the major groups. Those sessions we were able to release sold poorly, and we were unable to come even close to the achievements of the Strange Fruit or Band of Joy series, which is perhaps a lesson to be learned – but I have no answers. The only album to show any life was by Jethro Tull, which can hardly be deemed heavy metal. Ian Anderson pondered long and hard before saying yes. He recalled the recordings without pleasure, as they had taken place on the eve of an American tour that he had been forced to cancel on account of ill health. I wish we could have served him better.

A lot has been said about racism in the music business, and it does exist – but my experience has been the opposite of the accepted ideas. Probably responding to years of oppression, far too many black artists make unreasonable demands that can limit their opportunities. We managed very few releases by black acts and often regretted even those. We tried to release sessions by a number of black performers but were beaten back by suspicion and hostility. One of Peel's very favourite groups is Misty In Roots, who, when we were eventually able to track them down, demanded that we spend a quarter of a million on television advertising and only retain one penny in the pound of any proceeds. All out of an EP selling at £1.99! Yo!

Peel is still resistant to CDs and in a classic on-air quote said that he was aware of the fact that vinyl releases contained surface noise but 'so does life'. We, too, held out against the new technology for as long as possible, but it became irresistible and we were forced to seek session artists prepared to allow us to release full albums. This was a very difficult task, but again New Order came to our rescue and granted permission to release an album, with the sole proviso that the cover featured a photo taken by their friendly photographer who had created a career from following and snapping the group. Finding the photographer was almost as difficult as tracking down some of the more obscure bands, but eventually he was located and charged us several hundred pounds for a poorly lit and ill-defined shot of what I presume was a band entering a subway. No matter, the album was an artistic and commercial success as were those from Billy Bragg, Joy Division, the Chameleons, Soft Machine and many more. The manager of Soft Machine assured us that he had the full authority and approval of all members of the group and gave us a fairly hard time with the advance and contract negotiations. Then, as soon as the double album hit the streets, various band members surfaced to tell us that they knew nothing of the deal and threatening legal action. Even the beloved Robert Wyatt expressed his concern.

The Only Ones were pretty hard to find, but the response to that release was so positive that the band began discussions about re-forming. I think the discussions are still going on. We tried to get approval for a full Fleetwood Mac release but were not at the time able to make contact with founder member Peter Green, who was variously described as sleeping rough in Richmond or to be found outside a pub in Kingston. Our enquiries to the solicitor apparently representing his interests drew no response at all. It's good to see Peter back alive and healthy and performing again. A similar situation arose with our attempts to deliver a full album of T. Rex material. When an artist with a catalogue of songs or recordings dies the estate is often handled by a solicitor, as was the case with Marc Bolan. Despite strenuous efforts I was never able to make any headway with the lawyers, and the album never saw the light of day, which is a great pity since, as we have seen, Marc's early career was so dependent on John's encouragement and support. But that's lawyers again.

After three successful years our distribution contract with Pinnacle was due to expire and, owing in part to pique at Mason's attitude over the Hendrix release and the recent installation at Rough Trade of a key former Pinnacle employee, George Kimpton, plus a number of other factors, I made the critical mistake of switching distribution to Rough Trade. Having been a big fish in what was Pinnacle's relatively small pond of the early days, with all of the clout and attention that attracts, we had now become just one of several successful small labels they distributed, but our time at Rough Trade was an unmitigated disaster. Within months of our arrival they went into liquidation owing hundreds of thousands of pounds to ourselves and dozens of indie labels, including the company now owned and run by Bee and Chet, who had just spent everything on their first ever television campaign. In those circumstances the first thing to do is to retrieve your stock before the liquidator locks it away, and we all made several tiresome journeys to King's Cross, leaving with cars groaning under thousands of pounds' worth of records to be stored away in garages and flats.

Apart from trying to retrieve our money, there was an urgent need to find and negotiate a new deal with a new distributor and, with a couple of dozen labels suddenly available, the rush was on. As a collectors' label, our needs were not as urgent as the likes of Beggars Banquet, which had current hits to nurture, and Bee and Chet survived only by Chet selling his house and moving in with his girlfriend. Meanwhile the liquidating company was charging thousands of pounds an hour to inspect the books and tell us what we already knew. Many of the labels were fiercely independent and determined to stay that way, despite the approaches of the major companies with open chequebooks. So began a series of interminable meetings of a dozen or more label owners trying to find an alternative distribution outlet. This eventually resulted in the formation of a new company to handle the sales, with distribution back in the hands of Pinnacle, but it was a long and tedious process, during which I became even less popular since I held little brief for idealistic indie posturing. I just wanted to get back into the business of running a label and struck a deal with Polygram to distribute just the Strange Fruit label, as Band of Joy was still contracted to Pinnacle.

The former key employee who had moved to Rough Trade had now joined Polygram and, since he was familiar with our catalogue, I thought we would be in good hands. I also took this opportunity to ask Brian O'Reilly, our former label manager at

Pinnacle, to join us – which was possibly the only smart thing I did in that turbulent time. Between the three of us we managed to turn the situation around to some extent, but the edge of the interest had gone and I began to feel the draught.

We had licensed the catalogue in the USA, and sales were healthy but not out-standing. It is one of the great joys of the music industry, and possibly many others, to discover something you have created on sale in far-flung places. I was thrilled to hear an assistant in a record store in Arizona ordering further copies of 'the Banshees' Peel Session' on the telephone, unaware of my interest. It must be a sensational rush for a new artist. On the strength of the success of the label we managed to drum up support for an American radio series for John, but, despite massive and astonishingly kindly press coverage, we were unable to sustain the interest of a major advertiser and the series did not take off. John was disappointed, but he could never have found the time to develop it had it been successful.

France was an altogether different affair. As a general rule catalogue sales abroad are best handled by one of the many excellent export companies. That way you know exactly how many you sell and, assuming you get paid, the profits are comparable to home sales. It doesn't always work out, and a big American company, which went belly-up but continued trading, stiffed Bee and Chet for many thousands of dollars. The problem with dealing with US companies is that, as a general rule, they pay only when they need to order more product, which makes it imperative to have a stream of hit product.

However, back to France. We were quite happy to export to that country, but a major company with substantial interests in supermarkets and megastores persistently asked us to license the label to them on the basis that they would sell too many to make importing practical. The managing director telephoned personally and sent his top representative over to plead their case. Because we were too busy to take time out to inspect the organization, and driven partly by greed no doubt, I caved in and licensed Strange Fruit to them for a substantial advance and under a strict contract laying out the legal requirements. Of course, I completely forgot the French natural arrogance and disregard for the rules. The first notice of trouble came from a very heated call from Ita, who handled Fiction Records from whom we had obtained the Cure session. She had obtained a copy of the French release of that session, which had been released as a picture disc in a picture sleeve, and in both instances the photos used were of a different line-up. We were aghast and demanded an explanation from the French company together with an undertaking that the record would be withdrawn. No such under-taking was forthcoming, and we further discovered that a similar release had appeared with the wrong line-up of the Banshees on the cover.

Letters and faxes to the managing director, who had been so ingratiating, brought no response, and our only recourse was the law, which would have been expensive, time-consuming and, in this case, with the international aspect, very complex. Our own lawyer was not well versed in international law and suggested another company, which managed to put a stop to the nonsense at a cost of several thousand pounds and a couple of Paris trips for Brian. This was all very costly and annoying but, more important, it nearly cost us the goodwill of two major acts. Those illegal French releases are now probably worth a fortune to collectors, but it will be a very long time before I am tempted to deal with any French companies again.

With Radio 1 approaching its twenty-fifth birthday, we planned a special release to celebrate our connection. We again approached many of the artists who had earlier refused our blandishments and, racing against time, were proud to develop a double CD with thirty-six tracks from luminaries such as Dire Straits, Elton John, U2, Police, Simple Minds, UB40, Culture Club, Free, Erasure, Traffic, Joe Cocker, Soft Cell, Depeche Mode and Elvis Costello. Still no Bowie, Beatles or Stones, but a fabulous commemoration of the BBC's contribution to popular music. It barely sold enough to cover its costs and certainly not enough to merit the effort involved. We were in competition with Pinnacle, which was now presenting a similar compilation of commercially recorded tracks, and the monthly meetings at Radio 1, with Steve Mason in attendance as the deadline approached, were exercises in one-upmanship that I generally lost.

Though we had introduced the concept of commercially releasing session recordings and had an exclusive arrangement with BBC Enterprises, we discovered that the Corporation was not keeping to its side of the deal and was prepared to license session tracks to anyone who asked. On the strength of our apparent success many companies were getting into the act and, as so often happens, offering advances and deals that made no commercial sense. Even our former distributor, Pinnacle, had struck a deal with BBC Enterprises for the release of the 'In Concert' series, on which I had broken the ground for BBC Records briefly as a consultant. It is indicative of the degree of sophistication in BBC Records at that time that, having secured the agreement of three top artists for their work to appear, I suggested that it was time to start work on the design of a series of sleeves. It was suggested that I discuss the matter with the recently appointed sales director, who was a very upmarket young woman. She perused the artist details and potential track listings and enquired, in vowels plummy enough to make your nose bleed, as to whether I had arranged for the sleeve notes to be written, since she felt unable to consider suitable artwork without complete sleeve notes. This prompted John Walters to suggest that we write a set of clever sleeve notes and then go out in search of a suitable band. It was generally believed at the time, with some justification, that a job at BBC Enterprises was the last repository for the sons and daughters of admirals and wing-commanders who wanted a career in show business but couldn't cut it in the real world. Peel insists that he initially suggested releasing session recordings to BBC Records which, twenty years ago, dismissed the idea as having no commercial potential and then proceeded to release an album devoted to rose-growing. That was following a lunch with Richard Branson to discuss the same idea, at which, John remembers, Richard was more interested in going out to shoot something.

In the face of escalating costs and diminishing sales, we decided it was time to get off the treadmill and take the money and run. So began a tedious round of dealing with potential purchasers. This was somewhat complicated by the fact that the series could work only with the cooperation of BBC Enterprises, which would not reach agreement with any of the major players. Our American distributors were very keen to acquire the series, as were Phonogram, who were distributing us in Britain, but the

BBC would not consider either of them. We eventually sold the labels to Pinnacle, which is something that Shurley in particular would never wish to experience again. The detail required was unbelievable and entailed yet more sleepless nights poring over old contracts and royalty statements while dealing with endless calls and enquiries from accountants and lawyers.

Eventually a deal was agreed, and we met up with the Pinnacle team at their Kent headquarters in company with our own lawyer, who had informed us that at some point in the negotiations the opposition would make an unacceptable demand. He advised us that when this happened we should be prepared to get up and leave. We found this hard to believe after months of discussion and negotiation, but sure enough it happened just as he had predicted and, following his lead, we reluctantly called their bluff and headed for the door. We were called back, and the deal was concluded.

We had a truly terrific time; we created one of the world's great collectors' labels and made enough money not to have to worry. I am sure that we got out at the right time and have no regrets. But every time that telephone rings there is an instant when I wonder if it's Bowie or the surviving Beatles or maybe even the Stones.

ENDPIECE

Yes, it was a roller-coaster ride – and I hate roller-coasters. My youngest daughter Sam still chortles as she recalls me whimpering with fear on our last ride together at Disneyland.

These ramblings took a long time to write and an even longer time to live. As Sam Goldwyn is reputed to have said, 'We've all passed a lot of water since then' – but that was probably a quote dreamed up by a press agent to present him as a cuddly uncle rather than a ruthless mogul.

To load up yet another cliché, they do say that if you remember the sixties you probably weren't there. Well, I was there before, during and long after the fabled sixties and needed to make some kind of record of how it really was and may never be again. I cannot claim to remember all or even the majority of it, and my chronology may be suspect, but that, too, was how it was.

Since beginning this tome we have lost all too many of the main players, and the people running things now seem – at least to me – rather like the music, a little bland and less than memorable. Will we see another Sinatra, Elvis or Peggy Lee? Is there anyone on the horizon with the charisma of John, Jimi, Jim or Janis? Could the music establishment cope with another Obie? Is there still room at the BBC for a dedicated, witty iconoclast like Walters? I fear not, yet Peel goes from strength to strength while remaining out on the edge and steadfastly refusing to play the games. Perhaps there is hope.

Particularly among young people there is a hunger for a life more exciting, less predictable. The music business can provide this – but at a price. With the excitement comes much fear, sickening lurches of fortune and the danger of losing touch with friends, family and plain old common sense. It is not for the faint-hearted or those who prefer to separate work and relaxation. Achieving any kind of success demands total commitment and dedication. The rewards, however, are there for all to see.

I hope some of these jottings will further encourage the truly dedicated – who might spot the many career mistakes – dissuade the merely curious and amuse the vast majority who see us as a loony bunch of untalented mercenaries.

I am blessed with four intelligent and attractive children. They are all successful in their own ways. Daughter Sam is a promising writer with two plays already performed; eldest son Brod has just returned from a business trip to the USA where he was met by a stretch limo with all the trimmings and flown across the country in one of that company's private jets; and Bee and Chet – the only two who have picked up the music-biz baton – have achieved market leadership in their chosen field with a combination of very hard work, frightening risk-taking and great business acumen, coupled with brilliant creativity.

As these last words are written, it is almost springtime and we are about to leave our home in England, with beautiful views over the Sussex Downs, for our other home in Arizona with views over the mountains and horses in the corral. Was it worth it? You bet – but I'm still wondering what I'll do when I grow up.

Thanks for listening. See you on the charts?

AFTERWORD

They don't make 'em like they used to, do they?

Bollox.

'Course music should all be free . . . the internet will soon see to all you fat, cigar-chewing, rich music-business bastards . . . it's about time you got what you deserve . . .

I don't know. How much crap is there talked about the music business these days?

Ha! Look at EMI . . . what a mess . . . fancy having to bail out Mariah Carey for 38 million . . . or was it 58 million quid? See . . . told you so. The music industry is dying . . . they don't make 'em like they used to.

Hang on. What about Robbie Williams then?

Shite

Kylie?

Won't last.

Oasis?

Con artists.

How about the Hives?

Who?

Or the Strokes?

Never heard of 'em.

Then piss off and get out of my face. Come back when you've had a good hard think about the shite that's written about the music business every day in seemingly every paper you pick up. It's all bollox.

I love this poxy business almost as much as I love my dad.

Try as hard as I can, I can't get away from it. I suppose it's in my blood.

I live in the hard cut-throat world of the compilation album. This is commercially as fast as it gets. We have an idea, and it can be on the shelves in the shops four weeks later. One day after that you know if you have a winner, but by that time you're already working on the next two albums.

It's the ultimate drug. What a bang.

You put six weeks' furious work in for that ten-second high when you get the sales figs on Tues at 11 a.m. telling you what you sold on the first Monday.

Computers do that for you . . . speed . . . information . . . fact . . . no hiding place. You're a king or a prat come 11.01 a.m.

What a life.

It's all a far cry from how it was when me dad was riding high.

I remember spending endless hours in horrible recording studios with my brother and sister in the small hours, tired and bored. We used to try to sleep in the corner while Dad added a couple more strings or whatever. The stink of stale cigarettes, carpet tiles, bad coffee and leatherette couches will be with me for ever.

I didn't give a monkey's that he was doing all this great stuff. Didn't care a toss that he had fifteen out of the Top Twenty or whatever.

I liked Slade, Blue Öyster Cult, Status Quo and T. Rex. I'd play my dad's Occasional Word Ensemble to my mates for a giggle. Teenagers are like that – tribal – they know what they like and screw everything else.

But, hey . . . what a legacy he's left.

I always said that I'd never go into the music business because I saw what it did to me dad. You know, the stress – it nearly killed him.

But here I am.

Somehow, God knows why, I got roped into it, and I'm still here fifteen years later.

I just get that little sniff of a great album and the drug kicks in. You have to make the dream come alive . . . bust your ass to make a great album happen and put it out. When it hits the shops it's like closing your eyes, grimacing, turning your head forty-five degrees to your left with arms stretched straight out in front of you holding it . . . waiting for either the huge boot in the testicles or the warm glow of success. Hero or prat. A lottery.

One day I will get a few acts together and we'll take on my dad's legacy. One day . . . not yet maybe . . . but one day.

Dad, you are a hero.

Chet

xx